The Librarian's Guide to Genealogical Services and Research

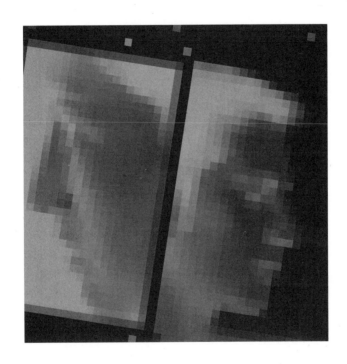

James Swan

Neal-Schuman Publishers, Inc.

New York   London

Published by Neal-Schuman Publishers, Inc.
100 William Street, Suite 2004
New York, NY 10038

ISBN 1-55570-491-3

Printed and bound in the United States of America.

The paper used in this publication meets the minimum requirements of American National Standard for Informational Sciences—Permanence of Paper for Printed Library Materials, ANSI Z39.48—1992

Cataloging-in-Publication Data for this book is available from the Library of Congress, record number 2004040152.

TABLE OF CONTENTS

LIST OF FIGURES

PREFACE

I learned genealogical reference service in a "sink-or-swim" experience. In 1964, knowing little about librarianship or genealogy, I found myself working the reference desk in the history and genealogical section at Brigham Young University Library. Like other opportunities in life, when my enthusiasm outweighed my knowledge, I jumped in with both feet and learned everything I could about genealogy and as fast as I could.

I began by researching my own genealogy in earnest. I went to the Genealogical Society (the forerunner to the Family History Library) in Salt Lake City. As I uncovered new information, I became more and more energized. Soon I realized I was hooked as a lifelong researcher. At the same time, I really began to love helping fellow researchers as a librarian.

Now, as someone who has spent more than forty years as a genealogist and a librarian, I hope that *The Librarian's Guide to Genealogical Services and Research* will convey my enthusiasm and know-how in both genealogy and librarianship. Having been on both sides of the genealogy reference desk, I feel I have a unique perspective to offer librarians and genealogists. I know what it feels like to be a novice researcher and not know where to turn for the right answers. I also know the frustration of being a librarian who lacks the skills or resources to deal with the difficult questions genealogists can ask.

The Librarian's Guide to Genealogical Services and Research is for librarians and others who guide genealogical researchers. It might also be used as a textbook or training manual. The reliable sources and practical advice will help librarians, archivists, family history workers, and family history researchers, skillfully navigate research through the ever-expanding sea of available materials. It will acquaint librarians and genealogists with the best sources and where to find them, so they can obtain and utilize the best information right away.

Many guides to genealogy are little more than links to this increasing supply of information sources. *The Librarian's Guide to Genealogical Services and Research* is designed not just to point readers to the door of resources, but to teach them how to select the best ones. It shows what to do with the material readers find and where to look for the next step. Naturally, it covers the broad view of genealogical research, but it also gets to the "nitty gritty," by providing the details you need actually to perform the tasks suggested.

Organization

Part I, "The Librarian's Guide to Genealogical Services," covers how to help genealogists get started, develop collections for genealogists, use technology, find out about other collections, provide instruction for genealogists, and stay current professionally. You develop expertise in genealogy, like so many other questions received in day-to-day practice, through experience. This is the short cut to becoming experienced at handling the needs of genealogists and family history researchers.

- Chapter 1, "Starting Research," covers the basics of genealogical research and how librarians can help beginning genealogists start their research. It also explores how to create a genealogy collection.

- Chapter 2, "Building the Genealogical Collection," contains sound advice for ways to develop a collection for the genealogical researcher.

- Chapter 3, "Defining the Technological Task," expands on collection development, but with a specific eye toward online databases and electronic resources essential to proper family history research; including subscriptions to online databases.

- Chapters 4, "Identifying and Accessing Major Genealogical Repositories," and Chapter 5, "Distinguishing Other Genealogical Resource Facilities," will familiarize librarians with the leading institutions and facilities for research. These chapters equip you to know where to send people when your library doesn't have the answers. No library or research facility can have every scrap of information researchers need. Librarians have to rely on their colleagues in other research facilities to help their patrons.

- Chapter 6, "Providing Instruction for Genealogists," will help to develop instruction programs for genealogists in the library.

- Chapter 7, "Staying Current Professionally," offers good advice for libraries and librarians, who want constantly to improve their genealogy reference service.

Part II, "The Librarian's Guide to Genealogical Research," is written to help librarians show patrons and help other researchers logically and systemically search for the best sources of information available. How do you start beginners on the right path? How do you direct them to finding significant sources, including databases and indexes? Should you ever suggest hiring a professional researcher? Part II includes descriptions and illustrations of the materials that you can give directly to users, so that they can become experienced and self-reliant researchers at your library.

- Chapter 8, "Starting an Organized Search," is a primer for getting research off the ground. It offers ways to search efficiently and effectively. It also provides an explanation of the forms in the "tool kits" available in the last part of this book.

- Chapter 9, "Finding Genealogically Significant Resources," contains an extensive list of potential sources librarians might recommend to researchers, including some of the more obvious documents that searches often overlook.

- Chapter 10, "Identifying Databases and Indexes," tackles the sometime intimidating, but always-key resources found in indexes and databases.

- Chapter 11, "Facilitating Research with Computers," shows the best ways to employ computers and the Internet in research.

- Chapter 12, "Getting Help from Professional Researchers," explains the value and (sometimes) necessity of a professional researcher, including why you may need one and how to do get that individual involved.

I have annotated the bibliography at the end of each chapter to describe not only what each resource contains, but also how it might fit into the library collection. Some of the materials are more appropriate for larger libraries with substantial budgets, and others belong in collections of any size—even in the personal research collection. To help you identify materials most appropriate for your collection, I have marked them as either "L" for libraries and "P" for personal. They are ranked from one letter for recommended, two letters for preferred, and three letters for essential.

Part III, "Handy Genealogical Resources and Worksheets," offers twenty-nine useful forms, guides, and keys to help any researcher begin a search, or help any librarian start researchers on their journey. Organized into Tool Kits, these resources include:

- Tool Kit 1 is a resource bibliography that can be used as a collection development tool for librarians or as a consulting page for researchers.

- Tool Kit 2 is a compiled list of leading research facilities—libraries, archives, and other collections—to help find important documents. The list provides the name of each institution, contact information, Web site address, Online catalog address, special features of the collection, the restrictions on access to the collection, and special services provided by the institution.

There are also many useful worksheets for the librarian providing aid to genealogists. The best group of worksheets comprises the "Getting Started Handouts" in Tool Kit 3. These sheets help you get research under way. They include:

- Ancestor Interview Form

- Pedigree Chart

- Checklist of Personal Genealogy Sources

- Family Group Sheet

- Ancestors and Descendants Chart

- Oral History Interview Checklist

- Request for Information Tracking Sheet

In Tool Kit 4 are the means to keep your research organized:

- Research Log

- Data Extraction Form

- Family Bible Extraction Form

- Cemetery Research Outline

- Biographical Sketch Outline

You will find the following checklists in Tool Kits 5 and 6:

- Before you start, you need to comlete the "Checklist for Planning a Research Trip."

- My "First Places to Look" checklists are tailored to each every half century, from 1750 through 2000. This focuses your searching in the most relevant and likely sources of information for the times.

- To prevent a wild goose chase, I give you a "Checklist for Accessing Printed Information in Distant Libraries."

- The worksheets on the Federal Censuses from 1790-1930 provide quick answers to questions like, "Did the 1790 Census record the addresses of respondents?" or "Did the 1830 Census count white females under 16 years?"

- The Federal Census Chronology is provided in two forms—1790-1860 and 1870-1900—to reflect the unique changes that occurred and to help researchers search smarter.

Finally, in Tool Kits 7 and 8, I provide means for requesting information and for targeting electronic resources on the Web and elsewhere. There you will find the following:

- Requesting Information Summary Chart

- Sample Letter to Social Security Administration

- Comparing Geneaology Software Table

- Libraries and Archives Web Directory

I've made all these tools even more useful by placing them on the CD-ROM so you can reproduce and customize them as your library and users need.

The CD-ROM is truly a genealogical treasure. In addition to the forms and sheets, there are hyperlinked Web addresses (URLs) to nearly 500 research institutions, catalogs, and Web sites. All of this information is available at your fingertips and will greatly help the pursuits of the researchers you are trying to help out.

Helping people find their ancestors can be very challenging for any librarian; but, it doesn't have to be overwhelming. Learning how to help genealogical researchers is a fascinating process— you can only learn to do it one step at a time. What is my recommendation for librarians? One of the best first steps is to start research on your own family tree. Use *The Librarian's Guide to Genealogical Services and Research* to get started on your own genealogy. In the process, you will gain valuable insights into the excitement and challenges your patrons face when their research brings them to your library.

As you become more experienced and expert, I hope you get something you can use to help create better service for the genealogists that come to your library. I hope this book will help you:

- Enhance the way you see the information needs of family history researchers;

- Develop a greater appreciation for your role as a librarian who helps genealogists;

- Discover some genealogical resources you have never seen before;

- Generate some good ideas for helping beginning genealogists;

- Empower you to contact other agencies for genealogical information;

- Teach your patrons the genealogical research process;

- Learn how the Internet can enhance family history research;

- Come across books you can't wait to order for your library;

- Consider offering classes to genealogical researchers; and

- Begin researching your own family tree.

Most of all I hope you will enjoy reading this book as you discover new ideas and new places to go for help.

PART I

THE LIBRARIAN'S GUIDE TO GENEALOGICAL SERVICES

CHAPTER 1
STARTING RESEARCH

You may not have been thrown into the role of genealogy reference librarian like I was, but you probably wish that you had received additional training before you faced your first genealogy question. After some experience at it, you probably feel fairly comfortable helping genealogical researchers in your library, but maybe you still need help to bring it all together. Take heart. The cavalry is on its way.

What to Look for in This Chapter

Chapter 1 gives librarians some basic tools for helping beginning genealogists. It details the genealogical research process, an understanding of which is critical to helping genealogists.

Finding out How to Help Genealogical Researchers

Our job as librarians is to help people find the information they want when they come to the library. When someone comes to the library and asks a reference question, we usually conduct a cursory reference interview. Without getting too nosy we try to get to the heart of the question.

Sometimes family history researchers will walk into a library or other research facility and ask, "Where are your genealogy books?" The easy answer is to show them the general area of genealogy collection and let them browse their way around the collection. Sometimes they find a birth or death date, without ever finding exactly what they really wanted to know. A better way is to conduct a detailed reference interview. You need to help them focus on one event for one person in a given place on a specific date. If the researcher has only a scrap of paper with a name and approximate date, you may have your work cut out for you.

When a patron comes to the reference desk and asks us to help her find her great great-grandmother, this is how the interview might go.

Librarian: "Tell me then what it is you really want to know about your great great-grand-mother."

Patron: "I want to know when and where she was born and who her parents were."

Librarian: "What was your great great-grandmother's name?"

Patron: "Her name was Polly Mitchell."

Librarian: "Is Mitchell her married name or maiden name?"

Patron: "I think it was her married name?"

Librarian: "What was her husband's name?"

Patron: "John Mitchell."

Librarian: "When did they get married?"

Patron: "That is one of the things I want to find out."

Librarian: "Do you know the names of Polly's children?"

Patron: "Her daughter, my great grandmother was named Janie."

Librarian: "How many children did she have?"

Patron: "As far as I know, maybe six."

Librarian: "Do you know any of their names?"

Patron: "I think she had twins named Billy and Bobby."

Librarian: "Where was Polly living when she died?"

Patron: "From what my grandmother says, Polly was living in Wisconsin."

Librarian: "Do you know about when she died?"

Patron: "Not for sure, but I'm certain it was after the Civil War. Her husband was killed in the Civil War and she died several years after that."

Librarian: "Where have you looked for information about your great great-grandmother?"

Patron: "Nowhere. I am just getting started."

Librarian: "Where did you get the information you have?"

Patron: "From my grandmother. She gave me this family tree a few years before she died."

Librarian: "When did she give you the family tree?"

Patron: "About six years ago. Some time in 1998."

Librarian: "Did She have any other family documents?"

Patron: "Not that I know of."

Librarian: "Have you asked other family members for genealogical information?"

Patron: "Yes, but none of them have any information about Polly Mitchell."

The patron has obviously consulted home and family sources and has come to the library to take her research to the next level, which is why she is in your library.

Synthesizing the Answers

The answers to the reference interview questions will give you clues to where to start looking, but first a summary of learnings from the case of Polly Mitchell is in order. Begin by asking questions to find out what you know. Then make assumptions to lead you to the facts you don't know. Lastly, test the assumptions by looking for the facts to prove or disprove what you think might be true.

Assumptions about Polly Mitchell:

- Mary or Mary Jane was probably her real given name. See a dictionary of nicknames, or the list of Nicknames and Naming Traditions at the Web site (Available: www.tngenweb.org/franklin/frannick.htm), for possible nicknames.

- Polly probably married John Mitchell about 1840. If they had six children before 1861 they would have had to be married no later than 1848, the twins notwithstanding.

- Polly was probably born between 1820 and 1830. Most women in those days married at between ages 18 and 20.

- Polly probably died between 1870 and 1890. She would have been between 50 and 60 in 1880.

Looking for the Best Sources First

Unless your library is near where great great-grandma Mitchell lived and died, your library may not offer very many resources to help the patron. So you are probably going to go outside your library to find the information. The easiest first stop is to check the online databases of compiled genealogies, like FamilySearch.org or Ancestry.com (see Chapter 3). The next place to look would be the 1850 Federal Census for Wisconsin. You might have the microfilm in the library, or you can borrow or rent it from another library. (Census images online are available at HeritageQuest Online and Ancestry.com) Also, look for a Wisconsin death index for the years 1860 to 1890. Check for Mary, as well as Polly. You should check for a Civil War Pension Application from a Mary Mitchell on her husband John Mitchell. If the ancestor lived in the county where your library is, I would send the patron to the county courthouse to look for a death, or marriage certificate. If the event occurred in a different part of the country, have her write to the courthouse where the ancestor lived.

There is only so much a librarian can do with the resources in his or her library. Online resources on the Internet can help researchers find information you don't have in your library, but eventually you will have to send them to other research facilities. The local Family History Center is the first place I would send them. It is the local link to the vast resources of the Family History Library (FHL) in Salt Lake City.

These suggestions represent only the tip of the iceberg. One piece of information could lead to another assumption that can be tested, and so on. I have created several checklists of research sites to look first. For computer access and printing, these checklists are on the CD-ROM that goes with this book.

If the researcher has brought a briefcase full of documents, you may find it difficult to get him or her to narrow the focus of the search to one event for one person at a particular place and time. You could start by asking to see his or her pedigree chart. After looking at the chart with the patron, you could ask, "Which of these individuals would you like to focus on today?" and "What would you like to find out about this person?"

Helping Researchers Get Started

Some researchers will know exactly what they need and what resources to consult. They may not even need help from the reference staff. However, many others will come in with little more than the name of one of their ancestors in their heads.

While some of the advice that follows may not apply to all of the genealogists who come to your library, there are enough genealogists who are just getting started to warrant a few words about the basic forms for documenting genealogical research. If they don't have their research organized, you need to help them by providing some basic forms. Whether you charge for the forms or not is your business. You might try giving them the first pages free and charging for additional copies. I have always felt that providing a printout or a blank form is one way of answering a reference question, which is part of our service to people who walk into the library.

Essential forms for genealogists are found on the CD-ROM that accompanies this book. The most basic forms are the Pedigree Chart, the Family Group Sheet and the Research Log, presented in Chapter 8, as well as in Tool Kits 3 and 4. Also included in Chapter 8 is a list of other tools the family researcher may need to acquire. These three forms allow researchers to record the family data they gather and to create a record of sources and questions that have been researched. This includes both successful and unsuccessful searches. The list of sources that did not have a particular piece of information are just as important to record as those that did—saving the researcher the time and effort required to repeat the same unsuccessful search at some point in the future. The advent of so much genealogical information on the Internet may cause researchers to rethink their use of a research log when searching online. It may be quicker and easier to redo the search than to take the time to write everything in the log. New information appears on the Internet all of the time, so a search done today with no result might have a positive result a week later.

Many other forms are available for a variety of other purposes. The book, *Unpuzzling Your Past Workbook: Essential Forms and Letters for All Genealogists*, by Emily Anne Croom (Croom, 1996), has many, many forms for genealogists.

Helping Researchers Get Organized

When genealogists come to a library with a name written on a scrap of paper, they need more help than putting a roll of microfilm on the reader and letting them find the information it contains. They need a little coaching. You could start by giving them a pedigree chart and suggesting that they take it home and fill it out. You could also give them the checklist of home sources of genealogical records. You could show them how to look up living relatives, who might have genealogical information they haven't seen. When they come back to the library, you can praise their efforts and help them use the information they have recently found.

Taking the Initiative

Sometimes we need to get a little proactive to help genealogists get more than they expect. A while back two women came into the library. They asked specifically for the Barton County Cemetery books, which we keep under lock and key. I opened the case and pulled the books for them. In a few minutes they had located the information they wanted and were ready to leave. I knew how limited the information in the cemetery book was so I offered to let them search the newspapers on microfilm for an obituary. They agreed and sat down at the microfilm reader/printer. Within 15 minutes they had two obituaries and left the library pleased with their success.

Documenting Sources

Librarians who help their patrons do a good job of documenting their sources are doing them a huge favor that will save them time in the future. The best book I have ever seen on documenting sources is *Evidence! Citation and Analysis for the Family Historian*, by Elizabeth S. Mills (Mills, 1997). It sets forth the correct style for source citation and the standard for reliable analysis of evidence. These two practices are inseparable in successful genealogical research. The author's keen observations and approach to this concept are insightful. Every library should have a copy of this book in circulation, as well as on the reference shelves. Some genealogists may have different standards or no standards at all for documenting and proving sources. Others may be seeking membership in a patriotic society such as the D.A.R. and they will have their own high standards of proof and documentation. Every library should have this book. As a librarian you could develop a one-page summary on how to document sources and include it in the packet for genealogists.

Genealogical Toolbox for Librarians

A plumber would never go to a job without a toolbox. Librarians who help genealogists need toolboxes, as well. Most traditional librarians think of books and microfilm as the tools of the trade. They are, but others are just as crucial to our efforts in genealogy research. Here are a few to ponder.

Important But Less Tangible Items

- A vision statement for the library that defines the scope of the library's genealogical service. This can be a sentence within the library's overall mission statement, or a separate statement just for the genealogy department.

- A materials selection policy that specifically addresses genealogical and local history needs. This is usually a sentence in the library's collection development policy that articulates the library's plans for developing the local history and genealogical collection. It should include a statement that will guide the librarian and board at budget time.

- A budget priority dedicating an appropriate share of the library's resources to genealogical and local history materials. Some library budgets have a specific line item for materials in the local history and genealogy section of the library.

- An interlibrary loan policy that is friendly to genealogists. It seems reasonable to circulate materials that can be replaced including microfilm. Many libraries will lend, through interlibrary loan, county histories or genealogies if they have a second copy.

- A staff that is trained to help genealogists. Some of the best-trained reference librarians still lack the skills to help genealogists. Even though they can usually do an adequate job, it is best if they can receive some special training on helping with genealogical research. They could attend regional or statewide genealogy conferences as part of their own professional development.

- Public relations support to promote the library's service to genealogists. Too often the library's service to genealogists is almost hidden. I found this to be absolutely true when I did the research for the list of libraries found in Chapter 4. When I checked the Web sites of several large libraries I was surprised when I could not find a link to the genealogy department from their main page. The Allen County Public Library in Fort Wayne, Indiana, knows how to use its service to genealogists to promote the whole library.

More Tangible Items for the Toolbox

- Forms and "Getting Started" handouts for beginning genealogists. New genealogists face what can be perceived as huge challenges. If you can give them a form to fill out or a checklist to complete, they will feel their trip to the library was successful in helping them advance to the next step in their research. Give them something they can use and they will keep coming back. Check out the forms on the CD-ROM that accompanies this book.

- A detailed brochure that outlines the library's resources for genealogical researchers. The library's catalog is usually the window to the collection, but if a genealogist does not know that a tool exists, he or she may miss it in the catalog. Include as many of the types of resources in your library as will fit in the brochure. If possible, keep it to four pages (11" x 17" folded). More people will read a concise but detailed brochure if you present is in this fashion. Follow up with single-page handout on specific topics.

- A way to control the lighting in the microfilm reading area. Microfilms are sometimes difficult to read if the ambient light is too bright, because bright room light prevents good contrast on the reading surface of the microfilm reader. Design the lighting and microfilm reading room area to reduce the glare from light sources.

Big Stuff for the Toolbox

- At least one microfilm/microfiche reader/printer. If the library has a significant microform collection and doesn't have a reader/printer, you are seriously limiting the use of the collection.

While these machines may cost a few thousand dollars, they make a good project for local fundraising.

- A photocopy machine in the genealogy room. If the library can afford to lease or purchase a second photocopier, your genealogists will greatly appreciate you putting it in the genealogy room.

- A computer with live connection to the Internet. Genealogy on the Internet is exploding. Researchers are putting their information on the Internet and sharing it with others. If you can afford it, invest in online access and let people know you have a computer for genealogists. Additionally you could put another computer in the genealogy room that is capable of reading CD-ROMs and/or DVDs, with our without Internet access. Also, install samples of genealogical software programs on this computer. Of all the things you could do for genealogist, having one or more computers in the genealogy department could be the most helpful. They will flock to the library to use it. In Chapter 11 we encourage researchers to purchase their own computer to take advantage of its multiple benefits.

- Subscribe to online genealogy databases like AncestryPlus and HeritageQuest for use in the library. Many researchers are reluctant to spend $200.00 for a personal membership in one of these services—especially if they are unfamiliar with the value of the information they could find.

Suggestions for Librarians

1. Attend a beginning genealogy workshop.
2. Publish a handout of local genealogical sources.
3. Fill your genealogy toolbox.
4. Offer formalized genealogical research classes.
5. Learn how to use at least one genealogy software program.

Summary

Helping patrons understand the research process could be the best thing you will ever do for them. You have to take your time when helping genealogists who are just getting started; but if you do a good job, you may witness great joy and excitement. They will return and share their successes with you.

Having the necessary forms is a great first step. Suggesting places to start looking may be the best thing you can do. Doing a good job on the reference interview will help your patron learn how to ask questions that lead to the information they seek. After you explore the many types of documents available for genealogical research, review the research process, and help the patrons get started, you can move to the next level, which is developing the collection in the local library and learning how to access the collections of other facilities.

Start by looking at your own mission statement to see where genealogy fits in the total picture. It also helps to understand the missions of other research facilities, because not all of them focus on the needs of genealogists. If you understand how they do business, you can shape your efforts to match more closely what they do best. You win, and your patrons win.

Bibliography (Ratings Guide explanation follows last citation)

Croom, Emily Anne. 1996. *Unpuzzling Your Past Workbook: Essential Forms and Letters for All Genealogists*. Cincinnati, OH: Betterway Books.

This is a good book for beginners. It has the reproducible forms they need and checklists to help organize their research, as well as suggestions to help with the transcription of data from public deeds, marriage record indexes, and the census Soundex. The forms for gathering information help save time and create a focus for interviews and research in books, documents, deeds, and census records. The tips on letter writing will make letters more effective. Sample letters provide ideas for letters to individuals, requests for copies of documents, and letters to relatives asking for answers to family history questions. **PP**

Croom, Emily Anne. 2003. *Unpuzzling Your Past: the Best Selling Basic Guide to Genealogy*. Cincinnati: Betterway Books.

This book is indispensable for beginners and not too technical. Easy to read and understand, it makes getting started with genealogical research interesting and fun. It is an exceptional guide that is beautifully printed. Make sure the library has copies both in reference and in the circulating collection. **PPP**

Galford, Ellen. 2001. *The Genealogy Handbook: the Complete Guide to Tracing Your Family Tree*. Pleasantville, NY: Reader's Digest.

Today it is easier for many people to do genealogical research. With the advent of computers, the Internet, and digital photography, thousands of people are successfully finding their ancestors. With two or three illustrations on every page, this book uses a popular approach to help beginning researchers find their ancestors. **PP**

Hunter, Julius K. 2000. *Digging for Family Roots: A Beginner's Guide to African American Genealogical Research*. St. Louis, MO: Julius K. Hunter & Friends African American Research Collection in the St. Louis County Library.

This 29-page book is a good starting place for anyone who wants to have fun as they start their research. It was not written for the professional or the seasoned researcher, but for the beginner. **P**

Mills, Elizabeth S. 1997. *Evidence! Citation and Analysis for the Family Historian*. Baltimore, MD: Genealogical Publishing Company.

This is the best book I have ever seen on documenting sources. It sets forth the correct style for source citation and the standard for reliable analysis of evidence. These two practices are inseparable in successful genealogical research. Every library should have a copy of this book in circulation, as well as in reference. **PPP**

Sperry, Kip. 2003. *Abbreviations and Acronyms: A Guide for Family Historians*. Provo, UT: Ancestry Publishing.

This book takes the guesswork out of deciphering abbreviations, and acronyms researchers find in their genealogical research. It gives the meanings for abbreviations, alphabetic symbols, initials, contractions and shortenings of words. This guide is a perfect reference tool for family researchers, historians, and reference librarians. **PP**

United States. National Archives and Records Administration. 2000. *Microfilm Resources for Research: A Comprehensive Catalog*. Washington, DC: National Archives and Records Administration.

Since 1941, the National Archives has microfilmed federal records of high research interest to make the records available for researchers, while preserving the originals from deterioration and damage due to repeated handling. Copies of these microfilmed records are sold to the public, making these federal records accessible to libraries, research centers, and individuals. This catalog is essential for any library that rents or buys microfilm from the National Archives. It lists more than 2,000 microfilm publications. (Distributed by: Scholarly Resources, Inc.) **LLL**

Ratings Guide

The ratings for each bibliography describe not only what each resource contains, but also how it might fit into the library collection. Some of the materials are more appropriate for larger libraries with substantial budgets, and others belong in collections of any size—even in the personal research collection. To help you identify materials most appropriate for your collection, each resource is marked as either "L" for libraries and "P" for personal. They are ranked from one letter for recommended, two letters for preferred, and three letters for essential.

CHAPTER 2

BUILDING THE GENEALOGICAL COLLECTION

On a Saturday when I was working the reference desk in the library, three people came in from a town about 60 miles away. They had come to sell our library a copy of their town history. It was nicely done in the style of a high school yearbook. They apologized for charging $25.00, but explained that it had cost them $23.75 to produce each copy. I bought the book, and was glad that I did because our service area extends to a 17-county area that includes their hometown. Had they not come to the library, I would probably never have had the opportunity to buy that book.

This story begs the question: How far from home should librarians collect and preserve materials pertaining to local history and genealogy? The answer is another question: How large is your umbrella? Or in other words, what is your perceived service area? Your library's collection policy will determine the local material you collect.

Underlying a quality genealogy collection you normally find a clearly articulated collection development policy, which outlines what the library will and will not collect. You have to decide how large the umbrella of your genealogy collection will be. Many libraries in the shadow of the Family History Library in Salt Lake City have decided to collect only those documents that pertain to the history of their town. It is a way of allocating scarce resources for other purposes in the library and referring serious genealogists to the Family History Library. Regardless of where you live, librarians have to ask: Do we collect materials that cover the state, or do we limit our collection development to our community? It is important for librarians to establish collection development policies that work for them, practically and economically. If they choose to collect research tools that reach beyond the boundaries of their own libraries, this chapter should give them some guidance and direction.

What to Look for in This Chapter

This chapter is primarily for librarians who are in charge of developing the genealogy collection for the library. You will get some ideas for developing your own policy for collecting and preserving local genealogical material. You will learn what kinds of materials to seek out and acquire for researchers who want local resources. You will also see recommendations for significant resources and guidebooks.

Developing a Policy for Local Collection Development

Every public library has an unqualified responsibility to collect and preserve local histories, newspapers, city directories, telephone directories, and the like. Beyond that, those who govern and administer the library have the authority to define the library's policies on the development of its genealogical collection. Check the *Librarians Serving Genealogists* Web site at www.cas.usf.edu/lis/genealib, for sample collection development guidelines.

Librarians may decide to buy readily available databases and indexes with a national scope to accommodate all researchers. These materials on CD-ROM or book format make it easier for patrons to research their family trees as they go back to the American colonies, Europe or other parts of the world.

It may not be possible to set aside a fixed amount in the budget for local history and genealogical materials, but local materials should not have to compete with bestsellers for funds. Local materials go out-of-print so fast that the collection developer that hesitates may miss the opportunity to buy them.

The first collection development decision a librarian needs to make is what role the library will have in collecting and preserving local history and genealogical materials. Local genealogists with roots in the area will use these records. Outsiders with ancestors that lived in the area will want access to these materials, as well.

It may be difficult to find some locally produced materials. They may have a weak binding or may not have an index, but they still contain unique information not available anywhere else. If the local library does not collect and preserve these materials, who will? Locally produced cemetery books, marriage records, or obituaries can be the mainstay of the local collection, because they will have specific names and dates for patrons who have local roots. Librarians need to know the type of information local materials contain, why they are important to genealogists, and where to find them.

Criteria for Selection of Genealogical Books

If it is a genealogical resource, consider these evaluation criteria for books:

- Does it meet the selection criteria for the level of genealogical research you want your collection to provide? Is your library a regional or statewide resource? You will want to collect and preserve any materials pertaining to your region or state.

- Will the purchase of the material/book fit within the budget for the genealogical collection? Don't spend the entire local history budget at the beginning of the fiscal year. Something may come along later for which you will need the money. Do not buy family histories unless they apply specifically to a family in the community. Acceptance of gifts from local citizens of family histories is appropriate. At least one family in the community has an interest. Others may, too. Do not be afraid to ask for gifts of family history books that are being published locally. Stay abreast of local publishing efforts, and then ask for a free copy when the book is published.

- Does the book contain information that could be of value to your patrons? Do not buy or even collect books that have lists of names that have been copied from a telephone directory.

- Has the book been produced in a useable format? Does it have an index? Genealogical reference tools without indexes are not totally worthless, but they are sure difficult to use.

Must-Buy List

Here is a prioritized list of locally published materials. The most important resources are on the top of the list and should be purchased and preserved regardless of the library's budget.

1. Microfilm Copies of All Local Newspapers

Newspapers may be the only extant records of a person's birth, death, or marriage. Obituaries can lead researchers to death records and probates. Anniversary features can lead us to other family members, especially children. Historical newspapers, if you do not already have them may be available from the state historical society or the local newspaper. The library should maintain a microfilm file of current copies of local newspapers—whether the library has to have the newspapers filmed or can buy them from a vendor that is making the copies on a regular basis.

2. City Directories and Telephone Books

Local libraries must have a collection of city directories and telephone books for as far back as the librarian can obtain them. Just keeping current directories from year to year is important. In 25 years, the directories I started collecting for my library 25 years ago will be 50 years old and an invaluable part of our collection. City directories also include the person's occupation or place of employment, which could lead to a search of other records.

Directories can be used to fill in the gaps between census years. They can also help researchers predict a death date, though death may not be the only reason a person may not be in a director from one year to the next. About the only way to collect directories is to obtain them as they are published. Sometimes companies that are going out of business will have some for sale, but don't count on it.

3. Cemetery Books for the County

Cemetery books provide a link to other records like official death records and newspaper obituaries, as well as probate records. When the Barton County Genealogical Society folded, they gave the public library the copies of the *Barton County Cemetery Records* they had left. Now we are faced with the job of preserving these records while making them available to the public. We offer lookups for a fee to people who live outside the county. This is just one way we extend the service to researchers outside our service area.

Cemetery books are like other locally produced records. You take what you get and you are just grateful you have them. If you do not accept such materials, they will be gone before you know it. The *Barton County Cemetery Records* were a labor of love by several dedicated people. They did the best they could with the resources they had. We are glad to have the records, because they are no longer in print, and have not been updated for 20 years.

4. Microfilmed Courthouse Records

If they are available, try to get copies of the courthouse records on microfilm. These records will include deeds, letters of intent to naturalize, early death records, marriage and divorce records, probate papers, and military records. Chances are the library is open more hours a week than the courthouse is, and the library often has better equipment for public access to the records.

For many years the Family History Library has been microfilming courthouse records and giving the county a copy of the microfilm. Some libraries have been able to obtain a copy of the microfilms at the same time. Find out if the courthouse records have been converted to film and ask for a copy for the library. You might have to pay a duplication fee.

5. A County Plat Atlas

Plat books will show property boundaries and give you the names of owners at the time the atlas was published. Plat atlases can be a link to land records, census records, and cemetery records. These large format books were published around the turn of the century and more recently in the 1970s and 1980s. Contact publishers to see what they have for sale. This type of publication can go out of print quickly. Rockford Map Publishers, of Rockford, Illinois (Available: www.rockfordmap.com), has published hundreds of them and now has some on CD-ROM.

If someone offers to give you a plat map of your county, take it. I recently drove half way across Kansas and back to pick up a copy of a 1911 Barton County plat book. The binding was shot and the pages were fragile, but we were glad to get it. We keep these books in a locked case.

6. Local High School and College Yearbooks

Some people only see their picture or name in print when they appear in the high school yearbook. A high school annual can lead to a birth record, a marriage record, or a school record. From the first day your local high school published an annual to the present your library should buy a copy of the yearbook, catalog it and keep it under lock and key. The same goes for college annuals. Even then your yearbooks may not be safe. Someone could take a razor blade to one while you are not looking.

The first priority is to collect yearbooks and annuals from institutions within the county, and then build the collection from outside the county with yearbooks that are donated. After all, something is better than nothing. If you collect yearbooks from the state or region, you could run out of storage space; a reality that you need to weigh carefully.

7. City and County Histories

Local histories come in two flavors—those written by serious historians and those put together by entrepreneurs, who were in it for the money. Both kinds are worth having in the library, but we need to understand the background of each.

Accounts written by historians tend to cover everything about the history of the town or county—even the dry boring stuff. They often lack the family details on which genealogists focus. The histories done by businessmen around the turn of the twentieth century are often referred to as "mug books," because if you paid the compiler enough money you could have your portrait in the book. For more money you could write a lengthy autobiography.

All of these histories are worth having in the library, because without them you would have no sources. They provide clues for further research. For proof of Revolutionary War ancestry, the DAR will only accept records from published histories if sources for the data are linked to the text.

State historical societies and others have reprinted some county histories. Others may be available on the used book market. It does not hurt to have multiple copies of city and county histories. That way you can circulate extra copies to patrons or on interlibrary loan.

8. County Heritage Books

A modern version of the mug book is called a heritage book. Local history groups sponsor the publication by guaranteeing the publisher a certain amount of money. They gather family genealogies and money from contributors to get the books published. All publications that claim to be city or county histories cannot mention everyone who ever lived in the county. Prominent and wealthy citizens dominate the pages of these books.

County heritage books are a commemoration of county history, places, and of the families who have lived in the county. Local residents write articles and genealogies. The county heritage book is a compilation of these articles. Some are gold mines of family histories and genealogy. Other articles are nothing more than an ego trip for the writer. County historical and genealogical societies generally work together to complete the project. They solicit articles, photographs, and other materials. In the end, the gathered materials are compiled, edited, organized, indexed, and printed. Production of the books is usually underwritten by the historical or genealogical society that put it together. They get their money back by selling copies of the books to those who submitted articles and others who may be interested in the history and genealogy of the county.

Contributors tend to filter events to put a good face on the history of their family. Consequently, everything you read in a heritage book has to be weighed against other corroborating sources. A county heritage book can be a valuable resource as a tool to point you in the right direction, but you have to be skeptical about it accuracy.

One way to use a heritage book is to locate other family members that may have research to share. A few years ago I bought a county heritage book that had something about one of my family lines in it. A cousin, who I didn't know, had written a paragraph that connected to my great grandmother. I contacted him and he was able to give me information that helped me extend one of my lines back several generations.

You can expect to find unique details in a county heritage. Typically you will find the following sorts of information:

• Summary of the county's beginnings

• Information about local governments and key political figures from the past

• Photographs of old and new buildings

- Town histories and details of lost communities

- Church photographs and histories

- Histories of educational institutions and significant attendees and graduates

- History of industries and their influence in the area

- Individual and family historical and genealogical accounts

Librarians will undoubtedly be aware of the compilation and production of a county heritage book for their county. They should buy several copies in case one or more of them is lost or stolen. Researchers will want to look for county heritage books when they visit other libraries.

9. Genealogical Society Newsletters

Local genealogical societies publish their own newsletters. They contain the genealogies of their members. When you catalog these newsletters it would be helpful to enter the family names with the bibliographic record. Individuals searching the online catalog could then find the information in your library. About the only way to acquire genealogical society newsletters is to subscribe to them and receive them as they are published.

10. Centennial and Bicentennial Books

These books take a snapshot of the community at the time of publication. Centennial books usually have a brief history and lots of advertising and articles about local businesses and current residents. Some include pictures with captions of families. You have to buy them fresh off of the press or lose the chance to own a copy forever, with rare exceptions.

11. County Marriage Books

Sometimes individuals will transcribe and compile marriage records found in the courthouse. I don't know if anyone has ever made much money from compiling and publishing a county marriage book, but they deserve high praise for their efforts. Librarians will know if their county has a published marriage book, because the library is a primary customer for this kind of publication.

12. Local Church Histories

Histories of local congregations are most widespread in colonial states, where some churches have been around for over 200 years. Local church histories are not as common in western states, but they may be just as valuable. When European immigrants settled in the Midwest and Plains, they brought their religions with them along with their traditions for keeping family records in the church. It is not uncommon to find church histories in Kansas that read like family genealogies. Local congregations often published a history of their congregation on a special anniversary date, such as their jubilee or centennial celebrations.

Locating local church histories can be tricky. Start with the church itself if it is still active. The current minister may have a copy of the published history. Individual members might have copies, but they may not be willing to give them up. In that case, ask them to let you copy it. There is no general bibliography for local church histories and even the Family History Library does not have a comprehensive collection of these works. The best thing librarians can do is to accept every published church history that is offered and be vigilant when copies are offered for sale and ask for a free copy for the library.

13. Federal and State Census on Microfilm

Regardless of how big or small your umbrella is your library should have microfilm copies of every state and federal census available for the county. These are primary source documents and contain valuable information for genealogists. The library may be the only place in the county the public has access to these records. Even though images of census records are becoming available on the Internet through Ancestry and HeritageQuest, you still need to have the microfilm. In Chapter 9 we discuss census records more thoroughly.

14. Family Histories

Family histories may contain the family information that is not available anywhere else. Histories of local families are prized acquisitions. Histories of families not connected to local families may be interesting, but not essential to a local collection. Typically, family histories include more biographical than genealogical information. Some publications will include both.

Genealogists like to have access to family histories, because they are rich with the kind of data for which they are looking. But, because family histories are normally compiled sources, they can be as problematic as they are helpful. While they contain much correct factual genealogical data, the information in family histories needs to be verified by other researchers.

Librarians will be lucky to acquire a few family histories relating to local families. You will find most family histories in the collections of other facilities. Start with the surname section of the Family History Library catalog. Additional family histories can be identified in the Library of Congress and the *American Genealogical-Biographical Index*.

15. Family, School, or Military Reunions

If a reunion is held in your town try to get a copy of the directory the organizers created to invite participants. If some of the people are old you will at least have the last known address for these people. Sometimes reunion organizers will prepare a photocopied book consisting of brief family or personal history since the individual left school or the military. Published reunion materials may not be accurate or complete but they may be the only clue available about some individuals.

If you hear of someone gathering information for a class reunion, ask for a copy of the director y of class members they have found, plus a list of those who have passed away. This is the kind of information you will not find in other sources and it could be priceless to the right researcher.

Using the List

For the above list of local materials, simply finding out what is available may be your biggest challenge. Some of the best genealogy books are written and published by dedicated people who want to make the fruits of their research available to others. Many authors and compilers end up self-publishing and marketing their own books, and for the librarian, finding self-published books is more difficult. Authors or self-publishers tend to lack marketing skills and the money to advertise broadly. You may be lucky enough to be personally acquainted with the people who are producing local histories.

Finding the Funding for the Genealogy Collection

Several librarians I know have kept careful statistics of the researchers whom have come from out of town to do research in their libraries. They ask everyone who uses the genealogy collection to register, asking what city they live in. The librarians also conducted a survey to estimate the value in tourism dollars the genealogy library had generated for the business community. They asked questions like:

How long did you stay in our city?

How many people were in your party?

What kinds of services, other than the library, did you avail yourself of?

How much do you estimate you spent on this trip?

Do you plan to return within the next year?

The survey enabled them to calculate the economic benefit to the community generated by genealogy researchers. Armed with solid data, they approached funding agencies and asked for the money they needed to continue offering good service to genealogical researchers.

Even more important than leveraging tourism created by the genealogy department is making sure the department gets its share of the annual funding the library receives through regular channels. In my book, *Fundraising for Libraries: 25 Proven Ways to Get More Money for Your Library* (Swan, 2002), I introduce the idea of keeping two lists.

On one side of a page make a list of key individuals, who control the library's budget. On the other side of the page make a list of all the people who use the resources of the genealogy library. How do the lists match? How influential are the people on the user list? Do they have pull with the board? Do they have pull with the library director? If not, look for ways to merge both lists. As the director of the Great Bend Public Library, I am the first one to admit that my avid interest in genealogy has helped the allocation of funds for the genealogy collection.

Beyond these two suggestions, I also recommend that you buy a few books on fundraising and grant writing, and look for some grants to help you develop the genealogy collection. See the bibliography at the end of this chapter.

Preserving Genealogical Materials

When a librarian spends extra effort and good money to collect and organize materials for the genealogical collection, it stands to reason that he or she will want to preserve the materials in usable condition. Unfortunately, materials wear out when we use them. Some of the logical perils include:

- mutilation (pages or picture ripped or cut out);

- vandalism (writing in books);

- deterioration because of poor-quality originals;

- deterioration due to age;

- damage from normal regular use;

- theft (disappearing from the shelves);

- theft (keeping/losing materials that have been checked out); and

- obsolescence of equipment used to read preserved material.

What we do to prevent these losses to our collections depends on the level of risk, how replaceable the items are, and the cost of preservation. If you have some bound newspapers from the 1800s, they are irreplaceable, but they could be available on microfilm. So, there is no need to put them under lock and key. High school yearbooks are another story—especially the older ones. You probably cannot replace them. I know of schools that do not even keep a copy of their own yearbooks. They are also at risk. One person with a razor blade can ruin one book in a matter of seconds. Keep your yearbooks in a locked case and restrict there use to a place in the library were a staff member can keep an eye on them.

Here are a few things librarians can do to protect and preserve their genealogy collection:

- Buy multiple copies of at-risk materials when you have the opportunity.

- Lock up the materials that are most at risk and irreplaceable.

- Check materials that have been circulated for condition before putting them back on the shelf. Repair damaged materials before reshelving them.

- Encourage staff and patrons to handle materials carefully.

- Improve the temperature and humidity conditions for storing materials.

- Photocopy one-of-a-kind items and bind them as a book if you can do it legally, or obtain permission to do so from the copyright holder.

- Put fragile materials in an archive storage box. This will lessen the wear and tear on the item.

- Require patrons to have and show their identification to gain access to these materials.

- Microfilm materials with brittle paper. This is a good option, because it will last several hundred years and additional copies can be made from the preservation negative.

- Put rare or fragile individual pages in acid free sleeves to preserve them.

- Digitized materials if they have sufficient intrinsic value to ensure ongoing use. No one can assure long-term access to digital resources; therefore, digital images cannot serve to replace original materials. Who remembers opaque "micro-cards."

- Organize and maintain a disaster response team to deal with floods and other crises.

This is not an exhaustive discussion on preserving library materials, but here are a few preservation activities librarians can use to maintain their collections for as long as possible. For more information on library material preservation see these sources:

Preservation of Library and Archival Materials: A Manual, by Sherelyn Ogden (Ogden, 1999);

Preservation: Issues and Planning, edited by Paul N. Banks and Roberta Pilette (Banks and Pilette, 2000);

Guidelines for Preservation, Conservation, and Restoration of Local History and Local Genealogical Materials (Available: www.ala.org/Content/NavigationMenu/RUSA/Professional_Tools4/ Reference_Guidelines/Guidelines_for_Preservation,_Conservation,_and_Restoration_of_ Local_History_and_Local_Genealogical_M.htm);

Check out the "Preservation Guidelines and Resources" at the Librarians Serving Genealogists Web site (Available: www.cas.usf.edu/lis/genealib/colldev.html), which has links to various preservation statements from the American Library Association (ALA), the Library of Congress, and the National Archives and Records Administration (NARA).

What Materials Should You Loan?

Some libraries have a policy that prohibits loaning anything from the genealogy collections. They really need to examine their collection and their policy to determine if they can risk loaning any of their genealogical materials. Reciprocal lending policies benefit all libraries. Here are a few resources that libraries need to consider lending on interlibrary loan:

- Extra copies of county histories

- Materials that can be replaced

- Microfilm copies of newspapers

- Materials in the circulating collection

What Materials Do You Put Under Lock and Key?

Some items should never leave the special collections room let alone the library. Here is my short list of materials that should be kept under lock and key.

- One-of-a-kind items

- High school yearbooks

- College annuals

- Diaries and journals

- Fragile first editions

- Irreplaceable items

Other Local Agencies and Resources

The first level of resources outside your library is the community. These resources include the courthouse, cemeteries, mortuaries, historical societies, newspapers, etc. You may be able to influence patron access to the information in these agencies by your involvement with the people who run them. If you have regular contact with them, your patrons may have an easier time getting information from them. You will know what they will find, if you go to the courthouse yourself and ask the same kinds of questions that they will ask.

Helping researchers find the genealogical resources within the community is just as critical to good service as having resources in the library. When I think of resources outside the Great Bend Public Library, the first places I think of are the courthouse and the local Family History Center. I also think of the manager of the local cemetery and the historical and genealogical society. You can probably come up with a list for your own community, and you should.

Creating a Handout

Try writing a one-page handout about other places that may have genealogical information. Include the organization's name, contact person's name, the address, telephone number, the hours of service, and a brief description of what researchers can expect to find or how to use the service. You can pave the way for them by establishing a relationship with the staff in some of these places. Find out what type of information they have and are willing to share. Tell them that you may be sending some genealogists to them from time to time. Only refer patrons who have questions you think the people in these other agencies can answer.

Here are a few places you might want to include on your list:

- Courthouse

- LDS Family History Center

- Funeral homes

- Newspaper offices

- Historical societies

- Churches (especially old ones)

- Local archives

- Bookstores

- Local professional genealogists

- Local historians

You may not have the county courthouse in your town. Mention it anyway. It is probably within easy driving distance. You may want to include selected businesses, especially mortuaries, in other nearby communities. You may be fortunate enough to have an agency like the State Historical Society nearby. Put them on the list. Do not underestimate the potential value for genealogical research of long-time residents of the area. They can sometimes provide clues to the past that can help genealogists. If cemetery records for your county have been put on the Internet, include the URL address for the Web page.

Reaching Beyond Local Materials

Once you get past local resources you need to think about what kinds of other materials will help your patrons. If your library is large enough you may be able to collect some of the research tools that cover the state or specific regions of the United States. These resources might include all of the federal census films for your state from 1790 to 1930; or the microfilms of major newspapers in your state. If you have a significant number of researchers with a specific ethnic background you may want to develop your collection along those lines.

Many of the people who live in our part of Kansas have ancestors from Germany, some of whom lived in Russia for a few generations. We also have researchers with Native American ancestors. To meet the needs of these customers we have collected passenger lists from Germany and the Dawes Rolls. If we listen, our patrons will tell us what they need.

So many genealogy guidebooks, similar to this very book, assume that the library is starting from scratch in developing a genealogical collection. That is probably not the case. Your library may already have many of the resources listed in this book. Go to Part III, Tool Kit 2, or the CD-ROM, for a list of all the resources we refer to in this book. You can check them off and feel good that you already own them. It will help you to identify where you want to add more resource materials.

Significant Resources

Certain significant resources need to be in all but the smallest genealogy collections. Below, I mention a few by category for your consideration.

Guidebooks

Family History Research Outlines—State-by-State

Each research outline offers research strategies for a specific state. The outlines also list major genealogical records available for specific geographical areas. They are available through FamilySearch.org at $2.50 per outline. To purchase them, click on "Order/Download Products," at www.familysearch.org. For the price every library ought to have a set for reference and one that patrons can check out.

The Researcher's Guide to American Genealogy, 3rd ed., by Val D. Greenwood, (Greenwood, 2000)is the standard text for genealogical research. It gives you enough detail to give you the help you need without giving up essential coverage. The third edition gives more complete coverage to computers and how technology has impacted the business of genealogical research. The new edition belongs in every library and on every researcher's bookshelf.

Military Histories

The War of the Rebellion: A Compilation of the Official Records of the Union and Confederate Armies, U.S. Department of War, 1901, is one of the most complete histories of the Civil War. This 128-volume set provides the most comprehensive, authoritative, and voluminous reference on civil war operations. Researchers can find it in many public and university libraries. You can also purchase it from out-of-print dealers, or find it online at the E-history Web site (Available: www.ehistory .com/uscw/library/or/index.cfm). This resource is also available on CD-ROM.

Suggestions for Helping Genealogists

1. Establish a policy for genealogy services and collection development.
2. Make a handout that identifies local cemeteries on a map of your county.
3. Organize volunteers to abstract or clip obituaries from your local newspaper.
4. Visit your county courthouse to see what vital records they have and learn how to gain access to them.
5. Buy a microfilm copy of every newspaper published in your county.
6. Visit with the people in local historical or genealogical societies.
7. Develop your own criteria for selecting genealogical materials.
8. Compare your collection to the "Must-Buy List."

Summary

Most libraries have a general materials selection policy. It should apply to the selection of materials for the genealogical collection, as well. Better yet, it should contain a special section for local history and genealogy, which should include collecting and preserving all available materials on local history. Some books that would be rejected for other parts of the collection, because of format, binding, appearance, or content, may be welcomed into the local history and genealogical collection because they are the only books available on the topic. There may be only one or two extant histories of your county. If another one is produced, you shouldn't reject it because it doesn't have an index, is produced by a photocopier, or has a plastic comb binding. So if it is local history; keep it, regardless of its condition. Never weed a local history/genealogy book from the library. Even if it falls apart, put it in a plastic bag and keep it.

Bibliography (Ratings Guide explanation follows last citation)

Banks, Paul N., and Roberta Pilette, eds. 2000. *Preservation: Issues and Planning*. Chicago: American Library Association.

Various experts in the field of preservation have contributed to this handbook. It covers topics like selection for preservation, preservation microfilming and photocopying, special collections conservation, digitization for preservation and access, and defining the library preservation program. Any library that is serious about preservation will have this book. **LLL**

Brewer, Ernest W. 1995. *Finding Funding: Grantwriting and Project Management from Start to Finish*. 2nd ed. Thousand Oaks, CA: Corwin Press.

This is a powerful book on applying for federal funding. It explains the components of a proposal, how it is reviewed, how it is implemented. **LLL**

Greenwood, Val D. 2000. *The Researcher's Guide to American Genealogy*. Baltimore, MD: Genealogical Publishing Company.

The author keeps this excellent textbook from being dry and boring by interjecting anecdotal material and personal accounts. This is probably the very best genealogy guidebook available. **PPP**

Hall-Ellis, Sylvia D., and Frank W. Hoffman. 1999. *Grantsmanship for Small Libraries and School Library Media Centers*. Englewood, CO: Libraries Unlimited.

Almost every librarian has faced the daunting task of writing a grant to get more money for his or her library. This book can lower the anxiety level for anyone who has to write a grant. The chapters take the grant writer through the process one step at a time. **LLL**

Melnyk, Marcia Yannizze. 2000. *The Weekend Genealogist: Timesaving Techniques for Effective Research*. Cincinnati, OH: Betterway Books.

This book is for the new genealogists with little time for research. The author talks about the blessings of tapping relatives for family information. She discusses the Internet along with ideas for using and assessing the value of electronic sources. She shares some timesaving methods she has used. Every researcher and librarian should read the chapter dealing with research etiquette. **PPP**

Melnyk, Marcia Yannizze. 2002. *The Genealogist's Question and Answer Book: Solutions and Advice for Maximizing Your Research Results*. Cincinnati, OH: Newton Abbot-Betterway.

With answers to more than 250 questions about genealogy methodology and inquiry, this book belongs at every library reference desk. The author cuts through the plethora of genealogical sources and gets us to the good stuff right away. **PPP**

Ogden, Sherelyn. 1999. *Preservation of Library and Archival Material: A Manual*. Andover, MA: Northeast Document Conservation Center.

This work is the bible for anyone who wants to preserve a library collection, but lacks expertise. First published in 1992 this loose-leaf formatted manual has experienced several incarnations. This most recent edition reflects new approaches to an age-old problem—preserving library materials. **LLL**

Swan, James. 2002. *Fundraising for Libraries: 25 Proven Ways to Get More Money for Your Library*. New York: Neal-Schuman.

I wrote this book to help librarians who need to improve their funding. It has lots of ideas for anyone who is looking for fundraising projects and how to make them happen. **LLL**

Ratings Guide

The ratings for each bibliography describe not only what each resource contains, but also how it might fit into the library collection. Some of the materials are more appropriate for larger libraries with substantial budgets, and others belong in collections of any size—even in the personal research collection. To help you identify materials most appropriate for your collection, each resource is marked as either "L" for libraries and "P" for personal. They are ranked from one letter for recommended, two letters for preferred, and three letters for essential.

CHAPTER 3

DEFINING THE TECHNOLOGICAL TASK

Technology and the Internet have forever altered the way we do genealogy. The way libraries deliver all kinds of information has changed, too. I remember the day FamilySearch.org went online. The Web site was so busy that some researchers could not access the site. Other online genealogy services were proceeding cautiously, though some visionaries knew what they were doing. Even though slow responses to their Web sites frustrated customers, they stayed the course and survived. I recently heard that genealogy research accounts for the second highest traffic on the Internet. I am not sure how accurate the statement is, but I know that thousands of organizations are spending millions of dollars to make genealogical data available on the Internet.

What to Look for in This Chapter

Chapter 3 considers some options and makes recommendations for librarians who take seriously access to all forms of genealogical resources. Just as we suggested a collection development policy in Chapter 2, we suggest that those in charge of the library decide how much technology the library will make available for genealogical research.

Getting the Hardware

Initially, you cannot expect every genealogist to have his or her own computer with access to the Internet at home. Eventually, though, most researchers will realize how indispensable a computer can be and purchase their own. In the meantime libraries should do what they can to provide public access computing for all of its patrons, including genealogists. You can also do fundraising, look for gifts, and write some grants to get the money you need to have enough computers in the genealogy department.

"Should the library designate a separate computer or several computers just for genealogical research?" My answer is, "Yes, and make sure each computer also has access to the Internet." The information needs of genealogists and the time requirements for research are sufficiently different from the needs of other patrons to warrant designating at least one computer exclusively for genealogical research. Internet access on the genealogy computer will also permit the researcher to e-mail data to his or her home computer.

Should the genealogy computer have its own printer? I think so. While using a single printer for a network of public access computers seems logical, it is just as reasonable to have a dedicated printer for the genealogy computer. The person sitting at the genealogy computer may need to change printer functions or print out long documents. Having a dedicated printer will avoid disrupting service to other patrons.

So many indexes and databases are primarily available on CD-ROM that a CD drive is essential to a genealogy computer. While I fully expect to see exponential growth in online resources for genealogical research, genealogy products on CD-ROM will be with us for some time to come. In fact, I recommend a CD-ROM tower or a multiple-disk changer that will let the computer access several CDs without changing them.

Most librarians do not like patrons messing with the library's hard drives, so the genealogy computer needs a high capacity disk drive like a CD-burner or a Zip drive. Standard floppy disks lack the capacity to download all but the smallest graphics or databases. Since both types of drives are currently used by lots of people, it may be necessary to have both types of drives in the computer. You should also have blank disks for each type of drive for sale at the library.

A flatbed scanner makes a nice addition to the configured genealogy computer. Patrons might find noncirculating print materials that have information or graphics they want to copy. Patrons will appreciate having a scanner connected to the genealogy computer.

Because of its cost a microfilm reader/printer used to be the unreachable fantasy acquisition of many small libraries—they just couldn't afford one. Today's digital reader/scanner/printers are even more expensive. But they make it possible to find an obituary or some other piece of data on a microfilm, scan it as an image, and e-mail it to the researcher's own e-mail account, or someone else's. If you do not already have this technology in your library it is worth considering. Maybe you can find someone to help pay for it.

Selecting the Software

Genealogists who are deciding which genealogy software programs to put on their computers will find it helpful if the library has several different programs on the genealogy computer for them to test before they buy. I recommend that the library have Personal Ancestral File, Family Tree Maker and two or three others—one more free or shareware version and others that seem to be popular in your area. Don't bother with demos or shareware versions. Spend the money and do it right. (I review available genealogy software in Chapter 11.)

Assessing CD-ROM Technology

Although its popularity seems to be waning, CD-ROM technology will not completely disappear in the near term, because of its stability as a storage medium. In the earlier days of CD-ROM technology, limited hard drive capacity made them very attractive. In fact, many products that required extremely large amounts of storage, like encyclopedias or very large databases like the International Genealogical Index, were ideally suited for CD-ROM production, but they were and still are cumbersome to use.

Different CD-ROM products require different software programs to run them. Software takes up disk space and is often not compatible with available hardware. Librarians need to check out the operating systems before buying a new CD-ROM product.

Some genealogical publishing companies have been commercially successful, because they placed their genealogical databases on CD-ROMs. Family Tree Maker, produced several databases on CD entitled *Family Archives*. They are reasonably priced for individuals or libraries. Eventually though, I expect to see online services take the place of CDs, for all but the largest static monographs.

These are a few of the CD-ROMs I would buy and make available on the genealogy computer.

AniMap

AniMap by the Gold Bug (Available: www.goldbug.com/AniMap.html). The map CD contains both AniMap and SiteFinder. AniMap Plus is an essential tool for any genealogist doing research in the United States. AniMap shows a map of each of the 48 adjacent states with county boundary changes from colonial times to the present. Use SiteFinder to locate any of hundreds of thousands of cities, cemeteries or historical sites, then plot them on the appropriate state maps of AniMap. Pick a year and see which county that site was located in at that time. Armed with this information, researchers can visit the correct county records repository to find information on their ancestors.

The Great Migration Begins: Immigrants to New England

Millions of American can trace their ancestry through the American colonies—especially New England. The purpose of this comprehensive resource is to provide concise, reliable information from past research on early immigrants to New England. It includes genealogical data for over 1,000 seventeenth-century immigrants to America. This remarkable resource is available on CD-ROM; also available in book form.

Individual sketches include origin of the subject, date of migration, and first New England residence. It also includes biographical data, birth, marriage, and death information for the family and descendants.

This data has been gathered from:

- passenger lists,

- lists of freemen,

- court, town, and land records,

- church and vital records, and

- journals and letters.

Freedman's Bank Records

The Freedman's Savings and Trust Company served former slaves from 1865 to 1871. The records of the bank continue to provide a source of genealogical research. The records, which were only available on several microfilms, are now available in a searchable database on CD-ROM. Searching for connections among 480,000 names of depositors is now an easy task. This resource is a true blessing to African American researchers. It is available through FamilySearch.org.

The African American Newspapers: The 19th Century CD-ROM

This collection is a gold mine of information for those who are researching the culture and history of African Americans in the 1800s. It contains about 90,000 records and over 50 million words. It also has many early biographies and vital statistics. The set is available on CD-ROM.

English Parish Records CD Collection (26 CD-ROMs)

Ancestry.com has published a set of 26 CDs covering records from 1538 to 1837 for English, Scottish, and some Irish parishes. While not totally inclusive of all records for all parishes for the period, the CDs are extremely useful to anyone who needs to find his or her ancestors in the British Isles for this period. Check with Ancestry.com for coverage.

Slave Narratives CD

This work is rich with the stories of African American life during the colonial period. It contains first hand accounts of over 2,000 slaves. The Works Progress Administration compiled these personal stories between 1936 and 1938. The CD-ROM is available from Ancestry.com.

Indexes

Pedigree Resource File

The Pedigree Resource File is compiled from linked pedigrees submitted by individuals who want to share their research. The online version is only an index. The complete file is stored on CD-ROMs and is available for purchase through FamilySearch.org. See Chapter 10.

PERSI Periodical Source Index 2003

The *PERSI Periodical Source Index 2003*, compiled by the Allen County Public Library, is the largest index of genealogical and historical periodical articles in the world. Every library that offers genealogical research materials should have access to this index—if not online access, then on CD-ROM. See Chapter 10.

Online Requests for Lookups

Books We Own (*Available:* www.rootsweb.com/~bwo)

This is a look-up resource for genealogical research. It lists resources owned by individuals who are willing to look up genealogical information and e-mail or snail mail it to others who request it. Operated by over 1,500 volunteers, who may request reimbursement for the cost of postage and copies.

Books and Publishing

Genealogical Publishing Company (*Available:* www.genealogical.com)

This is the electronic home of Genealogical Publishing Company, the largest commercial publisher of genealogical reference books, textbooks, and how-to books in the world. GPC and their subsidiaries have published more than 5,000 titles in genealogy and related fields.

Higginson Book Company (*Available:* www.higginsonbooks.com)

Higginson Book Company is a major reprinter of genealogies and local histories. This could be a good source for materials that are unavailable from other sources.

UMI Research Collections (*Available:* www.il.proquest.com/research)

UMI's Genealogy program provides a unique, ongoing collection of research materials for tracing family lineages, beginning with the thirteen original colonies. This extensive microfiche collection can meet the needs of all genealogists—amateurs and professionals alike. It gives them access to documents that might otherwise be inaccessible. For the benefit of individuals, titles from the first 30 units are available for single-title sale.

Online Databases with Free Patron Access

On the genealogy computer we need to create a page with quick links to the online databases that are free to individuals. Here is my top-10 list.

1. FamilySearch (Available: www.familysearch.org)
2. Worldconnect (Available: www.worldconnect.rootsweb.com)
3. RootsWeb (Available: www.rootsweb.org)
4. Cyndi's List (Available: www.cyndislists.com)
5. Social Security Death Index (Available: http://ssdi.genealogy.rootweb.com/cgi-bin/ssdi.cgi)
6. USGenWeb Project (Available: www.usgenweb.com)
7. Bureau of Land Management General Land Office Records (Available: www.glorecords.blm.gov)
8. Vital Records (Available: www.vitalrec.com)
9. RootsWeb Surname List (Available: www.vitalrec.com)
10. WWW Genealogical Index (Available: http://gendex.com/gendex)

Online Subscriptions for Patron Use

Pedigree databases can be some of the most fruitful places to search on the Internet. Albeit the data they contain is only as good as the researcher who uploaded the information and needs to be verified. Some researchers are very careful and provide extensive notes and sources that can be verified. Other researchers will piece together a pedigree from a variety of Web sites without even a hint of documentation.

HeritageQuest Online (*Available:* www.heritagequestonline.com)

This is a remarkable service offered to libraries for their patrons. It is not free, but licensing fees are not prohibitive for medium to large public libraries. Many state libraries offer this service to library patrons statewide. Content is growing every day.

From their own homes or libraries, beginning or professional researchers can access the images of millions of pages from census records and books with known genealogical content. The online collection of more than 25,000 genealogy and local history books provides unique access to researchers. The powerful search engine searches every word in every book and returns a list of hits. When researchers find significant content, they can easily download or copy the pages they find. Currently this collection consists of over 8,000 family histories, 12,000 local histories, and 250+ primary sources.

The U.S. Federal Census, 1790–1930 is the easiest to use of all census images on the Web. HeritageQuest has created all of the indexes to the censuses. Researchers have the ability to search by name, place of birth, ethnicity, and age. The search engine returns a list of individuals with their ages and the state of the census. You do not have to bring up every name if you know more or less when your ancestor was born. Access to the images is seamless, and the individual pages are easy to navigate.

In the future ProQuest/HeritageQuest plans to include newspaper obituaries, Revolutionary War pension and bounty land warrant application files, and the Freedman's Bank Records.

AncestyPlus

Thomson-Gale markets AncestryPlus to libraries on a subscription basis. It a companion site to Ancestry.com that is available by subscription to individuals. Though most of the databases are identical, some like historic newspapers are unique to Ancestry.com—supposedly to encourage personal memberships to Ancestry.com. Both sites include federal census images and indexes, the Social Security Death Index, American marriages before 1699, the Civil War Pension Index, and Revolutionary War Pension Index. Other unique online databases include Slave Narratives, Australian Convict index, 1788–1868, passengers and immigration Lists, and the Great Migration Index.

Best of all, both sites offer access to the Ancestry World Tree, which has almost 300,000 names. It is the largest database of its kind on the Internet. AncestryPlus also features Ancestry.com Research Registry, which allows researchers to share information.

The powerful search engine retrieves hits from all of the databases on the Ancestry site and presents a list of sources where the possible hits have occurred. While the researcher starts by entering a first name, a last name, and a location, the Ancestry World Tree lets the researcher refine the search at the end of the first page of hits. Generally a spouse of a father will narrow the search sufficiently to turn up any matches in the database.

From a personal standpoint, I like the user interfaces for the census images and the census indexes better on HeritageQuest Online than on AncestryPlus. They seem easier to use and more reliable.

Thomson-Gale bases its pricing structure for AncestryPlus on the number of simultaneous users. Licensing fees are within the budget capability of all but the smallest of libraries. We have a subscription for the Great Bend Public Library.

ProQuest Historical Newspapers

ProQuest's collection of historical newspapers includes digital reproductions of every page of every issue (Available: www.umi.com/products/pt-product-HistNews.shtml).

They have already completed the *New York Times*, the *Wall Street Journal*, the *Washington Post*, and the *Christian Science Monitor*. The *Los Angeles Times* and the *Chicago Tribune* are currently being digitized.

ProQuest uses the Portable Document Format (PDF) format by Adobe. Coverage for the newspapers that are currently available is from 1851 to 2001. (See their Web site for details.)

Genealogical researchers can use the database to find obituaries, birth announcements, and marriage announcements. The date-range searching tool lets researchers search on a specific date, before a specific date, or between two dates. Researchers can display the complete image of any page in any issue or browse the database and scan individual issues page by page.

Accessible Archives

This group started in 1990 with the purpose of making archival historical information available in an electronic format. Accessible Archives (Available: www.accessible.com/default.htm) has found the most significant primary source documents and digitized them for publication on the Internet. Their online full text search capability and digital imaging lets users search and manipulate information is some unusual ways. The databases are complete and allow full Boolean, group name, string, and truncated searches.

The current offerings include the following:

- *Godey's Lady's Book, 1830 to 1880*. Today this magazine is considered among the most important resources of nineteenth-century American life and culture.

- *The Pennsylvania Gazette 1728–1800*. Published in Philadelphia from 1728 through 1800, this periodical provides researchers with a first hand view of colonial America, the American Revolution, and the New Republic.

- *The Civil War: A Newspaper Perspective*. This database contains the full text of major articles gleaned from over 2,500 issues of *The New York Herald*, *The Charleston Mercury*, and the *Richmond Enquirer*, published between November 1, 1860 and April 15, 1865.

- *African American Newspapers*. This database has wealth of information about the cultural life and history during the 1800s, and is rich with first-hand reports.

- *American County Histories to 1900*. The full-text search ability, will permit the student/researcher to instantly explore all the publications of a particular county by using a single query. For genealogical researchers, this single database could be worth the price of the subscription.

- *The Pennsylvania Genealogical Catalogue*. This database is primarily a listing of marriages, deaths and obituaries from the *Village Record*, published in West Chester, Pennsylvania. 1809–1870

- *The Pennsylvania Newspaper Record.* This database documents the industrialization of predominantly agrarian culture established by Quaker farmers in the eighteenth century. It contains full-text transcriptions of articles and vital statistics.

African American Biographical Database (*Available:* http://aabd.chadwyck.com/infopage/feature.htm)

Biographies of African Americans that may not be found in any other source may be found in this resource. The *African American Biographical Database* (AABD) features the biographies of thousands of African Americans. The search engine allows researchers to retrieve several levels of information through searches of nine combinable fields. From the results page researchers can link to full-text narratives and photographic images.

Otherdays.com (*Available:* www.otherdays.com/homepage/default.asp)

This is a premier site for Irish research. The people at Otherdays.com believe that genealogy is much more than a list of names and dates on a family tree. Genealogy is an exploration of the landscape, lifestyle, and culture of our ancestors. The purpose of this site is to provide online access to primary sources relating to the history, culture, and genealogy of Ireland.

Featured databases at Otherdays.com include:

- *Griffith's Valuation 1847–1864.* The most used and useful of Irish genealogical sources, this database consists of a comprehensive listing of persons who rented land or property and from whom they rented in Ireland between 1847 and 1864.

- *Ordinance Survey 1824–1846.* This database includes detailed maps of Ireland for the period. These maps display the county, barony, parish, and townland boundaries. They are sufficiently detailed to allow identification of individual houses and other structures.

- Wills and Marriage Licenses, Dublin Diocese 1270–1857. The index of Wills, Marriage Licenses, Administrations, and Probates for the dioceses of Dublin from 1270 to 1857 has almost 500,000 names. This makes it one of the most significant Irish genealogical sources to become available online.

- Surname Reports. This is a must have product for those who trace their Irish ancestry, but are uncertain of their ancestor's county or parish of origin.

  This site also includes directories, cemetery listings and lists of clergy.

Biography and Genealogy Master Index (BGM)

The *Biography and Genealogy Master Index (BGM)* (Detroit: Gale Research, 1975–) is the major index to biographical sketches in printed works. The series features accumulations for a range of years with annual update volumes. *BGMI* is available in printed, microfiche, and electronic (CD-ROM or online) formats. It indexes more than 8 million names in current and retrospective biographical dictionaries, such as *Who's Who in America, Who's Who in Canada, Who's Who in the World,* and *The Dictionary of National Biography* (Great Britain). Most of the works indexed deal with individuals in the United States. *BGMI* does not index periodicals or books of biography about a unique individual only. *BGMI* and the biographical dictionaries it indexes are available at major research libraries. The online database is available through the Gale Group (Available: http://galenet.gale.com). Contact them for licensing information.

Reference USA Residential Database

The *Reference USA Residential Database* lists more than 120 million households in the United States. Contact the Gale Group (Available: www.galegroup.com/macmillan/about.htm) for subscription information.

America's Obituaries and Death Notices

America's Obituaries and Death Notices is a collection of obituaries and death notices in newspapers offered by NewsBank (Available: www.newsbank.com). The user-friendly search engine makes it easy to search by the name of the deceased, date range or text, such as residence, occupation, hobbies, or family members found in the death notice.

Digital Sanborn Maps, 1867–1970

Digital Sanborn Maps, 1867–1970 licensed by ProQuest Information and Learning (Available: http://sanborn.umi.com/HelpFiles/about.html) offers academic and public libraries digital access to more than 660,000 large-scale maps of 12,000 American towns. Users can manipulate the maps, magnify and zoom in on specific sections, and layer maps from different years.

NewEnglandAncestors.org

For an institutional membership fee libraries can have access to NewEnglandAncestors.org, which includes full text access to the *New England Historical and Genealogical Register, 1847–1994* and several other full text New England historical resources. Libraries, genealogical or historical societies can have multiple Internet users at single URL location. Contact the New England Historical and Genealogical Society (Available: www.newenglandancestors.org/rs1).

GRC National Index (*Available:* http://members.dar.org/dar/darnet/grc/grc.cfm)

This database indexes the records of Daughters of the American Revolution. For a fee, members and nonmembers can request copies of documents associated with proofs of their ancestor's participation in the Revolutionary War.

Other Internet Sources on Local History and Genealogy (*Available:* www.loc.gov/rr/genealogy/other.html)

This page has links to several of the most popular and productive genealogical research Web sites. It includes online library catalogs and archival and historical databases.

Local Cemetery Records Online

If local cemetery records are not online, the library staff could decide to recruit volunteers and take on the project. Make sure nobody else is engaged in a similar project. You do not want a turf battle with someone who has spent time and effort doing the work you plan to do.

Recently, newspapers are uploading current obituaries, but they don't usually go back more than five or ten years. Volunteers at the library could abstract older obituaries and put them online. The effort will require an HTML program and someone who knows how to create Web pages.

The librarian in Kanopolis, Kansas, compiled a paper copy of the graves in the local cemetery. I volunteered to create Web pages for the cemetery listing and put it on the Internet. I also created a map of the cemetery, so people could find the graves of their family members. About six months after we uploaded to pages, the librarian got a very nice letter from someone who had been stymied in her research until she found her ancestor in the cemetery listing. After finding the page she was able to take her genealogy back another seven generations.

Cataloging Local Obituaries

The Godfrey Memorial Library in Middletown, Connecticut, enters obituaries into their catalog and on OCLC from materials in their collection, which makes them bibliographically accessible from their online catalog and on OCLC. I see this as a way a library can use technology to help genealogists. Cataloging an obituary is like doing an analytic for one poem in a collection of poetry. The materials are in the library's collection so researchers could retrieve the obituary and read it in the library or a staff member could copy and send it to an out-of-town customer.

Tom Kemp from the Godfrey Memorial Library says, "Everything we catalog is in our collection so that our researchers can easily retrieve it. We catalog the obits that appear in professional journals. Journals like the *Transactions of the American Society of Chemical Engineers, Proceedings of the American Irish Historical Society*. We did experiment with cataloging the obits from area newspapers, but it was more than we could handle, so we've concentrated on just the professional journals for now. Other types of material for which we create analytics are the books of the 'war dead' published by various groups by companies, clubs or religious groups.

"Another strong category for us is clergy. Our catalog is filled with analytics for Baptists, Presbyterians, [and others]. These are both biographies and obituaries depending on the publications we used. These are very heavily used because we have a lot of researchers interested in finding Colonial clergy.

"I look for publications in our collection that researchers would never explore on their own, then create the analytics so researchers will find them easily in our catalog. By putting these obituaries in our online catalog anyone, anywhere can find the citation and use the resources of a library near them or by contacting us." [E-mail from Tom Kemp, 31 October 2003.]

Kathy Rippel of our reference staff recommends that librarians get involved with and use the Obituary Daily Times (Available: www.rootsweb.com/~obituary). Volunteers abstract obituaries from local newspapers and add them to the Web site. This is a good resource for finding obituaries for people who have died in the past few years.

Creating a Genealogy Web Page

Most libraries that offer resources to genealogical researchers will have a Web site for the library. It is a logical step for the person in charge of the genealogy collection to collaborate with the library's Webmaster to create one or more pages that spotlight the library's services to genealogists. The main purpose of the page is to help researchers who live outside the library's service area become aware of research potential at your library. Genealogy Web pages should include the following:

• A link from the main page for the library to the genealogy department's page (make sure that the words "Genealogy" or "Local History" or "Family Research" appear on the library's Home Page).

- A description of how out-of-county residents may request lookup services from the library (the Great Bend Public Library charges $5.00 to look up an obituary in a newspaper.)

- A list of unique resources that can only be found in your library like local newspapers and cemetery books

- A list of genealogical services in the county

- A list of electronic resources in the library CD-ROMs and local family databases

- Links to online genealogy databases available to local residents with instructions on how to access the service

- A link to the library's online catalog

- A cemetery map for the county

- Contact information to other community agencies that may have genealogy data

- Any genealogy classes offered by the library

- A page with links to the major free online genealogy databases

The genealogy Web pages will help local citizens, as well as people who live outside the area. If you decide to do a genealogy Web page, make sure researchers can get to your genealogy page from your library's main page.

HALINET Genealogy and Local History (Available: www.halinet.on.ca/library.lochist.htm) is a great example of what a local genealogy page can be. It has tons of online data from newspapers, birth records, death records, census records, court records, and just about any other type of document known to be genealogically significant. Check out this site if you are thinking about doing a local digitization project.

Suggestions for Librarians

1. Decide how large your technology umbrella will be when it comes to genealogy services.
2. Designate at least one public-access computer for the use of researchers doing genealogy.
3. Develop a policy for collection development of CD-ROMs and other software for the genealogy computer.
4. Try to meet the research needs of your local customers first. Just remember that not everyone in your town was born in your county, and may need research materials from other parts of the country or the world.
5. Review your budget for online database subscriptions to see if you can afford one or more online subscriptions.
6. Read *Internet Genealogy: What you can and cannot do*, by Jan McClintock (Available: www.leisterpro.com/doc/Articles/IntGen/InternetGenealogy.html). It has links to many sites that will point you in the right direction. You might even find a clue, a name, or a date of one of your ancestors.

Suggestions for Researchers

1. Check to see what electronic or computer genealogy services your library offers.
2. Recommend resources you need to the genealogy librarian.
3. Use the services the library offers.
4. Ask for genealogy classes at the library.

Summary

Every library has a level of responsibility to genealogical researchers and their technology needs. It is time for librarians to take seriously these responsibilities. In this chapter we offered some worthwhile options. You may have already implemented some of them. Some of the will be out of your library's financial reach. The rest may doable for you. Give these ideas some serious thought.

Technology for genealogical research will continue to expand and grow. Looking the other way and hoping the trend will go away will only leave your library behind in the future.

Bibliography (Ratings Guide explanation appears on page 26)

Crowe, Elizabeth Powell. 2001. *Genealogy Online.* New York: Osborne/McGraw-Hill.

This fully revised and updated edition explains how to begin and maintain a family history research project. It covers more than a hundred of the most useful genealogy Web sites. **L**

Howells, Cyndi. 2001. *Cyndi's List: A Comprehensive List of 70,000 Genealogy Sites on the Internet.* Baltimore, MD: Genealogical Publishing Company.

This is a monster of a book—16,652 pages worth. It is difficult to imagine a published book coming from the massive Web site known as Cyndi's List, but Cyndi Howells did it. The book includes links to every possible genealogical site on the Internet. They are categorized and cross-referenced into more than 140 categories. **PP**

Kemp, Thomas Jay. 2000. *The Genealogist's Virtual Library: Full-Text Books on the World Wide Web.* Wilmington, DE: Scholarly Resources.

This book is for anyone who wants to do his or her genealogy on the World Wide Web. Full-text books are becoming increasingly available and this book is a good guide to what you can find on the Internet. The book includes a CD-ROM that includes all of the links mentioned in the book. **LL**

Kemp, Thomas Jay. 2003. *Virtual Roots 2.0: A Guide to Genealogy and Local History on the World Wide Web.* Wilmington, DE: Scholarly Resources.

This book is essential to any researcher who uses the Internet to find his or her ancestors. The Web has changed the way we do genealogy. Virtual Roots 2.0 shows us just how much. This is an exhaustive directory of the top genealogy sites on the Internet. Surfing the Web without it is like finding information in a book without an index. **LL**

CHAPTER 4

IDENTIFYING AND ACCESSING MAJOR GENEALOGY REPOSITORIES

Every year hundreds of researchers come to the Great Bend Public Library to find out if we have anything that will help them. We do the best we can, but at some point in the research process we have to admit that local genealogical resources simply do not meet the needs of every researcher that comes to our library. It is time for us to look to other libraries and archives for our patrons.

What to Look for in This Chapter

In this chapter we identify major genealogical collections and tell you why they are mentioned in this book. Not every research facility can have every document every researcher needs. We will review other research facilities and tell you what they have and how to access the collection—even if it means paying someone to do the research.

The Process for Assessing Collections

Determining the Criteria for Inclusion

As I considered the libraries and archives to include in this chapter, I considered the following:

1. Bibliographic access to the collection: Do they have and online catalog?
2. Size of the genealogy collection: How many records of genealogical value do they have?
3. Uniqueness of the collection: Do they have records that no other library has?

4. Remote access to the information: How will researchers who live 1,000 miles away get access to the information? Do they have regional or local branches? Do they offer interlibrary loan for at least some of their collection? Do they offer in-house research services?

5. Not every genealogical research facility had to get a perfect score on all of these criteria to make the list, but they had to score high on one or more of the measurements.

Deciding What Information to Include

Making a decision about what to include requires a delicate balance. I want to include enough information to give researchers what they needed to know without overwhelming them with irrelevant material.

For each of the libraries listed I have included the following:

1. Contact information
2. Address for online catalog
3. Description of collection
4. On-site access to the collection
5. Remote access to the collection
6. Additional information or special services

Trimming the List

By the time all of the responses came back, I realized that I had more information than I could fit in this book. Besides that, there are already books on the market that list the libraries and archives and their addresses. If you want to find libraries with genealogical collections not included in this book, check out the *Genealogist's Address Book*, by Elizabeth Bentley (Bentley, 1999) or *America's Best Genealogy Resource Centers*, by Ronald Bremer and William Dollarhide (Bremer and Dollarhide, 1998).

Most Significant Libraries and Archives

For a library to be included in this chapter, it had to do more than just exist. Libraries that had very large or truly unique collections or offered some special service made the list, even if that service is only accessible through their online catalog.

1. The libraries and archives listed in this chapter are exceptional and should be considered first when researchers want to use facilities outside your library or community.

2. The library or archive had to have the quantity and quality of records that made their collection truly unique.

3. The facility needed to provide some sort of remote access. It could have been physically accessible to researchers from more than one location, for instance, regional centers or branches, like the Family History Library and its Family History Centers, or the National Archives and its regional centers. Or, the research facility needed to provide interlibrary loan or on-site research services.

4. The library had to have a catalog of its holdings that could be searched from a remote location like an online catalog available over the Internet.

This is not a top-ten list, but I have listed the libraries and archives, more or less, in the order I would recommend them to researchers.

The Family History Library

35 North West Temple Street
Salt Lake City, UT 84150-3400

Phone: 801-240-2331 or 800-453-3860, ext. 22331

Fax: 801-240-5551

E-mail: Available from Web page

Web site: www.familysearch.org

Online catalog: www.familysearch.org/Eng/Library/FHLC/frameset_fhlc.asp

Description of Collection

The Family History Library in Salt Lake City, Utah, is simply the biggest and best genealogical facility in the world. The collection covers the United State, Canada, the British Isles, Europe, Latin America, Asia, and Africa. Most records cover individuals who lived before 1920. Some 240+ cameras are currently microfilming records in over 40 countries.

On-Site Access

This library is open to the public for research, free of charge. The only costs associated with using the Family History Library are those of making copies and printouts.

Researchers who are planning to visit the FHL should consult the Family History Library Catalog, online at www.familysearch.org/Eng/Library/FHLC/frameset_fhlc.asp or the CD-ROM available for $6.00 through FamilySearch.org. The Family History Centers will also have the catalog on CD-ROM. Researchers will save research time if they print out a bibliography of materials they want to see before making the trip.

Access from a Distance

Family History Centers located in the United States and around the world are generally within an hour's drive for most researchers. For the cost of postage they can borrow microfilms listed in the Family History Library Catalog. Some other libraries have Family History Center status. Gaining such status doesn't happen automatically. The library director has to write a letter to the Family History Library and explain his or her reasons for being designated as a Family History Center. This is an opportunity worth exploring for local libraries.

Additional Information or Special Services: Microfilm Project

The Family History Library's primary purpose is to provide members of The Church of Jesus Christ of Latter-day Saints with access to information so they can trace their ancestry. About 40 years ago the Church started a coordinated plan to microfilm all available records in the United States. They started in the eastern United States and are moving west. They are now microfilming records in central Kansas.

Professional staff members and volunteers are in the library to help people develop search strategies and suggest additional resources. These professionals have been extensively trained and have years of experience. They are not there to do research for individuals, but they are very approachable and helpful. One clearly focused question from a researcher will help the professional staff member provide an answer that will give the patron a resource to check that could produce the desired result.

National Archives and Records Administration

700 Pennsylvania Avenue NW
Washington, DC 20408

Send mail to:
The National Archives and Records Administration
8601 Adelphi Road
College Park, MD 20740-6001

Phone: 866-272-6272

Fax: 301-837-0483

Web site: www.archives.gov/index.html

Online catalog: www.archives.gov/aad/index.html (to search the Access to Archival Databases [AAD] System); www.nara.gov/cgi-bin/starfinder/0?path=micfilm.txt&id=mfilm&pass=&OK=OK (to search the microfilm database)

Description of Collection

The most frequently used resources of the National Archives' collections are the federal censuses. They have all the censuses from 1790–1930 (accept for 1890) on microfilm. Other records include: Military Service Records, Immigrant and Passenger Arrivals Genealogical and Biographical Research, Federal Court Records, American Indians, and Black Studies.

On-Site Access

The National Archives (NARA) has the backing of the federal government and a constitutional mandate to preserve the records of our country. Its broad powers and vast resources have allowed it to build a network of research facilities and amass a collection that is second to none. NARA has printed catalogs of all its microfilms that are readily available to individuals and other institutions. For an institution this large, the National Archives epitomizes accessibility. The agency rivals the Family History Library in attracting genealogists.

Although the principle purpose of the National Archives is not specifically to help genealogists find their ancestors, the documents they have collected and preserved contain so much information genealogists need, we cannot overlook the research value of these records. The following information is a summary of what you can find at the NARA Web site (Available: www.archives.gov).

Going to the National Archives in Washington, DC, is the best way to get access to the collection. Genealogists make up the lion's share of researchers who use the Archives. Not only do they have a major research facility with several reading rooms in the Washington area, but they also have thirteen regional records service facilities strategically located around the country. While they are constantly working to make their records available electronically, it will be many years before a significant portion of their genealogical records will be online. In the interim, they have prepared finding aids, guides, and research tools to prepare researchers for a visit to one of their facilities.

Access from a Distance

If you can't get to Washington for access to these resources, try getting to one of the thirteen regional sites For most people a trip to one of the regional archives is a day trip. If you cannot get to one of the regional sites, you can use what is available on the Internet and rent films directly from NARA. Check Part III, Tool Kit 2 for a list of the regional collections.

Additional Information or Special Services: Microfilm Rental Program

The National Archives will rent microfilm to individuals. They claim the lowest prices around—as low as $2.25 a roll (if you rent 10 films at a time)—and they promise the best clarity and readability available. Films rent for a full 30 days. Individuals can rent official microfilm rolls by becoming a member of the National Archives Rental Program or they can order films through their local libraries. The membership fee is $28.00. New members receive a Startup Kit that contains everything researchers need to begin using the archives resources. Using the local library to access the National Archives If your library is not one of the more than 6,000 libraries nationwide that participate in the National Archives Microfilm Rental Program, find out what you need to do to offer this service to your patrons. Call 301-604-3699.

New York Public Library

The Irma and Paul Milstein Division of United States History,
Local History and Genealogy New York Public Library
Fifth Avenue and 42nd Street
New York, NY 10018-2788

Phone: 212-930-0828

E-mail: histref@nypl.org

NYPL Express: express@nypl.org (the library's fee-based research and copy service)

Web site: www.nypl.org/research/chss/lhg/genea.html

Online catalog: www.nypl.org/catalogs/catalogs.html
http://catnyp.nypl.org

Hours: www.nypl.org/research/hours/hsslhours.htm

The U.S. History, Local History and Genealogy Division of the New York Public Library is a major research center with 300,000+ volumes, 112,000 photos, 417,000 postcards. Interlibrary loan is very limited to Research Libraries Group and that only includes a few dozen major university and research libraries.

Up to ten photocopies are free to reciprocal libraries. Printed catalogs may be available in many research libraries. This collection is in this list because of its incomparable collection and the fact that the library will lend at least some of its materials to other libraries.

Description of Collection

The genealogical research collection includes many unique resources. Since the stacks are closed, researchers have to rely on their catalogs to identify the materials they want to use. Many of these research tools have been compiled from original records and will contain the type of data genealogists are seeking.

New York City Vital Records Indexes

These indexes enable researchers to acquire copies of vital records from the New York City Municipal Archives and Department of Health. The indexes themselves must be used on site. Indexes available:

- Index to Births, 1888–1982
- Index to Deaths, 1888–1982
- Index to Marriages, 1888–1937

Passenger Lists and Indexes

The Library acquires published passenger lists and indexes, including those available through the National Archives on microfilm.

Federal census records and extant Soundex indexes are available on microfilm in the Center for the Humanities for:

- New York,
- New Jersey, and
- Connecticut.

Newspapers and Indexes

The Library has an extensive collection of newspapers; however, there are few indexes to their contents. Among the available indexes are:

- *The New York Times Obituaries Index: 1858–1978*;
- *The New York Times, 1970–1980*;
- *Personal Name Index to The New York Times Index, 1851–1989*. 34 v.;
- Deaths taken from the *Brooklyn Eagle*, 1841–1880; Marriages taken from the *Brooklyn Eagle*, 1841–1880; *New York Evening Post*: Deaths, 1801–1890; *New York Evening Post*: Marriages, 1801–1890.

Family Histories

The Library's large collection of family histories, acquired by purchase and gifts, are accessed in the catalogs under the standard form of the family's surname. These compiled records are often rich in family anecdotes and genealogical data. Format and type of records available: The collections consist mostly of printed materials (books and periodicals) though some of their vital records and indexes are compiled from original documents.

On-Site Access

Patrons must rely on the catalogs, because most library materials are held in closed stacks. Patrons use CATNYP, the Library's online computer catalog.

Access from a Distance

The staff will respond to requests about Library holdings and for information on a subject within an area of the Library's responsibility, which *can be quickly answered*. Requests that require more in-depth research will be directed to the Library's fee-based information service, NYPL Express.

Library of Congress

Local History and Genealogy Reading Room
101 Independence Avenue SE
Jefferson Building Room LJ G42
Washington, DC 20540-4660

Phone: 202-707-5537

Fax: 202-707-1957

Web site: www.loc.gov/rr/genealogy

Online Catalog: http://catalog.loc.gov

The Library of Congress has one of the world's premier collections of United States and foreign genealogical and local historical publications. The Library's genealogy collection began as early as 1815 when Thomas Jefferson's library was purchased. These collections made it into my list in spite of the fact that researchers must go there to use the collection. Serious genealogists spend weeks, even months using this library.

The Library of Congress encourages genealogical researchers to use local libraries first. Researchers who have exhausted local and regional resources may direct specific inquiries to the Library of Congress by writing a letter to: Reference Referral Services, Library of Congress, 101 Independence Avenue SE, Washington, DC 20540-4660. Your inquiry should explain what resources you have already consulted. The Library is unable to handle extensive genealogy research project. The will refer researchers to professional researchers.

Description of Collection

Printed materials, primarily books, are the main strength of the Library's Local History and Genealogy Reading Room. The Library has more than 40,000 genealogies and 100,000 local histories. The collections are especially strong in North American, British Isles, and German sources. The Library's unsurpassed royalty, nobility, and heraldry collection further supports this international collection. While the Library's collection is strong in manuscripts, microfilms, newspapers, photographs, maps, and published material, it is not an archive or repository for unpublished or primary source materials.

On-Site Access

You really have to go there to use the collection. You begin by registering for a photo identification card, which allows you to request books to use in the library. It takes about an hour for the staff to retrieve requested materials. Their online catalog has the more recent publications, and the card catalog, which has been closed since 1980, covers the older materials., covers the older materials.

Access from a Distance

Users can access the catalog through the Web site to identify holdings, but there are no provisions for remote access to the collection except by hiring a professional.

Allen County Public Library

Reynolds Historical Genealogy Department
PO Box 2270
Fort Wayne, IN 46801-2270

Phone: 219-421-1225

Direct: 214-424-1330

Fax: 219-422-9688

Web site: www.acpl.lib.in.us/genealogy/index.html

Online Catalog: www.acpl.lib.in.us/Genealogy/genealogy.html

Description of Collection

The Historical Genealogy Department made it into this list because of their tremendous financial commitment to genealogists, their online public access catalog, and their unsurpassed periodical collection.

All the standard reference works are here, including the *American Genealogical Biographical Index* and the *National Union Catalog of Manuscript Collections*. County and town histories, vital, cemetery, church, court, land, probate and naturalization records can all be accessed through department catalogs. The department also has significant collections for Canada, the British Isles, and Germany. Resources are also available to aid in locating African American and Native American records.

Periodicals ACPL (Allen County Public Library) holds the largest English language genealogy and local history periodical collection in the world, with more than 3,200 current subscriptions and more than 4,100 titles. Individual articles may be accessed through a variety of indexes including the PERiodical Source Index (PERSI), compiled by department staff. (See Chapter 10 for more information about PERSI.) PERSI is available online by personal membership with Ancestry.com or organizational subscription through HeritageQuest Online.

Here is a list of their major records categories:

- Family histories
- Census records
- City directories

- Passenger lists
- Military records
- U.S. local records

On-Site Access

The collection is not available on interlibrary loan, but the library does provide research service. While some photocopying service is available for a fee, the best way to access the collection is to go there and use it in person. The department is so large you will need their free map. Then watch the orientation video. Librarians experienced in genealogical research are always on duty to answer questions. Groups planning to visit the library for research should notify the department in advance.

Access from a Distance

Interlibrary loan is not an option, but they will photocopy pages from their extensive periodical collection. Use PERiodical Source Index (PERSI). Request their form for requesting photocopies of articles. They charge $1.50 per sheet of periodical requests plus $0.20 a page for photocopies.

New England Historic and Genealogical Society

101 Newbury Street
Boston, MA 02116

Phone: 617-536-5740

Fax: 617-536-7307

E-mail: mtaylor@neghs.org

Web site: www.nehgs.org

Queries should be sent to:
Enquiries Service
c/o NEHGS
101 Newbury Street
Boston, MA 02116
Fax: 617-536-7307

If your genealogical research leads to the New England, this is the best research facility around. The library of the New England Historic and Genealogical Society is a major genealogical repository. It is open to the public, but is financed with private funds and membership fees. Nonmembers pay a fee to use it. Members can use the circulating collection for a fee. Photocopies are also available for a fee.

Regular members have unlimited searching of the NewEnglandAncestors.org Web site. This online database includes full text coverage of the New England Historical and Genealogical Register that was started in 1847. Members also have circulating borrowing privileges and discounts on research services.

Institutional membership is $150.00 and includes access to NewEnglandAncestors.org with multiple Internet users at a single location.

Description of Collection

While the primary focus of the collection is New England, it also has materials for the entire United States, Canada, the British Isles, Ireland, and continental Europe. The Canadian collection is especially impressive. The Manuscript and Rare Books section has over a mile of unpublished manuscripts, genealogies, and books. Since the 1850s, NEGHS has been the repository for the works of principal genealogists in America.

Over 200,000 books, one million microforms, plus a rapidly growing collection of CD-ROMs are available for on-site use.

On-Site Access

Members enjoy unlimited on-site use of the NEHGS Research Library, including access to the rare book and manuscript collections, and consultations with genealogical reference staff. In the Manuscript and Rare Book collections the stacks are closed and staff members retrieve materials from call slips. Manuscripts and rare books can be photocopied at the discretion of the librarian on duty. Nonmembers may use the main collection for a fee. My advice: If you are going to spend the money to travel to Boston to use this library, spend the money to become a member, too. Take the time to read the membership information or check out their Web site before making a trip to the library.

Access from a Distance

Members can borrow (rent) books from the 25,000-volume Circulating Library by mail. They have several skilled genealogists who will, for a fee, do research in the NEHGS library. This service was established to meet the demand for competent research in the New England area and elsewhere. They will only accept mail or fax requests. They ask people to write clearly and concisely, to provide all the information gathered so far, including citations for sources. They also ask questioners to specify the number of hours authorized to work on the project, and to send prepayment for services, excluding expenses, which will be billed later.

Additional Information or Special Services: Publications

Membership includes a subscription to *The New England Historical and Genealogical Register* and *New England Ancestors*. The *Register* is one of the oldest and one of the foremost genealogical periodicals in the world.

Daughters of the American Revolution

1776 D Street NW
Washington, DC 20006-5392

Phone: 202-628-1776

Fax: 202-879-3227

Web site: www.dar.org/library/default.cfm

Online catalog: www.dar.org/library/onlinlib.cfm

The library is open to the public. Unannounced closings may occur. Please check before planning a visit from a distance.

The DAR is one of the nation's premier genealogical research centers. It is one of my personal favorites of all the libraries on the list because the materials are so accessible. Incorporated by an act of Congress in 1896, the National Society of the Daughters of the American Revolution is a nonprofit, nonpolitical, volunteer service organization with nearly 180,000 members in some 3,000 chapters. The Society was founded in Washington, DC, in 1890 and has celebrated more than one hundred years of service through historic preservation, promotion of education and patriotism. The library is a "must go there" location for all family history researchers.

Description of Collection

The DAR has 150,000 volumes; 250,000 files; and 40,000 microforms. It is privately funded and open to members for free; nonmembers pay a daily fee. Most of the printed materials are in open stacks and organized by family surname or geographic regions, broken down to counties and then cities.

On-Site Access

The library is open to the public. The online catalog is very useful, especially with surname research. But browsing the stacks in the geographic section is also an effective way to find materials. Staff members make requested photocopies.

Access from a Distance

Orders for photocopies by mail must come to the Library's research service directly from the researcher. Telephone assistance is available for very specific questions and general information. NSDAR members pay $10.00 per request, which includes 10 pages. Nonmembers pay a flat fee of $15.00 for up five pages. The limit is two books or magazines per request. Check the Web site for current details.

The DAR Patriot Index contains names of Revolutionary patriots, whose service (between 1775 and 1783) has been established by the National Society, Daughters of the American Revolution. Anyone may request a free lookup to determine if the DAR has recognized the ancestor as a Revolutionary Patriot. Check the Web site to fill out the request form. Additional information available may include: dates and places of birth and death, name(s) of wife (wives) or husband(s), rank, type of service, and the State where the patriot lived or served. If pension papers are known to exist, the index will include that fact.

The National Genealogical Society

National Genealogical Society
4527 17th Street
Arlington, VA 22207-2399

Tel: 703-525-0050
Toll Free: 800-473-0060

Fax: 703-525-0052

E-mail: Ngs@genealogy.org

Web site: www.ngsgenealogy.org

Online catalog: http://64.7.52.99

The National Genealogical Society is the premier national membership organization for genealogists. Since 1903 it has been assisting its members trace their family histories. It provides leadership and education for individuals, societies, and institutions through programs, publications, and service to over 15,000 members. This library made it into the top-five list because they circulate materials through the mail for the cost of postage.

Description of Collection

The Society maintains a collection of family and local histories, genealogies, transcribed source materials, reference works, periodicals, Bible records, and manuscripts. Format and type of records available primarily include printed materials (books and periodicals), though they also have some primary source documents like Bible records and manuscripts. Most of what they have are compiled records.

On-Site Access

The circulating collection of the National Genealogical Society is located at the St. Louis County Library (SLCL) in Missouri. The collection consists of 20,000+ books and new titles are being added daily. Every book in the NGS Special Collection at St. Louis is available for use on site or through interlibrary loan to NGS members and nonmembers alike.

Interlibrary loan requests may be submitted to the St. Louis County Library in one of the following ways.

1. OCLC—the symbol is ZAE
2. ALA forms using regular mail to:

    St. Louis County Library
    1640 S Lindbergh Boulevard
    St. Louis, MO 63131-3598

3. E-mail to scollections@slcl.org. Include your library's mailing address, phone number and contact person.

The Glebe Collections are housed at NGS Headquarters in Arlington, Virginia. This collection does not circulate. Members may use the collection on site, or use the NGSearch option to access information. The fee for this option is $5.00 per title and includes the first five pages copied. Additional copies are $0.25 per page. Nonmembers pay a $5.00 surcharge.

The Society collects, preserves, and disseminates genealogical information and source materials and provides education and training in genealogical research. The NGS encourages excellence in genealogical writing and serves as a nucleus for family research at the national level.

This is a membership organization with membership categories for individuals and families.. Most genealogical societies have a publication that is included with the membership benefits, but if they have a library or research facilities members have to travel to the location of the library to take advantage of library services. The lending service to members and nonmembers makes the National Genealogical Society unique. They also offer member discounts for enrollment for training seminars and home study courses.

Another valuable benefit is the Members' Ancestor Charts (MAC) File. This unique collection is designed to help members contact other members interested in the same families. New members are asked, as a contribution to the society, to complete, as far as possible, a chart for each of their four great-grandfathers. These charts on three generations, including the parents and children of each of their great-grandfathers are made a permanent NGS record. Since 1969, approximately a million names with their vital statistics have been submitted. Members are encouraged to file as many other charts pertaining to their ancestors as they wish. Members may request up to four surname searches at one time. There is no charge for this service.

Additional Information or Special Services: Research Services

Genealogists may request that NGS researchers devote one to two hours to a specific research problem. They will use their experience and judgment, based on the information provided. The fee for this service is $40.00. Up to 30 pages of photocopies and computer printouts are included. They will clear additional pages with the client before engaging in additional work.

The National Genealogical Society has acquired the American Medical Association's card file of deceased American physicians, amounting to some 350,000 records. The cards provide birth and death information for physicians who died between 1906 and 1964. For a fee they will search the card file and send a report. In most cases they can find the record knowing no more than the name of the physician.

Mid-Continent Public Library

Genealogy and Local History Department
Mid-Continent Public Library
317 West 24 Highway
Independence, MO 64050-2747

Phone: 816-252-7228

E-mail: ge@mcpl.lib.mo.us

Web site: www.mcpl.lib.mo.us/branch/ge

Online catalog: http://opac.mcpl.lib.mo.us

The Mid-Continent Public Library has a circulating collection they lend to the public free and on interlibrary loan. They also have a tremendous online catalog. They only lend microfilm to Missouri libraries.

Description of Collection

The collection consists mainly of books. Also worth noting is their collection of the UMI Genealogy and Local History Series on microfiche. The Circulating Collection began in 1984 with a small set of books donated to the library by the American Family Records Association (AFRA). Kermit Karns, then President of AFRA, envisioned a genealogy collection available to researchers nationwide through local public libraries. The collection has grown to almost 5,000 volumes. Last year the library lent 3,612 books to researchers in 43 states and Canada.

On-Site Access

Anyone can walk in and use the collection. They have professional librarians on duty to help with reference questions. The online catalog is user friendly and will lead the researcher easily to the documents needed. They have printed catalogs and supplements available, and their online catalog is available through the Internet at: www.mcpl.lib.mo.us/disclaim.htm. Researchers that are visiting as a group are encouraged to call ahead to give the library a chance to have adequate staff available to assist patrons.

Access from a Distance

Over 5,000 genealogy and local history books available are on interlibrary loan to researchers nationwide. Interested individuals should write for a free copy of *Genealogy from the Heartland, A Catalog of Titles in the Mid-Continent Public Library Genealogy Circulation Collection* (1992–1994 Supplement, 1996 Supplement). This catalog lists the books available on loan through local public libraries. The 1994 and 1996 supplements may be downloaded from the Web page.

The staff does not conduct extensive genealogical research, but they will check indexed materials as time permits. Requests may be submitted by telephone, e-mail, and through the post. There is no charge for these services, but donations are always appreciated. Photocopy charges are 15¢ per page. Invoices for copy charges will be sent with copied materials. The library has a list of local researchers who will do research for a fee.

American Antiquarian Society Library

185 Salisbury Street
Worcester, MA 01609

Phone: 508-755-5221

Web site: www.americanantiquarian.org/generali.htm

Online catalog: http://catalog.mwa.org

The American Antiquarian Society was founded in 1812 in Worcester, Massachusetts as an independent research library. The collection includes books, pamphlets, newspapers, periodicals, broadsides, manuscripts, music, children's literature, graphic arts, genealogy and local histories— depicting America's people from the colonial era through the Civil War and Reconstruction.

Description of Collection

The Local History collection includes 55,000+ volumes published after 1820. This collection is one of the most frequently used resources at the library. The library also has solid genealogical research collection with over 17,000 family histories. Almost 30,000 biographies constitute a significant source for researchers.

The American Antiquarian Society is well known for its collections of early American newspapers. The main purpose for the collection is to acquire, preserve, and make available for research newspapers published in the eighteenth and nineteenth centuries in the United States, Canada, and the English-speaking West Indies. The society has accumulated over 15,000 newspaper titles in 20,000 volumes.

On-Site Access

This is truly a research library and only serious researchers are encouraged to go there to use it. The library is open, free of charge, to experienced researchers who are working on projects that require use of the collections. New readers must complete an application describing their research project and must have available two forms of identification (one bearing a photo, e.g., a driver's license or passport). As part of their orientations to the library, all new readers meet with a senior staff member to discuss their research interests and to review reading room policies.

All stack areas are closed. Researchers must request items by using call slips after consulting the card catalog and the online catalog. Only pencils may be used in the library.

Access from a Distance

The society rents microfilm, when a service copy exists. Master negatives of any item or collection are never rented or loaned. For specific questions about services from a distance contact:

Reference Services Department
185 Salisbury Street
Worcester, MA 01609

Phone: 508-471-2171

Fax: 508-753-3311

E-mail: mlamoureux@mwa.org

Planning a Trip to a Major Research Facility

Every year after we moved to Kansas we used to make a trip to Utah to visit my wife's parents. If I planned it right I could squeeze in a day of research at the Family History Library. At first, about all I could do was to toss my genealogy briefcase in the car as we were packing to leave. Later on, I had access to the Family History Library catalog on CD-ROM. Looking up titles ahead of time made my research time when I got to the FHL more effective.

Planning ahead for a visit to any research facility will make the precious time you spend in the research facility more productive for you. Here are a few tips that could help you prepare for your trip.

• Compile a checklist of ancestors you want to find.

• Prepare note cards that include what you already have and suggest places to look for more information.

• Take a copy of your pedigree chart with you in case you come across some names that could be related to your ancestors.

- Use the online catalog to get access to library's holdings and identify materials you want to search before making the trip.

- Conduct a place search to find out what is available in the area of your research.

- Conduct a surname search to learn if any records are available on your family names. You could get lucky searching a person's first and last name.

- Print out the records for the books or films you want to search.

- Prioritize the printouts by assessing the potential value of each resource you want to look at.

- See my "Checklist for Planning a Research Trip," Part III, Tool 5.1, and on the CD-ROM that comes with this book.

The collections of the research facilities in this chapter are vast. Visiting one or more of libraries or archives could be a valuable experience if you plan ahead.

Suggestions for Librarians

If a patron from your library needs research in another state, this list will give you a starting point for the research. Here are some ideas you can use to help your patrons:

1. Call the staff at the other institution and ask about their services.

2. Visit that library's Web site, if they have one, to learn more about their genealogical collection.

3. Check the library's online catalog to see what materials they have in their collection.

4. Send a request to that library for your patron.

5. Give your patron the information so they can make a request.

6. Compare and contrast the services provided by these libraries, using the ones you like as models for your own program.

Summary

We have some amazing genealogical research facilities around the country. In this chapter we have tried to mention only the best of the best. Only those with the most significant or unique collections and user-friendly services made the list. We tried to tell you why they were unique and how to access the collection by visiting the place or from a distance. All of the facilities had online catalogs of their holdings. Some provide for lending materials through a local library. Some even provided online access to digitized images.

I have been impressed with the quality of genealogical research material available around the country and the willingness of staff members to help researchers find the information they are looking for.

Bibliography (Ratings Guide explanation follows last citation)

Bentley, Elizabeth Petty. 1999. *The Genealogist's Address Book*. Baltimore, MD: Genealogical Publishing Company.

This book brings together an incredible amount of disparate data. *The Genealogist's Address Book* provides names, addresses, phone numbers, hours, and publications for genealogical organizations in five broad areas. Any serious researcher will want to have a copy. **PPP**

Dollarhide, William, and Ronald Bremer. 1998. *America's Best Genealogy Resource Centers*. Bountiful, UT: Heritage Quest.

This book lists, by state, selected research repositories. It describes the collections and mentions unique features. Helpful to genealogy librarians and researchers who travel to remote locations. **L** [Out of Print]

Neagles, James C. 1990. *The Library of Congress: A Guide to Genealogical and Historical Research*. Salt Lake City: Ancestry Publishing.

This is a comprehensive guide to the Library of Congress. It is a must read for anyone who plans to go there for genealogical research. With maps and full descriptions of the collections, this book says it all. **LLL**

United States. National Archives and Records Administration. 1995. *Guide to Federal Records in the National Archives of the United States*. 3 vols. Compiled by Robert B. Matchette, et al. Washington, DC: National Archives and Records Administration.

This supersedes both the 1974 edition and the 1987 reprint. It includes descriptions of federal records in the National Archives of the United States as of September 1, 1994. **LLL**

United States. National Archives and Records Administration. 1999. *Holocaust-Era Assets: A Finding Aid to Records at the National Archives at College Park, Maryland*. Washington, DC: Published for the National Archives and Records Administration by the National Archives Trust Fund Board.

This aid to locating records in the National Archives focuses primarily on efforts to identify, recover, and restitute assets hidden or stolen by Nazi Germany during World War II. However, it also covers such additional topics as World War II economic warfare and provides a starting point for those interested in other aspects of the Holocaust era, including refugees and war crimes. **LL**

Warren, Paula Stuart. 2002. Navigating the National Archives. *Family Tree Magazine* (October 2002): 40.

The author opens up the resources of the National Archives to help us understand how these records help genealogists. She gives us a glimpse of the vast holdings of this warehouse of our nation's historical records.

Warren, Paula Stuart, and James W. Warren. 2001. *Your Guide to the Family History Library.* Cincinnati, OH: Betterway Books.

This up-to-date guide is a welcome resource for anyone who is planning a research trip to Salt Lake City. The authors start with the basics and move to how to access the collection. They describe the records, tell researchers how to do on-site research, and suggest how to make the most of a research trip to Salt Lake City. They give you a layout of the building and the locations of various collections.

Anyone who is planning his or her first trip to the Family History Library needs to read this book before leaving home. **PPP**

Ratings Guide

The ratings for each bibliography describe not only what each resource contains, but also how it might fit into the library collection. Some of the materials are more appropriate for larger libraries with substantial budgets, and others belong in collections of any size—even in the personal research collection. To help you identify materials most appropriate for your collection, each resource is marked as either "L" for libraries and "P" for personal. They are ranked from one letter for recommended, two letters for preferred, and three letters for essential.

CHAPTER 5

DISTINGUISHING OTHER GENEALOGICAL RESOURCE FACILITIES

In the previous chapter you were introduced to ten outstanding genealogical research facilities. They were included in that chapter because not only did they have outstanding collections with many unique items, but also they were user-friendly. They took extra steps to make what they had accessible to researchers everywhere. Thousands of researchers spend lots of money and time to access these collections. Not everyone can get to one of these facilities, because of distance or resources. Every state in the United States has at least one facility that collects, preserves, and makes available to the public, documents that have recorded the major events of its residents. Some states have more than one truly exceptional genealogical research facilities, dedicated staff members anxious to help visitors.

What to Look for in This Chapter

In this chapter we look at a larger group of libraries and archives, some of which could have been included in Chapter 4. The purpose of this chapter is to identify some of the best genealogy collections in each state. Here again some extraordinarily strong collections may have been omitted, while other less notable libraries and archives have been included. I am sorry if your favorite library didn't make the list. I had to make some difficult choices to keep the long list as short as it is.

Selection Process

No list can possibly include every library that has a good genealogical collection; thus, some libraries with excellent collections may have been overlooked. I hope I haven't missed any truly outstanding genealogical collection in the United States.

To start with, I sent out a global message to my colleagues on the Librarians Serving Genealogists mailing list, (GENEALIB), genealib@mailman.acomp.usf.edu, asking them to identify the top five genealogical research facilities in their state. Genealogy librarians from about 35 states responded. I compared this list to the list created by William Dollarhide and Ronald A. Bremmer in their book, *America's Best Genealogy Resource Centers* (Dollarhide and Bremmer, 1998). Next, I turned to the Internet to look for Web sites for the libraries on the list.

The Internet helped me narrow the list. If the homepage of their Web site didn't mention their service to genealogists, they didn't make the list. I believe that every credible genealogical research facility, even at the state level, needs to have a first page presence on the World Wide Web. An online catalog provides a higher level of access to the contents of the material that has been cataloged. Catalogers can now give additional points of access (analytics) to significant individuals or surnames mentioned in a work, even if they are not the main subjects of the book. Researchers can search for a name in the online catalog and get a hit that will turn into a match. While not every research facility on the list has an online catalog, this component was an important consideration for those that made the list. See Part III, Tool 8.2 for URL addresses and look at the CD-ROM that accompanies this book for hyperlinks to library Web sites.

Using the Internet to narrow the field I identified between three and seven genealogy resource agencies per state that I wanted to include in the book. I am sure some public libraries with excellent genealogy collections are not on the list. They are not on my list because I could not find the genealogy collection mentioned right away on their Web page. On the other hand some relatively small collections made the list, because their collections are unique to a particular group of people, and I believed they needed to be spotlighted.

Even though small libraries may have a wealth of genealogically valuable material, they may not get mentioned in a book like this. The best that librarians can hope for is that these institutions will have an online catalog that we can search from our libraries. Then we can show these sites to researchers who come to us to for help.

Before we can look for an online catalog we need to find the library. That is why I like the Library Index (Available: www.libdex.com). From there you can check the catalog to see if the library's genealogy collection has anything you can use.

For example if a researcher knew one of his or her ancestors died in the area, he or she could do a search on "cemetery records" in the online catalog of a distant library. If he or she found a book or some other record that might have valuable information, he or she could check the library's Web page to find out what services they offer to people who live too far away to come to the library. The library might charge a fee to look up the information, make a copy, and mail it, but that would be cheaper than traveling to the library in person.

Organization of the List

To make the list as useful as possible, repositories are organized first by state, then in alphabetical order. You will find four types of information about each library or archive included here. First, you see the name of the organization in bold. Beneath the name is the organization's contact information. I want you to get to the "good stuff" as directly as possible, which is why I supply the phone number of the genealogy department. Third, to decide how relevant this particular source might be to your needs, read the description of collection information. It contains some of the unique information that might help you find specific references that you could otherwise easily overlook, like materials on an ethnic group or country of origin. The last bit of information explains how best to access the materials in this facility. Granted, access to some collections will require a trip to where they are and conducting research on site. But for a reasonable fee, many of the libraries and archives will look up the information you request, make a copy and send it to you. Some of the other options for access include: hiring a professional who lives in the area to do the research for you; paying the researchers in that library or archive to do the research; or calling the person in charge of the collection and asking him or her to suggest some options. I include some ideas I thought you could use to good advantage.

Using the List

Here is an example of how a person could use this list. If I were doing research in Chenango County, New York, I would find the nearest library to Chenango County and call the librarian there. I know there are a lot of helpful people all over the country with an incredible amount of goodwill. On one occasion I called a library in Wisconsin and asked for two obituaries. Within four days I had copies of the obituaries I wanted. I had the exact death dates for both individuals and I know that helped. It might have been easy to assume that they wouldn't have helped me, but if I had not asked I would never have gotten the obituaries.

If the person you speak to does not know the answer or have the information you need, maybe she or he can give you the name and number of someone who can help you. Think of this list as an invitation to ask for specific assistance. You will be surprised at the helpfulness of others.

Alabama

Birmingham Public Library

Linn-Henley Research Building
Tutwiler Collection of Southern History and Literature
2100 Park Place
Birmingham, AL 35203-2794

Phone: 205-226-3665

Collection Information: The collection is remarkable for its family folders, and its significant book collection.

Access: If you have a bibliographic citation, the staff will respond to specific requests.

Anniston Public Library

Alabama Room
108 East 10th Street
Anniston, AL 36201

Phone: 256-237-8501

Collection Information: They have the published collection of Leonardo Andrea representing a lifetime of work by a professional researcher in South Carolina.

Access: Researchers from all over the country travel great distances to use this collection.

Huntsville-Madison County Public Library

Archives and Heritage Room
Third Floor
915 Monroe Street
Huntsville, AL 35801

Phone: 256-532-5969

Collection Information: The collection is unique for its historic newspapers on microfilm dating from 1816.

Access: Open and free to public. Fee-based research.

Mobile Public Library

Local History and Genealogy Department
704 Government Street
Mobile, AL 36602-1403

Phone: 251-208-7093

Fax: 251-208-5866

Collection Information: Collection specializes in early settlers of Alabama, Spanish, French, and Anglos. This is the best genealogy collection on the Gulf Coast.

Access: On-site access is free and open to the public. Contact the library for remote services.

Wallace State Community College

Wallace State Library
PO Box 2000
801 Main Street
Hanceville, AL 45077-2000

Phone: 256-352-8000

Collection Information: The collection is significant and growing. It is also the host for a local Family History Center.

Access: Access is free and open to the public. Microfilms available from the Family History Library.

University of Alabama

William Stanley Hoole Special Collections
Box 870266
Mary Harmon Bryant Hall
500 Hackberry Lane
Tuscaloosa, AL 35487-0266

Phone: 205-348-0500

Fax: 205-348-1699

Collection Information: Collection includes maps, microfilm, newspapers, photographs, and electronic records.

Access: Special Collections and Alabama Collection materials do not circulate. Photocopying is at the discretion of the library staff.

Alaska

Alaska Historical Library

State Office Building
PO Box 110571
Juneau, AK 99811-0571

Phone: 907-465-2925

Collection Information: They have photographs, manuscripts, records, newspapers, and maps.

Access: Most resources are readily available to researchers.

Alaska State Archives

Archives
141 Willoughby Avenue
Juneau, AK 99801-1720

Phone: 907-465-2270

Fax: 907-465-2465

Collection Information: Collection includes documents relating to history and culture of Alaska.

Access: Open and free to the public. The best way to access the collection is to visit the archives.

University of Alaska Library Anchorage

Archives and Manuscripts Department
3211 Providence Drive
Anchorage, AK 99508

Phone: 907-786-1849

Fax: 907-786-1845

Collection Information: They have original documents relating to Native Alaskans plus Alaskan genealogy.

Access: Patrons wishing to visit the archives and/or use the department's collections are urged to contact the department staff prior to their visit.

University of Alaska Fairbanks

Rasmuson Library
PO Box 756808
Fairbanks, AK 99775-6808

Phone: 907-474-7224

Collection Information: Collection features oral histories and Alaska pioneers.

Access: Open and free to the public. Contact the library for access from afar.

Arizona

Arizona State Library

Archives and Public Records
Genealogy Collection
1700 West Washington, Ste. 342
Phoenix, AZ 85007

Phone: 602-542-4159

Fax: 602-542-4402

Collection Information: They have photos, territorial prison records, birth and death records.

Access: Staff will do limited research requests free. For lengthy searches contact a professional researcher.

West Valley Genealogical Society Library

Genealogy Library
12222 North 11th Avenue
Youngtown, AZ 85363

Phone: 623-933-4945

Collection Information: Strengths include obituaries and index of books.

Access: Collection is noncirculating. Nonmembers pay $5.00 per visit.

Arizona State University Libraries

Arizona Collection
PO Box 871006
Tempe, AZ 85287-1006

Phone: 602-965-6164

Collection Information: They have a large collection of books, periodicals, CDs, microfilm, microfiche and maps.

Access: All material in the Arizona Collection is available for scholarly use. Contact them for access.

University of Arizona

Special Collections
Main Library, Bldg. 55

1510 East University Boulevard
Tucson, AZ 85720

Phone: 520-621-2101

Collection Information: The collection is strong on southwestern American history and borderlands.

Access: Access is primarily on-site. Contact the library for remote access or research services.

Arkansas

Arkansas State History Commission Archives

Archives
One Capitol Mall
Little Rock, AR 72201

Phone: 501-682-6900

Collection Information: They have 13,000 historical images, and Confederate records.

Access: They do not accept research requests from the public.

Fort Smith Public Library

Genealogy Department
61 S 8th Street
Fort Smith, AR 72901-2480

Phone: 501-783-0229

Collection Information: Local birth and death records, cemetery index, mortuary records, city directories, family files, and Civil War records.

Access: Open to the public. Research fee $10.00 per hour.

University of Arkansas Library

Special Collections
365 N Ozark Avenue
Fayetteville, AR 72701-4002

Phone: 501-575-5577

Fax: 479-575-6656

Collection Information: Collections features county records, newspapers, manuscripts, church records, state history, and genealogies.

Access: Open to students, faculty, and staff and the general public. Researchers may request specific materials from the manuscript collections.

Pine Bluff/Jefferson County Library

Genealogy Collection
200 E 8th Avenue
Pine Bluff, AR 71601

Phone: 870-534-4802

Collection Information: Collection includes records for the whole state, plus indexes, surname folders, and genealogies.

Access: The library staff will make photocopies for a small fee. Exact dates required.

California

California State Library–Sutro Library Branch

Sutro Library Branch

480 Winston Drive
San Francisco, CA 94132

Phone: 415-731-4477

Fax: 415-557-9325

Collection Information: They have over 7,000 family histories, 35,000 local histories, and a huge city directory collection.

Access: Non-rare materials may be lent to libraries within California, or to California residents.

California State Library–Sacramento

California History Room
900 N Street, Rm. 200
Sacramento, CA 94327-0001

Phone: 916-654-0176

Collection Information: The collection has specialized publications and materials that support genealogical research.

Access: They provide a list of private researchers for those who are unable to visit the library.

Tuolumne County

Genealogical Society Library
158 West Bradford Avenue
PO Box 3956
Sonora, CA 95370-3956

Phone: 209-532-1317

Collection Information: They have extensive local vital records including voter registers and census records.

Access: On-site researchers are welcome.

Los Angeles Public Library

The History and Genealogy Department
630 W Fifth Street
Los Angeles, CA 90071

Phone: 213-228-7400

Fax: 213-228-7409

Collection Information: This library contains over 200,000 volumes in the history book collection.

Access: They furnish a list of genealogical researchers for hire for those who are unable to visit the library.

Huntington Beach Public Library

Genealogy Collection
7111 Talbert Avenue
Huntington Beach, CA 92648

Phone: 714-842-4481, ext. 2227

Collection Information: They have an extensive collection of 16,000 genealogical books and periodicals.

Access: Contact the library for the best way to access the collection from a distance.

Carlsbad City Library

Genealogy Division
Georgina Cole Library
1250 Carlsbad Village Drive
Carlsbad, CA 92008

Phone: 760-434-2931

Collection Information: This is the largest genealogy collection in southern California on the 17th, 18th, and 19th centuries in the United States.

Access: On-site researchers are welcome. They have a small circulating collection of duplicate books.

Sons of the Revolution Library

Library
600 South Central Avenue
Glendale, CA 91204

Phone: 818-240-1775

Collection Information: This is a repository for books and reference materials relating to the American Revolution; and genealogy.

Access: Use of the library is free to anyone in keeping with the purpose of the society.

Colorado

Colorado State Archives

Archives
1313 Shennan Street, Rm. IB-20
Denver, CO 80203

Phone: 303-866-2358

Fax: 303-866-2257

Collection Information: The archives have territorial, and county records This is *the* place for Colorado genealogical research.

Access: Out-of-State Requests: $25.00 per search or name to include 3 pages of copies with additional pages of copy work at $1.25 per page.

Colorado Historical Society

Stephen H. Hart Library
1300 Broadway
Denver, CO 80203

Phone: 303-866-2305

Fax: 303-866-5739

Collection Information: The collection has documents on wagon trains, stage lines, cowboys, early land grants, and homesteaders.

Access: Most resources available on request to library visitors.

Colorado State Library

Library
201 E Colfax
Denver, CO 80203-1799

Phone: 303-866-6900

Fax: 303-866-6940

Collection Information: Colorado histories, biographies, county and town histories, and genealogies.

Access: On-site researchers are welcome. Contact the agency for availability of research services.

Denver Public Library

Western History and Genealogy Department
10 W 14th Avenue Parkway
Denver, CO 80204

Phone: 720-865-1821

Collection Information: The Western History and Genealogy Department is a very good Colorado collection.

Access: The Genealogy Collection is primarily a U.S. research collection and does not circulate.

Boulder Public Library

Carnegie Library for Local History
1125 Pine Street
Boulder, CO 80302

Phone: 303-441-3110

Collection Information: This is a strong collection on Boulder city and county histories, historical photographs.

Access: On-site researchers are welcome. Contact the agency for availability of research services.

Pikes Peak Library District

Regional History and Genealogy Resources
20 N Cascade Avenue
PO Box 1579
Colorado Springs, CO 80903

Phone: 719-531-6333

Collection Information: They have Census, DAR lineage books, PA Archives, and more.

Access: Contact the agency for availability of research services.

Connecticut

Connecticut State Library

History and Genealogy
231 Capitol Avenue
Hartford, CT 06106

Phone: 860-757-6580

Fax: 860-757-6677

Collection Information: This is an extensive collection of local histories and genealogies, with particular emphasis on Connecticut.

Access: This is a user-friendly library. On-site use of materials is encouraged.

Connecticut Historical Society

Museum, Library and Education Center
One Elizabeth Street at Asylum Avenue
Hartford, CT 06105

Phone: 860-236-5621

Fax: 860-236-2664

Collection Information: Printed genealogies, Connecticut directories, vital and church records, and cemetery inscriptions.

Access: CHS Members may borrow materials from the Genealogical Loan Collection.

Godfrey Memorial Library

Genealogy Collection
134 Newfield Street
Middletown, CT 06457

Phone: 860-346-4375

Fax: 860-347-9874

Collection Information: The history collection of pre-1875 genealogical materials and includes mostly New England, New York, and Pennsylvania.

Access: For membership of $35.00 a year they will give you access to several fee-based commercial databases.

New Haven Colony Historical Society

Library
114 Whitney Avenue
New Haven, CT 06510

Phone: 203-562-4183

Fax: 203-562-2002

Collection Information: They have the best of earliest records of southern Connecticut.

Access: Call the society for the availability of remote access.

Stamford Historical Society

Research Library
1508 High Ridge Road
Stamford, CT 06903

Phone: 203-329-1183

Fax: 203-322-1607

Collection Information: Collection focuses on the history of Stamford, Connecticut, from presettlement to the present.

Access: All material is available for use on site only. Check with the library for a list of professional researchers.

Delaware

Historical Society of Delaware

Library
505 N Market Street
Wilmington, DE 19801

Phone: 302-655-7161

Collection Information: The collection includes colonial records, church, state, Civil War records, and Delaware histories, and genealogies.

Access: Open and free to the public. Materials may not be removed or checked out.

Delaware State Archives

Hall of Records
Delaware Public Archives
121 Duke of York Street
Dover, DE 19901

Phone: 302-739-5318

Collection Information: The collection has good coverage of colonial records for every hundred years and every county.

Access: Check the Web site for on-site access.

Wilmington Institute Library

Library
10th and Market Street
PO Box 2303-19899
Wilmington, DE 19801

Phone: 302-571-7400

Fax: 302-654-9132

Collection Information: They have 250,000 volumes; 375 periodicals; 25 newspapers; 7,000 microfilms; 6,669 audiovisuals.

Access: Photocopier access and interlibrary services available.

Hagley Museum and Library

Research Library
298 Buck Road
Wilmington, DE 19807

Mailing address: PO Box 3630
Wilmington, DE 19807-0630

Phone: 302-658-2400

Collection Information: They have original manuscripts, rare books, which document the history of American business not in the State Archives.

Access: Hagley's research collections are open to the public. First-time readers must obtain a research card in order to use the resources.

Dover Public Library

Delaware Room
45 S State Street
Dover, DE 19901-3526

Phone: 302-736-7030

Circulation: 302-736-7030

Reference: 302-736-7077

Children: 302-736-7034

Collection Information: Collection is strong on Delaware and Delmarva Peninsula, Delawareana, local histories and genealogies.

Access: On-site researchers are welcome. Contact the library for availability of access from a distance.

District of Columbia

Historical Society of Washington, DC and City Museum

Kiplinger Research Library
801 K Street NW
Washington, DC 20001

Phone: 202-383-1800

Fax: 202-383-1870

Collection Information: Collection includes photograph, prints, negatives, archives, manuscripts, maps, books, pamphlets, yearbooks and thesis.

Access: Photocopies may be requested by mail or e-mail if full bibliographic references are provided. Check the online catalog.

District of Columbia Public Library

Washingtoniana Collection
Rm. 307

Martin Luther King Jr. Memorial Library
901 G Street
Washington, DC 20001

Phone: 202-727-1213

Collection Information: The collection includes city directories from 1822 to 1973, telephone directories from 1907 to present. Newspapers from 1800 to present.

Access: On-site researchers are welcome.

Historical Society of Washington, DC

Library of Washington History
1307 New Hampshire Avenue NW
Washington, DC 20036-1503

Phone: 202-785-2068

Fax: 202-331-1079

Collection Information: This facility is like a state archives for the District of Columbia, containing many original documents.

Access: Admission fee for nonmembers is $3.00. Staff does photocopying of materials upon patron request.

Florida

Orange County Library System

Genealogy Department
101 E Central Boulevard
Orlando, FL 32801

Phone: 407-835-7323

Collection Information: They have Florida vital records indexes, city directories, and birth and death records for Orlando from 1910 to 1922.

Access: Open and free to the public. Check with the reference department for services to out-of-state patrons.

Miami-Dade Public Library System

Genealogy Department
101 W Flagler Street
Miami, FL 33130

Phone: 305-375-5580

Collection Information: They have publications on nearly every state in the Union, with emphasis on eastern Atlantic states.

Access: The collection is open to the public. Most materials do not circulate.

Tampa-Hillsborough County Library System

Genealogy Department
900 N Ashley Drive
Tampa, FL 33602-3704

Phone: 833-273-3652

Collection Information: Excellent Web page. Most comprehensive indexes on the family history of Florida.

Access: Microfilm and microfiche reader/printers copies are $0.25 per page.

Jacksonville Public Library

Genealogy Collection
122 N Ocean Street
Jacksonville, FL 32202

Phone: 904-630-2409

Collection Information: The collection is strong on Florida and the southeastern United States, with particular emphasis on Jacksonville.

Access: The collection is open to the public. Most materials do not circulate.

Florida Department of State

Division of Library and Information Services
Florida State Archives
500 S Bronough Street
Tallahassee, FL 32399-0250

Phone: 904-487-2073

Collection Information: They have private manuscripts, local government records, and photographs.

Access: The collection is for on-site use only. Contact the archives for research services.

Indian River County Main Library

Florida History and Genealogy Department
1600 21st Street
Vero Beach, FL 32960

Phone: 772-770-5060, ext. 108

Fax: 772-770-5066

Collection Information: Large collection on Virginia, Alabama records, marriage indexes for Texas, and a genealogical card file on Georgia.

Access: Mail requests - use e-mail or regular mail. Minimum charge: $2.00, photocopies $0.10.

Georgia

Georgia Department of Archives and History

Archives
5800 Jonesboro Road
Morrow, GA 30260

Phone: 678-364-3700

Collection Information: They have property records and other legal documents.

Access: Archives and manuscripts are meant to be used on site.

Georgia Historical Society Library

Library and Archives
501 Whitaker Street
Savannah, GA 31401

Phone: 912-651-2125

Library: 912-651-2128

Fax: 912-651-2831

Collection Information: Collection includes diaries, personal letters, ledger books, church records, and many primary sources related to Georgians.

Access: There is a $5.00 admission fee for nonmembers.

Macon-Bibb County Public Libraries

Washington Memorial Library
1180 Washington Avenue
Macon, GA 31201-1790

Phone: 478-744-0800

Collection Information: One of the most outstanding reference collections of its type in the South.

Access: The staff provides general assistance. Reference service is available in person or by mail.

Augusta Genealogical Society Library

AGS Library
PO Box 3743
1109 Broad Street
Augusta, GA 30914-3743

Phone: 706-722-4073

Collection Information: Unique to the collection are ancestor charts and surname files. They also have the Mims and Mealing Microfiche Collections.

Access: Due to the limited number of volunteers, they do not conduct research or answer inquiries for nonmembers.

Atlanta-Fulton Public Library System

Georgia Local and Family History Collections
One Margaret Mitchell Square
Atlanta, GA 30303

Phone: 404-730-1700

Collection Information: Substantial genealogical collection with good coverage of the Southeastern U.S.

Access: Open and free to the public. The reference staff will answer brief telephone questions.

Ellen Payne Odom Genealogy Library

Research Library
PO Box 2828
204 5th Street SE
Moultrie, GA 31776

Phone: 229-985-6540

Fax: 229-985-0936

Collection Information: Fine collection for the eastern seaboard of the U.S. and Civil War archival and genealogical information for 120 Scottish Clans.

Access: On-site access only. Contact the library to find out what they can do for researchers who cannot visit their library.

Huxford Genealogical Research Center

Huxford Research Library
PO Box 595
Homerville, GA 31634

Phone: 912-487-2310

Fax: 912-487-3881

Collection Information: Unique genealogical collection of the late Judge Folks Huxford, F.A.S.G.

Access: Members have free use of the library. For nonmembers, initial visit is free, then $10.00 per day after that.

Hawaii

Hawaii State Archives

Historical Records Branch

Kekauluohi Bldg.
Iolani Palace Grounds
Honolulu, HI 96813

Phone: 808-586-0329

Fax: 808-586-0330

Collection Information: Government records from the monarchy on, private collections, historical photographs, and maps.

Access: Research/Translation: $17.00 per hour.

Hawaii State Library

Hawaii and Pacific Section
478 S King Street
Honolulu, HI 96813-2901

Phone: 808-586-3500

Collection Information: The largest genealogy collection in Hawaii. Newspapers, maps, and the book collection are outstanding.

Access: Information is made available to the public through the public libraries.

Hamilton Library, University of Hawaii

Genealogy
2550 The Mall
Honolulu, HI 96822

Phone: 808-956-8111

Collection Information: Manuscripts on Hawaiians, Japanese, Chinese, and early Americans. A good place to find immigrants to Hawaii.

Access: The best way to use this collection is go there and use it.

Bishop Museum Library

Research Library
1525 Bernice Street
Honolulu, HI 96817-2704

Phone: 808-848-4148

Fax: 808-847-8241

Collection Information: A primary source collection, which documents cultural and natural history in the Pacific.

Access: Call the library to find out how they can help with your Hawaii-based research.

Hawaiian Historical Society Library

Library Services
560 Kawaiahao Street

Honolulu, HI 96813

Phone: 808-537-6271

Collection Information: Many documents of Portuguese, Chinese, Japanese, and Polynesian significance. Strong on pre-American era.

Access: For use by scholars, historians, serious students, and society members interested in Pacific Island area.

Idaho

Idaho State Historical Society

Library and Archives
1109 Main Street
Boise, ID 83702

Phone: 208-334-2682

Fax: 208-334-2774

Collection Information: Idaho materials include vital records, cemetery records, church records, family folders, and the Idaho death index, 1911–1932

Access: Check their Web site for "Information Requests" to find out how to access information from a distance.

University of Idaho Library

Special Collections and Archives
Rayburn Street
Moscow, ID 83844-2350

Phone: 208-885-6534

Collection Information: Unique data on mountain men and early settlers. The collections include Idaho-Northwest histories, rare books, and many documents relating to Idaho.

Access: Visitors to the Special Collections and Archives are always welcome, but it is helpful to call or writes first.

North Idaho College

Library
1000 West Garden Avenue
Coeur d'Alene, ID 83814

Phone: 208-769-3355

Fax: 208-769-3428

Collection Information: Strong on oral histories, Idaho and county histories, and biographies. This is one of the better genealogy collections in the state.

Access: They offer special services to distance learners.

Brigham Young University-Idaho

Arthur Porter Special Collections
240 McKay Library
525 South Center
Rexburg, ID 83460-0405

Archives: 208-496-2986

Family History Lab: 208-496-2386

Collection Information: This library combines the resources of the university library and a Family History Center.

Access: The library maintains several Idaho databases and offers copies of documents to those who request them.

Illinois

Arlington Heights Memorial Library

Kathrine Shackley Room for Local History and Genealogy
500 N Dunton Avenue
Arlington Heights, IL 60004-5966

Phone: 847-392-0100

TTY: 847-392-1119

Collection Information: Newspapers; birth, marriage, death, and obituary indexes; maps; Illinois death and marriage indexes; and passenger lists—a remarkable resource.

Access: Staff will answer genealogy queries by telephone, e-mail, and regular mail if an exact name, place, and date are given.

South Suburban Genealogical and Historical Society

Library
3000 West 170th Place
Hazel Crest, IL 60429

Phone: 708-335-3340

Collection Information: Local histories, genealogies, naturalization records, Pullman Car Works personnel records, obituary files, and church histories.

Access: Materials are used in the library only. Use of the library is free for members; non-members pay $3.00. Donations are encouraged.

Illinois State Archives

Norton Building
Capitol Complex
Springfield, IL 62756

Phone: 217-782-4682

Fax: 217-524-3030

Collection Information: For genealogists, this is one of the best state archives I n the country—lots of online data and good remote access. Check out their Web site.

Access: Nonresidents must prepay $10.00 to request copies of documents.

Lincoln Library

Sangamon Valley Collection
326 S 7th Street
Springfield, IL 62701

Phone: 217-753-4900, ext. 234

TDD: 217-753-4947

Collection Information: Strong genealogical collection including the Sangamon County Obituary File, computer indexes of local newspapers, and Springfield city directories.

Access: Materials do not circulate. Contact them for remote access.

Peoria Public Library

Genealogy Department
107 NE Momoe Street
Peoria, IL 61602-1070

Phone: 309-497-2000

Collection Information: State census, passenger lists, local cemetery indexes, Peoria city directories, U.S. Pension books, county histories, and biographies.

Access: They will check the Peoria newspapers for an obituary if you have an exact death date.

The Newberry Library

Research Library
68 W Walton Street
Chicago, IL 60610-3394

Phone: 312-255-3512

Collection Information: Renown for coverage of colonial America, and noble families of the British Isles. Comprehensive collection of New England town histories.

Access: Everyone needs a reader's card to use the library. Photo identification and proof of current address required.

Indiana

Indiana State Archives

Family History Department
6440 East 30th Street
Indianapolis, IN 46219

Phone: 317-591-5222

Collection Information: One of the best facilities for African American research.

Access: Subject to limitations and fees, they provide access to all of their collections.

Indiana State Library

Genealogy Division
140 N Senate Avenue
Indianapolis, IN 46204-2296

Phone: 317-232-3689

Fax: 317-232-3728

Collection Information: Collection includes family histories, cemetery transcriptions, federal census, Indiana county records, passenger lists, and military pensions.

Access: Researchers can visit the Indiana State Library or they can write, call, or e-mail their questions about the collections.

Kokomo-Howard County Public Library

Department of Genealogy and Local History Services
220 N Union Street
Kokomo, IN 46901-4614

Phone: 765-457-3242

Fax: 765-457-3683

Collection Information: Strong emphasis on Indiana's counties, mostly Howard County, and Caroll, Cass, Clinton, Grant, Tipton, and Miami Counties.

Access: Materials do not circulate. They charge $10.00 per hour plus $0.20 per page copied.

St. Joseph County Public Library

Local History/Genealogy
304 South Main Street
South Bend, IN 46601

Phone: 574-282-4630

Collection Information: Collection strengths include newspapers, local yearbooks, passenger lists, family histories, and vital statistics index.

Access: See the Web site for "Request for Information Search."

Willard Library

Regional and Family History Department
21 First Avenue
Evansville, IN 47710

Phone: 812-425-4309

Fax: 812-421-9742

Collection Information: A strong genealogy collection. They maintain online indexes for marriages, biographies, and companies.

Access: The library is open to the public. See their Web page for remote access.

Iowa

State Historical Society of Iowa–Des Moines

Library Archives Bureau
Capitol Complex
600 E Locust Street
Des Moines, IA 50319

Phone: 515-281-6200

Collection Information: Iowa local history materials include: city directories, plat maps, cemetery surveys, state gazetteers, trade catalogs, and county and city histories.

Access: This is the starting point for genealogical research in Iowa.

State Historical Society of Iowa–Iowa City

Centennial Building
402 Iowa Avenue
Iowa City, IA 52240-1806

Phone: 319-335-3916

Collection Information: This site does not duplicate the resources of the Des Moines archives. It has manuscripts, newspapers, government, business, biographies, and genealogies.

Access: Contact the archive to find out about services to researchers from a distance.

Kansas

Kansas State Historical Society

Research Library and Archives
6425 SW Sixth Avenue
Topeka, KS 66615-1099

Phone: 785-272-8681

Fax: 785-272-8682

TTY: 785-272-8683

Collection Information: Collection strengths: census records, newspapers, vital records, and county histories.

Access: Staff research fee is $15.00 payable at the time the request is made.

Johnson County Library

Genealogy Department
9875 W 87th Street
PO Box 2933
Shawnee Mission, KS 66201-1333

Phone: 913-495-9131

Fax: 913-295-2460

Collection Information: Special strength: Obituaries from local newspapers for Johnson County, Kansas, residents from 1977–present.

Access: Access is free and open to the public.

Wichita Public Library

Genealogy Department
Kansas Reference, and Local History Collection
223 S Main Street
Wichita, KS 67202

Genealogy Phone: 316-261-8509

Local History Phone: 316-261-8566

Fax: 316-262-4540

Collection Information: Collection includes photographs, manuscripts, directories, newspaper clippings, and maps.

Access: Open and free to the public. Research via mail is limited. The fee is $5.00 per half hour plus copy charges, with a maximum of one hour.

Iola Public Library

Raymond L. Willson Genealogy Collection
218 E Madison Avenue
Iola, KS 66749

Phone: 620-365-3262

Fax: 620-365-5137

Collection Information: Collection strengths: census records, county histories, and obituaries.

Access: They will do simple requests, such as asking for a photocopy of an obituary when you have the date of death.

Riley County Genealogical Society

Library
2005 Claflin Road
Manhattan, KS 66502

Phone: 785-565-6495

Collection Information: Great pre-Civil War records, histories for earliest Kansas settlers, family folders, and obituaries.

Access: They will do research for researchers who do not have access to their library.

Kentucky

Kentucky Department of Libraries and Archives

Library and Archives
300 Coffee Tree Road
Frankfort, KY 40601

Phone: 502-564-8300

Collection Information: Birth and death records from 1852, land records, marriage records, tax records, and estate records/wills.

Access: Out-of-state customers must submit a $15.00 nonrefundable research fee with genealogical reference request.

Daviess County Public Library

Kentucky Room
450 Griffith Avenue
Owensboro, KY 42301

Phone: 270-684-0211

Fax: 270-684-0218

Collection Information: Focus of collection: west central Kentucky, history of Kentucky and its families, and the settlement of Kentucky.

Access: They will answer requests for information through U.S. mail, e-mail, or by phone. Otherwise use a professional researcher.

Kentucky Historical Society

History Center
100 W Broadway
Frankfort, KY 40601

Phone: 502-564-1792

Fax: 502-564-4701

Collection Information: Collection strengths: manuscripts, maps, oral history tapes, photographs, and rare books.

Access: These collections do not circulate. Researchers are encouraged to visit the center.

Western Kentucky University

Kentucky Library
1 Big Red Way
Bowling Green, KY 42101-3576

Phone: 270-745-6125

Collection Information: Material about religious denominations (including the Shakers), state, county, and town histories, and genealogical compilations.

Access: Contact the library for remote access.

The National Society of the Sons of the American Revolution

Library
1000 S 4th Street
Louisville KY 40203

Phone: 502-589-1776

Fax: 502-589-1671

Collection Information: Family histories, genealogical materials, federal census, and Revolutionary War pension applications on microfilm.

Access: Open to the public. Nonmembers pay $5.00 per day.

Louisiana

New Orleans Public Library

Louisiana Division
219 Loyola Avenue
New Orleans LA 70112-2044

Phone: 504-596-2614

Collection Information: Focuses on New Orleans, Louisiana, the Southeast United States, Nova Scotia, France, and Spain.

Access: Copies of documents will be photocopied for a fee.

Louisiana State Archives

Archives
3851 Essen Lane
Baton Rouge, LA 70809-2137

Phone: 225-922-1000

Collection Information: Confederate pension applications index database; New Orleans ship passenger lists, church and vital records.

Access: Contact the archives for access from a distance.

State Library of Louisiana

Louisiana Section
Reference Desk
PO Box 131
Baton Rouge, LA 70821

Phone: 225-342-4914

Fax: 225-342-2791

Collection Information: Louisiana telephone and city directories; maps; and major Louisiana newspapers on microfilm.

Access: In-person, telephone, mail, and e-mail reference/referral services.

Diocese of Baton Rouge

Historical Archives
PO Box 2028
1800 South Acadian Thruway
Baton Rouge, LA 70808-1998

Phone: 225-387-0561

Fax: 225-242-0299

Collection Information: Sacramental holdings include baptisms, marriages, and burials by local chapel within each civil parish dating from 1722.

Access: Follow the procedures outlined on their Web page.

East Baton Rouge Parish Library

Bluebonnet Regional Branch
Genealogy Department
9200 Bluebonnet Boulevard
Baton Rouge, LA 70810

Phone: 504-763-2283

Collection Information: This is one of the finest collections in Louisiana; "Census of the Five Civilized Tribes."

Access: Open and free to the public. Contact library for remote services.

Maine

Maine State Library

State House Station #64
Genealogy Resources
Augusta, ME 04333-0064

Phone: 207-287-5600

Collection Information: Native American, Acadian and Huguenot records. This is the best collection in the state.

Access: Genealogy materials are not available for loan. They must be used at the Maine State Library.

Maine State Archives

Research Room
84 State House Station
Augusta, ME 04333-0084

Phone: 207-287-5795

Fax: 207-287-5739

Collection Information: Original records from all Maine counties and towns, plus court records dating back to the 1600s, military records through World War I.

Access: For researchers unable to visit, they provide a list of professional genealogists.

University of Maine

Fogler Library
5729 Fogler Library
Orono, ME 04469

Phone: 207-581-1661

Collection Information: Excellent collections of early Maine settlers, fisheries, Acadians, ships, and shippers.

Access: On-site research is the best way to access this collection.

Maine Historical Society

Research Library
485 Congress Street
Portland, ME 04101

Phone: 207-774-1822

Collection Information: This is a great collection for genealogists. It has over 100,000 books and pamphlets and two million pages of manuscripts from the 1400s.

Access: They offer a fee-based service ($25.00 minimum) for anyone who cannot visit the library in person.

Penobscot Maritime Museum

Stephen Phillips Memorial Library
PO Box 498
Church Street at U.S. Route 1
Searsport, ME 04974-0498

Phone: 207-548-2529

Fax: 207-548-2520

Collection Information: An important biographical index of Maine people, plus shippers, ship registers, logbooks, journals, and more.

Access: Send inquiries to the library by mail, by phone, or by e-mail. They charge $25.00 to cover research and inquiry response time.

Maryland

Maryland State Archives

Family History Research
350 Rowe Boulevard
Annapolis, MD 21401

Phone: 410-260-6400

Fax: 410-974-3895

Collection Information: Records date from 1634 to the 1990s. Documents of genealogical values include county probate, land and court records; and church records.

Access: Professional archivists will assist researchers. All requests from a distance must be submitted by mail, fax, or e-mail. No phone requests.

Frederick County Public Libraries

C. Burr Artz Public Library
Maryland Room
110 East Patrick Street
Frederick, MD 21701

Phone: 301-631-3764

Maryland Room: 301-694-1368

Collection Information: Collection strengths include census records, primary sources, newspapers, and personal papers. The Linton Obituary Collection is unique to this library.

Access: You really have to visit this library to appreciate its vast resources.

Maryland Historical Society

Research Library
201 W Monument Street
Baltimore, MD 21201-4674

Phone: 410-685-3750

Fax: 410-385-2105

Collection Information: Unique items include journals, manuscripts, newspapers, and oral histories.

Access: Admission to the library is $6.00 for nonmembers. Contact the library for access from a distance.

Enoch Pratt Free Library

Special Collections
400 Cathedral Street
Baltimore MD 21201-4484

Phone: 410-396-5430

Fax: 410-396-1441

TTY: 410-396-3761

Collection Information: Collection strengths are historically significant documents, rare books, and ephemera.

Access: Reference can be obtained through walk-in, e-mail, and telephone requests.

Dorchester County Public Library

Central Library—Genealogy/Local History
303 Gay Street
Cambridge, Maryland 21613

Phone: 410-228-7331

Collection Information: Strong on Dorchester County history, newspapers, and census records.

Access: The best way to use this collection is to go there and use in person.

Massachusetts

Massachusetts Archives

Archives at Columbia Point
220 Morrissey Boulevard
Boston, MA 02125

Phone: 617-727-2816

Fax: 617-288-8429

Collection Information: The Archives holds the registration books of births, marriages, and deaths for all Massachusetts cities and towns, 1841-1910.

Access: Access to these materials is provided through the research room.

Massachusetts Historical Society Library

Research Library
1154 Boylston Street
Boston, MA 02215

Phone: 617-536-1608

Fax: 617-859-0074

Collection Information: They have a large collection—117,000 books plus letters, diaries, and personal papers of people from Massachusetts, and their families.

Access: First time researchers must register and present current photo identification.

Connecticut Valley Historical Museum Library

Library and Archive Collections
220 State Street
Corner of State and Chestnut Streets
Springfield, MA 01103

Phone: 413-263-6800

Collection Information: The Springfield Families Database documents the lives of 15,000 Springfield residents who were enumerated on the 1880 U.S. Federal Census.

Access: Contact the library for the best way to access the collection.

Plymouth Public Library

History/Genealogy
132 South Street
Plymouth, MA 02360

Phone: 508-830-4250

Collection Information: You can find most of the published records that relate to Mayflower Pilgrims.

Access: The collection is accessible to the public during library hours. Volunteers can help you if you are unable to visit the library.

Michigan

Detroit Public Library

Burton Historical Collection
5201 Woodward Avenue
Detroit, MI 48202

Phone: 313-833-1480

Collection Information: Genealogical materials include: family histories, cemetery inscriptions, church records of baptisms, marriages, and deaths, and military records.

Access: Materials must be used in the reading room. A list of researchers is provided to those needing extensive research.

Michigan Library and Historical Center

Library of Michigan
702 West Kalamazoo Street
PO Box 30007
Lansing, MI 48909-7507

Phone: 517-373-1580

Fax: 517-373-4480

Collection Information: They acquire genealogical materials for the states in these areas: Great Lakes, New England, Mid-Atlantic, Southern states, Ontario, and Quebec.

Access: Researchers should come prepared to ask for specific information. Staff members will help in the use of the collection.

Michigan Library and Historical Center

State Archives of Michigan
702 West Kalamazoo Street
PO 30740
Lansing, MI 48909-8240

Phone: 517-373-0510

TDD: 800-827-7007

Collection Information: The archives publishes circulars on the Internet to identify and explain the records held by the State Archives of Michigan.

Access: Researchers need to read the circulars to learn how to access the collection.

Clarke Historical Library

Central Michigan University
Mount Pleasant, MI 48859

Phone: 989-774-3352

Fax: 989-774-2160

Collection Information: They have an obituary index for Mount Pleasant newspapers plus other resources unique to central Michigan.

Access: An on-site visit is the best way to access the collection. Staff assistance is limited.

University of Michigan

Bentley Historical Library
Reference Unit
1150 Beal Avenue
Ann Arbor, MI 48109-2113

Phone: 734-764-3482

Fax: 734-936-1333

Collection Information: Census schedules, city directories, county histories, residence and land ownership records, and Washtenaw Abstract Office.

Access: You really have to visit this library to appreciate the important resources they offer genealogists.

Minnesota

Minnesota Historical Society

Library and Collections
345 Kellogg Boulevard W
St. Paul, MN 55102-1906

Phone: 651-296-6126

Collection Information: This 500,000-volume collection is strong in early Minnesota publications, histories, directories, atlases, and plat books.

Access: Prepaid photocopies can be ordered in person, by **Phone:** 651-297-4706, **Fax:** 651-297-7436, or e-mail.

University of Minnesota

Immigration History Research Center
University of Minnesota
311 Andersen Library
222 21st Avenue S
Minneapolis, MN 55455-0439

Phone: 612-625-4800

Fax: 612-626-0018

Collection Information: Strong on eastern, central, and southern European and Near Eastern ethnic groups—those associated with the epic transatlantic migrations.

Access: Refer to Patron Research Services and Fees for on-site and remote access: www1.umn.edu/ ihrc/patron.htm.

Iron Range Research Center

Research Center
PO Box 392
801 SW Highway 169, Ste. 1
Chisholm, MN 55719-0392

Phone: 218-254-7959, ext. 2

Collection Information: City and telephone directories, death records, marriage records, and naturalization records.

Access: Research services for people all over the world via mail, e-mail, fax, and electronically through their Web site.

Minnesota Genealogical Society Library

Research Library
5768 Olson Memorial Highway
Golden Valley, MN 55422-5014

Phone: 763-595-9347

Collection Information: They collect, preserve and publish genealogical and historical records relating to Minnesota and its people.

Access: There is a $5.00 fee for nonmember use of the library. The collection does not circulate and is available for research only at the library.

Minneapolis Public Library

Resources for Genealogical Research
250 Marquette Avenue
Minneapolis, MN 55401

Phone: 612-630-6000

Collection Information: Minneapolis Ward maps, passenger list indexes, county histories, Sanborn maps, and military records.

Access: Their genealogy materials and services available for free public use.

Mississippi

Mississippi Department of Archives and History

Archives and Library
P. O. Box 571
200 North Street
Jackson, MS 39201-0571

Phone: 601-576-6850

Archives Fax: 601-576-6964

Historic Preservation Fax: 601-576-6955

Collection Information: Mississippiana, maps, government records, and personal papers. Public access to the archival holdings is provided in the search room.

Access: Contact the agency for access from a distance.

Evans Memorial Library

Research Library
150 North Long Street
Aberdeen, MS 39730

Phone: 622-369-4601

Fax: 622-369-2971

Collection Information: They have cemetery records, marriage indexes, photos, 1,600 plus surname file, and family histories.

Access: Open and free to the public. Contact the library to find out how to access the collection if you cannot do research in person.

Mississippi State University

Mitchell Memorial Library
Special Collections Department
PO box 5408
Mississippi State, MS 39762-5408

Phone: 662-325-7668

Fax: 662-325-9344

Collection Information: Genealogies, manuscripts, family histories, maps, Civil War diaries, letters, muster rolls, and other original materials.

Access: The best way to access this collection is to go there and use it. Otherwise contact a professional researcher.

Missouri

St. Louis County Library

Julius K. Hunter and Friends African American Research Collection
St. Louis County Library
1640 South Lindbergh Boulevard
St. Louis, MO 63131-3598

Phone: 314-994-3300, ext. 208

Fax: 314-994-9411

Collection Information: This is one of the most important collections for African American research in the country. Plantation and post-Civil War, and slavery records.

Access: The collection is designed to be used on site. Contact the library for alternative access.

St. Louis County Library

Local History and Genealogy
1640 South Lindbergh Boulevard
St. Louis, MO 63131-3598

Phone: 314-994-3300, ext. 208

Fax: 314-994-9411

Collection Information: They have the holdings of the St. Louis Genealogical Society and the National Genealogical Society Book Loan Collection.

Access: The St. Louis Genealogical Society will search other sources.

Missouri State Archives

Archives
600 W Main Street
PO Box 1747
Jefferson City, MO 65102

Phone: 573-751-3280

Collection Information: They collect and preserve records and make them available to state government officials, historians, genealogists, and the general public.

Access: Access to the Archives is provided through the research room. The reference staff will answer written requests.

State Historical Society of Missouri

Research Library
1020 Lowry Street
Columbia, MO 65201-7298

Phone: 573-882-7083

Fax: 573-884-4950

Collection Information: County and town histories, city directories, complied cemetery records, and indexes to local records.

Access: Out-of-state nonmembers are charged $25.00 per hour for research services.

Montana

Montana Historical Society

Library and Archives
225 N Roberts Street
PO Box 201201
Helena, MT 59620-1201

Phone: 406-444-2681

Collection Information: This is the place to start with Montana research. They have historical documents for all counties, including histories and early publications.

Access: If you are not able to visit the library to conduct your own research, our staff may be able to assist you with your research for a small fee.

Montana State Library

Library
1515 East 6th Avenue
PO Box 201800
Helena, MT 59620-1800

Phone: 406-444-3115

Fax: 406-444-5612

Collection Information: They have a solid collection of early historical publications and a good collection of newspapers on microfilm.

Access: Contact them to figure out the best way to access the records.

Parmly Billings Library

Library
510 North Broadway
Billings, MT 59101

Phone: 406-657-8257

Collection Information: This library has a comprehensive collection on the history of eastern Montana, plus indexes to cemeteries, biographies, and newspapers.

Access: If they have materials of value in your research, contact the reference desk to determine the best way to access their materials.

Great Falls Genealogical Society Library

High Plains Heritage Center
422 Second Street South
Great Falls, MT 59405

Phone: 406-727-3922

Collection Information: They have, passenger lists, coroner's records for Cascade County, cemetery transcriptions, probate records, and obituary files.

Access: Visitors are welcome to use the library. Volunteers staff the library. Call them to find out how to access the collection.

Butte—Silver Bow Public Library

Library
226 West Broadway
Butte, MT 59701

Phone: 406-723-3301

Fax: 406-723-1825

Collection Information: The collection has genealogies, county histories, and biographies with many old and rare books.

Access: The library provides information in person, by phone, or in writing.

Nebraska

Nebraska State Historical Society

Library/Archives
PO Box 82554
1500 R Street
Lincoln, NE 68501-2554

Phone: 402-471-4771

Fax: 402-471-8922

Collection Information: They have newspapers, telephone directories, city and county directories, county atlases, plat books, and maps.

Access: They welcome all researchers interested in the history of Nebraska and its people. Reference staff will do limited searches for a fee.

Nebraska State Genealogical Society Library

Beatrice Public Library
100 North 16th Street
Beatrice, NE 68310-4100

Phone: 402-223-3584

Fax: 402-223-3913

Collection Information: County and state histories, plus family histories and microfilm.

Access: Members may rent up to four reels of microfilm at a time and pay $2.50 per roll. Nonmembers pay $5.00 and must go through interlibrary loan.

Omaha Public Library

Genealogy Department
215 South 15th Street
Omaha, NE 68102

Phone: 402-444-4826

Collection Information: Obituary file, newspapers, maps, city directories, genealogical databases, indexes for vital records, census schedules, cemeteries, and family genealogies.

Access: The Omaha Public Library will perform some limited research on specific Omaha topics for a fee beginning at $10.00 + $0.50 per photocopy. Check their Web site.

American Historical Society of Germans from Russia

Research Library
631 D Street
Lincoln, NE 68502-1199

Phone: 402-474-3363

Fax: 402-474-7229

Collection Information: They specialize in the heritage of Germans from Russia. Their Web site is a gold mine of information and research links.

Access: The archive is open to the public at no charge. They participate in interlibrary loan through OCLC. Photocopies are $1.00 per page.

Nevada

Nevada State Library and Archives

Genealogical Resources
100 North Stewart Street
Carson City, NV 89701

Phone: 775-684-3310

Fax: 775-684-3311

TDD: 775-684-3338

Collection Information: The Web page is designed to point researchers in the right direction for genealogical resources in the state.

Access: They encourage researchers to call them for more information.

Nevada Historical Society

Research and Reading Room
1650 North Virginia Street
Reno, NV 89503

Phone: 775-688-1190

Fax: 775-688-2917

Collection Information: Materials available to the public include books, newspapers, maps, government documents, and subject files.

Access: Out-of-town researchers need to hire a professional to make copies that will take a long time. They will help you find a professional researcher.

New Hampshire

New Hampshire State Library

Genealogy Section
20 Park Street
Concord, NH 03301

Phone: 603-271-6823

Fax: 603-271-2205

Collection Information: They have early town records, tax inventories, federal census schedules, newspapers, city and county directories, and military indexes.

Access: The staff will assist patrons in using the collection. They accept mail requests up to about 10 pages for $0.20 per page.

New Hampshire Department of State

Division of Vital Records Administration
29 Hazen Drive
Concord, NH 03301

Phone: 603-271-4650

Fax: 603-271-3347

Collection Information: Online directory of New Hampshire city and town clerks. New Hampshire vital records are considered to be private, and access to them is restricted.

Access: Genealogist may visit the Genealogical Research Center, or write to request information for a fee. Contact the library for details.

New Hampshire Historical Society

Tuck Library
30 Park Street
Concord, NH 03301-6394

Phone: 603-228-6688

Fax: 603-224-0463

Collection Information: The most comprehensive genealogical resource in northern New England. They have unpublished cemetery records and a card index of 30,000 names.

Access: Members and full-time students use the library free. Others pay $6.00 per day. Copy charges are $0.20 and $0.25. Mailing or fax fees are $6.00.

Manchester Public Library

New Hampshire Room and Genealogy
405 Pine Street
Manchester, NH 03104

Phone: 603-624-6550

Collection Information: They have city and town histories, biographies, genealogies, and New Hampshire families.

Access: For $5.00 they will do a limited amount of research—no census or vital records searches. No telephone requests.

New Jersey

Rutgers University Libraries

Special Collections
Genealogical Resources
169 College Avenue
New Brunswick, NJ 08901-1163

Collection Information: This is the home of the Archibald S. Alexander collection—one of the most significant genealogical resources in the country.

Access: New Jersey's best genealogy resource.

New Jersey State Archives

Archives
225 West State Street, Level 2
PO Box 307
Trenton, NJ 08625-0307

Phone: 609-292-6260

Fax: 609-396-2454

Collection Information: They have marriage bond before 1795, wills and estate inventories, deeds before 1785, military records, naturalization records, some county marriage records, plus other records.

Access: The collection is open to researchers during their business hours. They can also request copies of indexed documents through the mail.

The New Jersey Historical Society

Library
52 Park Place
Newark, NJ 07102

Phone: 973-596-8500

Fax: 973-596-6957

Collection Information: Tax records, city directories, genealogical card indexes, maps, military records, newspapers, and other sources.

Access: Researchers are encouraged to use their card catalogs and then ask a reference if they still have questions.

Newark Public Library

The New Jersey Information Center
5 Washington Street
PO Box 630
Newark, NJ 07101-0630

Phone: 973-733-7775

Fax: 973-733-7835

Collection Information: This is a research-level collection for New Jersey, Essex County, and Newark. Books, newspapers, original documents, photos, and archives.

Access: They are open and free to the public. Check with the staff for access and copying fees.

Joint Free Public Library of Morristown-Morris Township

Local History and Genealogy Department
1 Miller Road
Morristown, NJ 07960

Phone: 973-538-3473

Collection Information: Published military and pension records, New Jersey tax lists, 1773–1822, church records, early town records, and significant family papers.

Access: All material has to be used in the local history reading room. They will answer specific queries that take less than an hour, checking indexed sources. They charge a minimum of $5.00 per question.

New Mexico

New Mexico State Records and Archives

Archival and Historical Services Division
1205 Camino Carlos Rey
Santa Fe, NM 87507

Phone: 505-476-7908

Fax: 505-476-7909

Collection Information: Best place to start research for New Mexico ancestors. They have lots of original records and early documents.

Access: Do your homework before going to the archives.

Rio Grande Valley Library System

Special Collections Library
423 Central Avenue NE
Albuquerque, NM 87102

Phone: 505-848-1376

Collection Information: Special Collections supports researchers concentrating on Hispanic genealogy.

Access: All materials are available for in-house use only. Photocopying is allowed.

New Mexico State Library

Library Services
1209 Camino Carlos Rey
Santa Fe, NM 87507

Phone: 505-476-9700

Fax: 505-476-9701

Collection Information: They have a large book collection including government documents, maps, bibliography of biographies and vertical files, and family histories.

Access: The southwest room is a serious reference collection for on-site use by serious researchers.

Carlsbad Public Library

Library
101 South Halagueno Street
Carlsbad, NM 88220

Phone: 505-885-0731

Fax: 505-885-8809

Collection Information: They have a great genealogy collection with resources for all parts of the U.S., thanks in part to the many winter visitors/residents.

Access: Check with the reference librarian to see how they can help with research from a distance.

University of New Mexico Zimmerman Library

Center for Southwest Research
General Library
University of New Mexico
Albuquerque, M 87131

Phone: 505-277-4241

Collection Information: The collection consists of books, etc. emphasizing New Mexico, and Oklahoma—including very early Mexican and Anglo records.

Access: Most volumes are housed in closed stacks. Researchers are encouraged to call ahead with specific needs to arrange for access to the collection.

New York

New York Genealogical and Biographical Society Library

Family History
122-126 East 58th Street
New York, NY 10022-1939

Phone: 212-755-8532

Fax: 212-754-4218

Collection Information: They have a solid book collection and an impressive manuscript collection. This is one of the best colonial period resources in the country.

Access: The collection is open to the public for a suggested donation of $10.00. Volunteers will do a record search for $35.00. A mini search consisting of 12 indexes is $5.00 for members.

New York State Archives

New York State Education Department
Cultural Education Center
Albany, NY 12230

Phone: 518-474-8955

Collection Information: They have indexes to older birth, marriage and death certificates. Staff members will assist researchers in finding the records they need.

Access: A local town, city, school, or county will often have the record you need before going to the New York State Archives.

Rochester Public Library

Monroe County (NY) Library System
115 South Avenue
Rochester, NY 14604

Genealogy Phone: 585-428-8370

Collection Information: Large holdings of upstate resources census, newspapers, and vital statistics index.

Access: Call the reference department to determine the best way for you to access the collection.

North Carolina

North Carolina State Archives

Public Services Branch
4614 Mail Service Center
Raleigh, NC 27699-4614

Physical address:
109 East Jones Street
Raleigh, NC 27601

Phone: 919-807-7310

Fax: 919-733-1354

Collection Information: They have bonds, census records, court records, land records, estate records, marriage records, tax records, and wills.

Access: The search and handling fee for out-of-state requests is $20.00 per inquiry. See their fee schedule page for additional services and products.

State Library of North Carolina

Genealogical Services
4641 Mail Service Center
109 East Jones Street
Raleigh, NC 27601

Phone: 919-807-7460

Collection Information: They have a significant collection of the colonial and post-colonial periods.

Access: Genealogical materials do not circulate. Though researchers may ask questions by e-mail, following the guidelines.

Public Library of Charlotte and Mecklenburg County

Carolina Room
310 North Tryon Street
Charlotte, NC 28202

Phone: 704-336-2725

Collection Information: The department focuses strongly on North and South Carolina, Tennessee, Virginia, and Georgia.

Access: Contact them for the best way to access the collection.

Olivia Raney History Library

History Library
1460 Carya Drive
Raleigh, NC 27610

Phone: 919-250-1196

Collection Information: County histories, vital records, maps, directories and military records.

Access: Contact the library for access to the library and the services they offer.

Rowan Public Library

History Room
201 W Fischer Street
Salisbury, NC

Phone: 704-638-3021

Collection Information: They have a unique in-house index to Rowan County birth certificates.

Access: Birth certificates can be accessed through the Rowan County Register of Deeds Office.

North Dakota

North Dakota State Library

Research Library
604 East Boulevard Avenue—Dept. 250
Bismarck, ND 58505-0800

Phone: 701-328-2492

Fax: 701-328-2040

Collection Information: The North Dakota State Library has a collection of county histories, which can be useful to genealogical researchers.

Access: The collection is available to residents of the state. The staff will not do research. They refer researchers to the North Dakota Historical Research Library.

State Archives and Historical Research Library

North Dakota Heritage Center
612 East Boulevard Avenue
Bismarck, ND 58505-0830

Phone: 701-328-2091

Fax: 701-328-2650

Collection Information: Historical Data Project (WPA) Biography files, biographical index, Oral History Project, naturalization records, and vital records.

Access: No general or surname searches will be attempted. A list of genealogical researchers can be provided if desired.

University of North Dakota Chester Fritz Library

Family History and Genealogy Room
University Avenue and Centennial Drive
PO Box 9000
Grand Forks, ND 58202

Phone: 701-777-2617

Fax: 701-777-3319

Collection Information: Federal Manuscript Population Census Schedules, American Lutheran Church records, plus extensive Norwegian local history books.

Access: The collection is open to the public. Check with the staff for access from a distance.

Bismarck Mandan Historical and Genealogical Library

Library
PO Box 485
Bismarck, ND 58502

Phone: 701-223-6273

Collection Information: Excellent collection of North Dakota biographies, family folders, and genealogies.

Access: You have to visit this place if you have North Dakota Ancestors. Call or write them to find out how to access the collection from a distance.

Ohio

Public Library of Cincinnati and Hamilton County

Genealogy Department
800 Vine Street
Third Floor—South Building
Cincinnati, OH 45202-2071

Main Phone: 513-369-6900

Genealogy Phone: 513-369-6905

Collection Information: This is one of the oldest and largest genealogy collections in the country—260,000 print volumes—covering all 50 states, plus some foreign countries.

Access: The staff provides in-person reference service, ready-reference by phone, and limited research in response to mail requests.

Rutherford B. Hayes Presidential Library

Spiegel Grove
Fremont, OH 43420

Phone: 419-332-2081

Fax: 419-332-4952

Collection Information: They have an online index to over 300,000 obituaries, death and marriage notices and other sources from Northwest Ohio.

Access: Open to the public and free of charge. Remote access is limited to mail and e-mail requests. Fee is $12.50 an hour in advance, plus copies.

Ohio Historical Society

Archives and Library
1982 Velma Avenue
Columbus, OH 43211

Phone: 614-297-2300

Collection Information: Access to birth records, death records, land entry records, marriage records, and African American records, 1850–1920.

Access: The Ohio Historical Society accepts requests submitted by members of the public who cannot visit the society's archives/library.

Ohio Genealogical Society

Library
713 S Main Street
Mansfield, OH 44907-1644

Phone: 419-756-7294

Fax: 419-756-8681

Collection Information: They have the best family folder collection in Ohio, plus an ancestral card file submitted by OGS members.

Access: Nonmembers pay $4.00 per day to use the library. They have a small lending collection of duplicate titles they will circulate to members.

Ohio State Library

Genealogy Services
274 East First Avenue, Ste. 100
Columbus, OH 43201

Phone: 800-686-1532

Fax: 614-728-2789

Collection Information: They emphasize the importance of Ohio as the Gateway to the West. They have records that cover individuals from Ohio, as well as other states.

Access: The library is open for unrestricted use by the public. Genealogy materials do not circulate and are not available for interlibrary loan.

Oklahoma

Oklahoma Historical Society

Research Division
2100 N Lincoln Boulevard
Oklahoma City, OK 73105-4997

Phone: 405-522-5248

Fax: 405-522-5402

Collection Information: For researchers of Native American and Anglo American ancestry. This is the best place to start Oklahoma genealogical research.

Access: They require a research fee of $20.00 for out-of-state inquiries before research can begin. The in-state fee is $5.00.

Oklahoma Department of Libraries

Allen Wright Memorial Library
200 Northeast 18th Street
Oklahoma City, OK 73105-3209

Phone: 405-521-2502

Fax: 405-525-7804

Collection Information: A massive of materials on Oklahoma history, specializing in county histories, government publications, and a vertical file.

Access: Most materials can be borrowed by interlibrary loan through a local public library.

Tulsa City-County Public Library

Genealogy Center
2901 S Harvard Avenue
Tulsa, OK 74114

Phone: 918-746-5222

Collection Information: They have one of the largest genealogy collections in Oklahoma.

Access: The staff can answer short questions by phone or letter. The staff cannot do look-ups or extensive research.

Lawton Public Library

Family History Room
110 SW 4th Street
Lawton, OK 73501

Phone: 580-581-3450

Collection Information: One of the largest book collections in the state. Specific materials cover Kiowa, Comanche, and Apache peoples.

Access: Open and free to the public. Contact the library for remote access.

Tulsa Genealogical Society

Library
9072 East 31st Street
Tulsa, OK 74145

Phone: 918-746-5222

Collection Information: Funeral Home Records of Tulsa, Oklahoma, Native American research in Oklahoma.

Access: Write them a letter to request research services.

Oregon

Genealogical Forum of Oregon

Library
1505 SE Gideon Street
PO Box 42567
Portland, OR 97242-0567

Phone: 503-963-1932

Collection Information: Specific research areas include Native American records, Oregon census, African American genealogies, and Multnomah County records.

Access: A small volunteer staff will search library resources for individuals who live outside the Portland area. The fee is $10.00 plus the cost of copies and an ASAE.

Oregon State Archives

Genealogy Records
800 Summer Street NE
Salem, OR 97310

Phone: 503-373-0701

Fax: 503-373-0953

Collection Information: Specific resources include adoption records, census records, land records, military records, naturalization records, and probate records.

Access: Open and free to the public. Check with agency for remote access.

Oregon Historical Society

Museum and Research Library
1200 SW Park Avenue
Portland, OR 97205

Phone: 503-222-1741

Photo/Map reference: 503-306-5250

Manuscript reference: 503-306-5258

General Reference: 503-306-5240

Collection Information: They have a government documents collection that is especially strong on early territorial and statehood periods.

Access: Adult admission to the library is $6.00. The staff will do research in response to inquiries subject to the research assistance fee of $50.00 per hour.

University of Oregon

Knight Library
1299 University of Oregon
Eugene, OR 97403-1299

Phone: 541-346-3056

Genealogy section: 541-346-1818

Collection Information: A solid genealogy collection with print materials, manuscripts, city directories, census films, newspapers, and a vital records index.

Access: Open and free to the public. Contact the library for remote access.

Rogue Valley Genealogical Society

Research Library
95 Houston Road
Phoenix, OR 97535-1468

Phone: 541-512-2340

Collection Information: This is one of the best collections in southern Oregon. It includes vital records, and local burial records.

Access: Staff members will help individuals with their research. The research fee is $10.00 per hour per request.

Pennsylvania

Historical Society of Pennsylvania

Research and Collection
1300 Locust Street
Philadelphia, PA 19107

Phone: 215-732-6200

Fax: 215-732-2680

Collection Information: This is one of the largest family history libraries in the United States. It includes some 600,000 printed items and over 19 million manuscript and graphic items.

Access: Skilled staff researchers will research and answer questions from the resources of the library and archives.

Genealogical Society of Pennsylvania

Research Room
215 Broad Street, 7th Floor
Philadelphia, PA 19107-5325

Phone: 215-545-0391

Fax: 215-545-0936

Collection Information: Included are wills, census and tax lists, church registers, funeral, cemetery, and family Bible records, and correspondence.

Access: Hour rate for requests from nonmembers is $35.00 plus cost for photocopies.

Library Company of Philadelphia

Research Room
1314 Locust Street
Philadelphia, PA 19107

Phone: 215-546-3181

Fax: 215-546-5167

Collection Information: This is a nonprofit independent research library, with nearly a half million holdings, including manuscripts and artifacts.

Access: Open to the public free of charge. No materials circulate. Photocopies may be ordered if the condition of the material permits.

Carnegie Library of Pittsburgh

Pennsylvania Department
4400 Forbes Avenue
Pittsburgh, PA 15213

Phone: 412-622-3154

Fax: 412-578-2569

Collection Information: This library has an extensive book collection, plus newspapers, county histories, and manuscripts.

Access: For $10.00 the staff will search the death notice index for up to five names. They will also search up to two Pittsburgh newspapers if an exact date is provided.

Lancaster County Historical Society

Research Library
230 N President Avenue
Lancaster, PA 17603

Phone: 717-392-4633

Fax: 717-293-2739

Collection Information: Deeds, genealogies, family files, marriage and death records and newspapers.

Access: If you seek information about a Lancaster County ancestor you should submit a research order form.

Historical Society of Western Pennsylvania

Library and Archives
1212 Smallman Street
Pittsburgh, PA 15222

Phone: 412-454-6364

Fax: 412-454-6028

Collection Information: Some 35,000 individual archives of personal and family papers, organizational records, and industry records.

Access: Requests for research should include a phone number and a mailing address and enough information to pin point the research requested.

Rhode Island

Rhode Island Historical Society

Research Library
110 Benevolent Street
Providence, RI 02906

Phone: 401-331-8578

Fax: 401-351-0127

Collection Information: This is the largest collection in Rhode Island. It includes original manuscripts, family Bibles, church records and family folders.

Access: Research fees are $45.00 per hour for nonmembers. The staff is unable to offer extensive research service.

Rhode Island State Library

Library
State House, Rm. 208
Providence, RI 02903

Phone: 401-222-2473

Fax: 401-222-3034

Collection Information: The collection has copies of all published Rhode Island town histories, plus biographies and genealogies.

Access: The library is open and free to the public. Contact the library for remote access.

Providence Public Library

Rhode Island Collection
225 Washington Street
Providence, RI 02903

Phone: 401-455-8000

Collection Information: Providence city directories, family biographies, Arnold's Vital Records, and regimental histories of the Civil War.

Access: Primary access to the collection is through the Rhode Island Index—a subject listing.

Rhode Island State Archives

State Archives and Public Records Administration
337 Westminster Street
Providence, RI 02903

Phone: 401-222-2353

Fax: 401-222-3199

Collection Information: The Rhode Island State Archives has the earliest of all town and county records.

Access: Fill out the probate request form and send it in. they will tell you their fees.

Westerly Public Library

Memorial and Library Association
44 Broad Street
Westerly, RI 02891

Phone: 401-596-2877

Collection Information: Specific strengths include Seventh-Day Baptist Church Index, family genealogy vertical files, and Revolutionary War pension applications.

Access: Requests for genealogy research must include a nominal fee of $10.00 per query (name) plus copy charges.

South Carolina

South Carolina Department of Archives and History

Archives and History Center
8301 Parklane Road
Columbia, SC 29223

Phone: 803-896-6100

Fax: 803-896-6198

Collection Information: This is an independent state agency that houses one of the most significant state archival collections in the United States.

Access: The staff will answer questions about the records and provide specific information from them if the amount of research time is reasonable.

South Carolina Historical Society

Library
100 Meeting Street
Charleston, SC 29401

Phone: 843-723-3225

Fax: 843-723-8584

Collection Information: This is one of the most significant private repositories of South Carolina history in the world.

Access: There is a $5.00 daily access fee for nonmembers. They recommend professional researchers.

Heritage Library Foundation

The Heritage Library–Hilton Head
The Courtyard Building, Ste. 300
Hilton Head Island, SC 29928-4640

Phone: 843-686-6560

Collection Information: Holdings include vertical file genealogies, plus a large local genealogical database.

Access: Call or e-mail the library for services or remote access.

Camden Archives and Museum

Library/Research Collections
1314 Broad Street
Camden, SC 29020-3535

Phone: 803-425-6050

Fax: 803-424-4053

Collection Information: This is one of the best genealogical research libraries in the state. It houses a broad-based collection of books, microfilms, and maps.

Access: Query letters should be specific. A $5.00 fee is required as advance payment . The research fee is $10.00/hour payable in advance plus copies and postage costs.

The Huguenot Society of South Carolina

Library
138 Logan Street
Charleston, SC 29401-1941

Phone: 843-723-3235

Fax: 843-853-8476

Collection Information: The collection is dedicated to the tracing of Huguenot ancestry.

Access: Professionals are available to help members and nonmember researchers. Nonmembers pay a minimal daily use fee.

South Dakota

South Dakota State Historical Society

South Dakota State Archives
900 Governors Drive
Pierre, SD 57501-2217

Phone: 605-773-3458

Fax: 605-773-6041

Collection Information: Government records, Indian archives, manuscripts, newspapers, city directories, yearbooks, local histories, family histories and county atlases.

Access: They lend microfilm and staff development items through interlibrary loan. Researchers may write to the South Dakota State Archives with specific research questions and expect to pay a fee for the search.

South Dakota State Library

Genealogy Research
800 Governors Drive
Pierre, SD 57501

Phone: 605-773-3131

Collection Information: They have the most significant book collections in the state, which includes county histories, biographies, and genealogies.

Access: South Dakota residents may contact the state library directly for research assistance.

Rapid City Public Library

Library
610 Quincy Street
Rapid City, SDa, 57701-3655

Phone: 605-394-6139

Collection Information: Obituaries, family folders, biographies, genealogies, and South Dakota families.

Access: Open to the public. Contact the library for remote access.

Siouxland Libraries

Sioux Falls Public Library
201 N Main Avenue
Sioux Falls SD 57104-6002

Phone: 605-367-8799

Fax: 605-367-4312

Collection Information: This library has a superb genealogy collection with indexes and family folders.

Access: Call or write the library for services or remote access.

Alexander Mitchell Library

Special Collections
519 S Kline Street
Aberdeen, SD 57401

Phone: 605-626-7097

Collection Information: The collection is strong on South Dakota history, genealogy, and Germans from Russia.

Access: Call them before making a research trip.

Tennessee

Tennessee State Library and Archives

Tennessee History and Genealogy
403 Seventh Avenue North
Nashville, TN 37243-0312

Phone: 615-741-2746

Collection Information: Extensive public records, original county records, records of Confederate soldiers.

Access: Copies of documents may be ordered by mail for $10.00.

Memphis-Shelby County Public Library

History Department
3030 Popular Avenue
Memphis, TN 38111-3527

Phone: 901-725-8855

Collection Information: The library has a very large collection that specializes in southeastern United States and Tennessee resources.

Access: The library will conduct limited historic and genealogical reference service for a fee of $25.00 per hour and $5.00 for shipping.

Knox County Public Library

McClung Collection
314 West Clinch Avenue
Knoxville, TN 37902

Phone: 865-215-8801

Collection Information: The library has a strong Tennessee collection and has a significant collection for other states in the southeastern United States.

Access: The staff will answer basic genealogical and historical questions for a basic fee of $15.00. Contact the library for a detailed fee schedules.

Chattanooga-Hamilton County Public Library

Local History and Genealogy Department
1001 Broad Street
Chattanooga, TN 37402

Phone: 423-757-5317

Collection Information: The library has a strong Tennessee collection, plus extensive holdings for the rest of the Southeast.

Access: For a fee the library will make copies of documents and send them to individuals who request them.

Tennessee Historical Society

War Memorial Building
300 Capitol Boulevard
Nashville, TN 37243

Phone: 615-741-8934

Fax: 615-741-8937

Collection Information: The Tennessee Historical Society is a nonprofit, membership organization.

Access: Contact the society for services and access to the collection.

Texas

Texas State Library and Archives Commission

Library and Archives
1201 Brazos Street
PO Box 12927
Austin, TX 78711

Phone: 512-463-5463

Collection Information: The state archives include newspapers, journals, manuscripts, maps and photographs.

Access: Call 512-463-5480 for access from a distance.

Houston Public Library

Clayton Library, Center for Genealogical Research
5300 Caroline Street
Houston, TX 77004-7896

Phone: 832-393-2600

Collection Information: This is one of the top genealogical research libraries in the United States. It is particularly strong on Texas and Tennessee resources.

Access: If you live in Texas, get a Houston Public Library Power Card and use it for access to genealogical materials.

Dallas Public Library

History and Social Science
Genealogy Section
1515 Young Street
Dallas, TX 75201-5499

Phone: 214-670-1433

Collection Information: The collection covers Texas well and is among the best at covering the rest of the states, especially those in New England, the mid-Atlantic, and the South.

All holdings in the collection are for in-library use only.

Carnegie Center of Brazos Valley History

Bryan College Station Public Library System
111 South Main Street
Bryan, TX 77803

Phone: 979-209-5630

Collection Information: Strong on local history and Texas.

Access: Contact them for remote access.

The Fort Worth Public Library

Genealogy, Local History and Archives
500 W 3rd Street
Fort Worth, TX 76102-7305

Phone: 817-871-7740

Collection Information: The focus is on Texas and the South, but also includes material on the Midwest and the original thirteen states.

Access: Write, call or e-mail for information about access and their services.

The Grapevine Public Library

Genealogy Resources
1201 Municipal Way
Grapevine, TX 76051

Phone: 817-410-3400

Fax: 817-410-3080

Collection Information: They have an extensive collection of genealogical reference and county histories.

Access: Call them to find out what they have before making a research trip.

Utah

Marriott Library, University of Utah

Special Collections
295 S 1500 E
Salt Lake City, UT 84112-0860

Phone: 801-581-8558

Western Americana Collection: 801-581-8863

Collection Information: Western Americana includes newspapers, serials, maps, and clipping files.

Access: This is a collection you really have to visit to appreciate. Contact them for remote access.

Utah State Archives and Records Services

Archives
PO Box 141021
State Capitol, Archives Building
Salt Lake City, UT 84114-1021

Phone: 801-538-3012

Fax: 801-538-3354

Collection Information: Birth and death records, naturalization records, court and probate records, publications, and other agency mission-related series.

Access: Microfilms of public records in the custody of the Utah State Archives may be purchased or borrowed.

Utah State Historical Society

Family History Resources
300 South Rio Grande Street
Salt Lake City, UT 84101-1143

Phone: 801-533-3500

Fax: 801-533-3503, or 3504

TDD: 801-533-3502

Collection Information: Collection has books, periodicals, pamphlets, maps, manuscripts, photographs, and microfilm.

Access: You really have to visit the Historical Society to appreciate what they have.

Brigham Young University

Utah Valley Regional Family History Center
Level 2 Harold B. Lee Library
Provo, UT 84602

Phone: 801-422-6200

Collection Information: They have thousands of family history microfilms on indefinite loan from the Family History Library.

Access: If you cannot get to the FHL in Salt Lake City this is a good alternative.

Vermont

Vermont Historical Society

Library
60 Washington Street
Barre, VT 05641-4209

Phone: 802-479-8500

Collection Information: The largest genealogical library in the state. Vital records, cemetery inscriptions, and town histories.

Access: Volunteers respond to genealogy inquiries to the library. There is a $15.00 research fee for up to 20 minutes of work.

Vermont State Archives

Archives
Redstone Building
26 Terrace Street
Drawer 09
Montpelier, VT 05609-1101

Phone: 802-828-2363

Collection Information: The online catalog, ArcCat, describes archival and manuscript collections held by Vermont institutions.

Access: Photocopying is available. Limited staff will help guide researchers in person.

Vermont Department of Libraries

Library
109 State Street
Montpelier, VT 05609-0601

Phone: 802-828-3216

Fax: 802-828-2199

Collection Information: They have a noteworthy historical reference collection.

Access: Access is free and open to the public. Contact library for services from a distance.

Brooks Memorial Library

Genealogy and Local History Room
224 Main Street
Brattleboro, VT 05301

Phone: 802-254-5290

Fax: 802-527-2309

Collection Information: Family Bibles, town directories and histories, newspaper clipping files, for Vermont and New England.

Access: You really have to visit this library to appreciate its resources.

Virginia

Library of Virginia

Genealogical Research
800 E Broad Street
Richmond, VA 23219-8000

Phone: 804-692-3777

Fax: 804-692-3556

Collection Information: Collection includes state, county, and city government records, personal papers, genealogical notes and charts, and maps.

Access: The Library of Virginia provides a list of professional researchers who specialize in Virginia history.

Virginia Historical Society

Research Collections
428 North Boulevard
Richmond, VA 23220

Phone: 804-358-4901

Collection Information: Seven million items in manuscript collection, including family and personal papers, and Bible records.

Access: Maximum of one-hour research costs $20.00, prepaid. The fee includes limited photocopies.

Fairfax County Public Library

Virginia Room
3915 Chain Bridge Road
Fairfax, VA 22030-3995

Phone: 703-293-6383

TTY: 703-324-8365

Fax: 703-385-1911

Collection Information: Collection is strong on local history, Confederate military history, manuscripts and local newspapers.

Access: The collection is freely open to the public. Check with the staff for the availability of someone to do research.

University of Virginia

Manuscripts and Rare Books Collection
PO Box 400111
Charlottesville, VA 22904-4111

Phone: 434-924-7261

Fax: 434-924-1431

Collection Information: Strong emphasis on Virginia history, letters, diaries, and other documents, especially about Virginia and southern families.

Access: Collection open to serious researchers. Check with staff for research services.

Jones Memorial Library

Library
2311 Memorial Avenue
Lynchburg, VA 24501

Phone: 434-846-0501

Fax: 434-846-1572

Collection Information: Genealogy and local history of central Virginia including county histories, court records, family histories, and genealogies.

Access: They can offer only minimal assistance for those who cannot use the library in person.

Washington

Fiske Library

Research Library
1644 43rd Avenue E
Seattle, WA 98112

Phone: 206-328-2716

Collection Information: Private library. Probably the best New England collection on the West Coast.

Access: One-day use of library $5.00, Evening use is $3.00. Yearly: single $40.00, couple $60.00

Tacoma Public Library

Northwest Room
1102 Tacoma Avenue South
Tacoma, WA 98402

Phone: 253-591-5666

Collection Information: Death indexes for Washington, Oregon, and California; local obituary indexes and city directories.

Access: Library staff will assist in learning to use the resources. Contact the library for access from a distance.

Spokane Public Library

Genealogy Research
906 West Main Avenue
Spokane, WA 99201

Phone: 509-444-5300

Collection Information: Spokane city directories, newspapers obituary indexes, family histories, and vertical files.

Access: Genealogy room staff will answer questions and assist researchers. Beginning researchers are encouraged to visit.

Washington State Archives

Archives
PO Box 40238
1129 Washington Street SE
Olympia, WA 98504-0238

Phone: 360-586-1492

Collection Information: Death records index 1907 to 2000, county histories, and marriage records 1968 to 1999, plus lots more.

Access: The best way to access this outstanding collection is to go there and use the resources there.

Seattle Genealogical Society

Research Library
PO Box 15329
6200 Sand Point Way NE, #101
Seattle, WA 98115-0329

Phone: 206-522-8658

Collection Information: They have Washington State death index, 1907 to 1989.

Access: Guests pay $4.00 per day to use the collection. They offer fee-base research services.

West Virginia

West Virginia Division of Culture and History

Archives and History Section
Capitol Complex
1900 Kanawha Boulevard East
Charleston, WV 25305-0300

Phone: 304-558-0220

TDD: 304-558-3562

Fax: 304-558-2779

Collection Information: They have original manuscripts, tax records, land records, and biographies.

Access: This is the place to start with West Virginia research.

West Virginia and Regional History Collection

West Virginia University (Morgantown)
PO Box 6069
1549 University Avenue
Morgantown, WV 26506-6069

Phone: 304-293-3536

Fax: 304-293-3981

Collection Information: Genealogies, census, public, and military records, photographs, and manuscript materials.

Access: Circulating materials available through interlibrary loan. Alternative is to hire a local researcher.

Marshall University

James E. Morrow Library, Special Collections
One John Marshall Drive
Huntington, WV 25755

Phone: 304/696-2343

Fax: 304-696-2361

Collection Information: Regional collection of published materials that deal with West Virginia.

Access: Closed stack area—not available for public browsing.

Berkeley County Historical Society

Genealogical Resources
PO Box 1624
126 East Race Street
Martinsburg, WV 25402

Phone: 304-267-4713

Collection Information: They concentrate on the old Berkeley County area. They have the extensive files of Don C. Wood.

Access: No charge to use the Belle Boyd House for personal research. Staff will conduct research for $13.00 per hour.

Wisconsin

Vesterheim Genealogical Center

Naeseth Library
415 W Main Street
Madison, WI 53703

Phone: 608-255-2224

Fax: 608-255-6842

Collection Information: Important for Norwegian research and is connected to Vesterheim Museum in Minnesota.

Access: Daily use fee for nonmembers: $10.00. Professional researchers available.

Wisconsin Historical Society

Library-Archives
816 State Street
Madison, WI 53706

Phone: 608-264-6535

Fax: 608-264-6520

Collection Information: Nearly 4 million published sources on the history and prehistory of North America.

Access: Many items may be borrowed for personal use by requesting an interlibrary loan through your local library.

Milwaukee County Historical Society

Research Library
910 North Old World Third Street
Milwaukee, WI 53203-1591

Phone: 414-273-8288

Fax: 414-273-3268

Collection Information: Materials on the history of the City of Milwaukee and Milwaukee County, including naturalization records from 1836 to May 1941.

Access: All materials are for in-library use only. Nonmembers user fee: $3.00.

Milwaukee Public Library

Library
814 W Wisconsin Avenue
Milwaukee, WI 53233

Phone: 414-286-3000

Web site: www.mpl.org

Collection Information: A huge collection focusing on German immigrants to Wisconsin.

Access: Check with the library for access to the document collection.

Brown County Public Library

Local History and Genealogy
515 Pine Street
Green Bay, WI 54301
920-448-4400, ext. 394

Collection Information: French Canadian collection of marriage indexes. Green Bay's early history as a fur-trading outpost.

Access: The collection is open and free to the public. Check with the staff for access from a distance.

Wyoming

Laramie County Library System

Genealogy and Local History
2800 Central Avenue
Cheyenne, WY 82001

Phone: 307-635-1032

Fax: 307-634-2082

Collection Information: A special feature of the collection is the surname index, which is cataloged.

Access: The collection is open to the public. Also a Family History Center.

Wyoming State Archives

Barrett Building
2301 Central Avenue
Cheyenne, WY 82002

Phone: 307-777-7826

Fax: 307-777-7044

Collection Information: The archives house a large collection of documents on Wyoming history and microfilms of most Wyoming newspapers.

Access: The archives are open to the public for on-site use. Check with them for fee-based research services.

Wyoming State Library

Library
2301 Capitol Avenue
Cheyenne, WY 82002

Phone: 307-777-6333

Fax: 307-777-6289

Collection Information: The Wyoming State Library offers a collection of state and federal government documents and history of the West.

Access: You really have to visit this library to discover their resources for genealogists.

Albany County Public Library

Wyoming Room
310 S 8th Street
Laramie, WY 82070

Phone: 307-721-2580

Collection Information: Historical information about Laramie, Albany County, and Wyoming.

Access: Contact them for help in accessing the data.

Suggestions for Librarians

1. Use this list to begin a list of genealogical research libraries and archives for your state. Then create a handout for the researchers who come to your library.

2. Study some of the genealogy Web pages you see and use the ideas to create a Web page for your library. See Tool 8.2 in Part III for a list of Web sites.

3. If your genealogy resources are not on an online catalog, create a list of your holding and publish it on the library's Web page.

4.   Prepare a class to demonstrate some of the outstanding Web sites and present it to researchers in your library.

5.   Think of ways to make your genealogy collection more accessible to people whom live outside of your service area.

Suggestions for Researchers

1.   Study the third column of the foregoing table to learn if any of the research facilities have some unique collections that could help with your research.

2.   Check out the online catalogs of some of the libraries on the list. Do a search on one of your ancestors to see if they have a book with something you can use.

3.   Try asking for assistance from a distant library to see how they can help you.

4.   Check out the Web site, "Directory of Genealogy Libraries in the U.S." (Available: www.gwest.org/gen_libs.htm), for other libraries that didn't make the list.

Summary

In this chapter we bring together an incredible amount of information about genealogical research facilities. The information makes it easier to get access to the resources of each facility. The contact information could change, but not in very many cases. If it does, you can use the Internet to update the listing.

Bibliography (Ratings Guide explanation follows last citation)

Bentley, Elizabeth Petty. 1999. *The Genealogist's Address Book*. Baltimore, MD: Genealogical Publishing Company.

This book brings together an incredible amount of disparate data. *The Genealogist's Address Book* provides names, addresses, phone numbers, hours, and publications for genealogical organizations in five broad areas. Any serious researcher will want to have a copy. **PPP**

Crume, Rick. 2002. Leaders of the Stacks. *Family Tree Magazine*. (October 2002): 26.

This is a great article on the best public libraries for genealogical research. The author talks about collection size, geographical scope, census records, special collections and accessibility.

Dollarhide, William, and Ronald Bremer. 1998. *America's Best Genealogy Resource Centers*. Bountiful, UT: HeritageQuest.

This book identifies the best genealogical research facilities at local, state, regional, and national levels. The authors are two of the most traveled genealogists in America. They have visited all of the centers described in this book. This is an indispensable tool for librarians who help their patrons locate other genealogical collections. **L**

Smith, Juliana Szucs. 2003. *The Ancestry Family Historian's Address Book: A Comprehensive Lists of Local, State, and Federal Agencies and Institutions and Ethnic and Genealogical Organizations.* Orem, UT: Ancestry Publishing.

This directory of contact information is an updated version of the 1997 edition. It tells researchers where to find organizations and agencies that can help them. It contains online contact information as well as traditional means of contact. It is indispensable for any researcher who has to do most of his or her research from a distance. **LLL**

Ratings Guide

The ratings for each bibliography describe not only what each resource contains, but also how it might fit into the library collection. Some of the materials are more appropriate for larger libraries with substantial budgets, and others belong in collections of any size—even in the personal research collection. To help you identify materials most appropriate for your collection, each resource is marked as either "L" for libraries and "P" for personal. They are ranked from one letter for recommended, two letters for preferred, and three letters for essential.

CHAPTER 6

PROVIDING INSTRUCTION FOR GENEALOGISTS

Every day someone new decides to search for his or her ancestors. You can make the task less daunting for them by offering classes for beginners. They say, "I just don't know where to begin." Your library is a good place for them to start, but they need a little more guidance than they can get by asking the reference librarian a question and getting a response. They need to be shown some of the basics and then turned loose to find their ancestors on their own. The more they know how to do research, the better their chances for success. That is one reason for offering formalized instruction on genealogical research.

What to Look for in This Chapter

This chapter gives you some tips on how to organize and teach classes for genealogists. Even if all you do is to hold up some of the resources you have in the library and tell people what kinds of information they contain and how to use them, you will be doing your genealogists a big favor. Going beyond that will be even better.

Learning for Life

If you offer story hour programs for children, and you believe that libraries are the citadels of life-long learning, then you need to offer classes for genealogists. Most genealogists are hobbyists. They come to the task with little if any formal training, so they rely on the library staff to teach them what they need to know about finding their ancestors. This could be a daunting task for a reference librarian who has limited experience or formal education in genealogical research. Nevertheless, we have an obligation to help everyone who comes to us with an information need. We may never be able to close the gap completely, but classes for genealogists can help. At the very least we need to show researchers how to use the library's online catalog.

Demonstrating the Library's Online Catalog

Most libraries with resources worth calling a genealogy collection have an online catalog. Even if your library still uses a card catalog, patrons need to know how to find genealogical resources in the library. This class could be the first one in a series of classes for genealogists, who want to use your library for research. Other classes on the research process and strategies for finding ancestors could follow.

You will want to demonstrate a subject and keyword searches, as the primary ways to find materials in the collection that contain the information genealogists will seek. Part of this instruction will include an advanced search that narrows the parameters to return only the best potential resources. You will also want to demonstrate how to create and printout a bibliography of potentially relevant resources to check. This bibliography will help the researcher avoid returning to the OPAC every so often. This instruction may not be worth a class by itself, but will probably be the beginning part of a class on general library resources.

Showing Off the Collection

When I was in library school the instructors used to load a book truck with reference books and bring them to class for show and tell. The instructor would hold up a book and tell the class about it. For homework we were expected to find the book in the library, examine it and write an abstract. Researchers may not want to be that thorough, but they will want to know how to use the book and enough information about the book to determine if it has information they can use. Preparing a bibliography ahead of time of the resources will provide an outline for the class to give the participants a chance to make notes.

The rest of this chapter is dedicated to helping librarians organize and plan for classes on genealogical research.

Giving Computer Classes

With the advent of so much genealogy on the Internet and the use of genealogy programs for computers, teaching computer classes is a prerequisite to teaching a class for genealogists. Before we can teach them how to look for their ancestors on the Internet, we need to teach them how to use Windows, how to use a browser, how to use a search engine, and how to narrow a search. Don't assume that people who have computers at home know how to use them.

In 2000 I was asked by a library system to give a genealogy workshop to a group of about 60 librarians in Michigan. I showed them how to use "Control+F" to bring up a dialog box to search for a word string on the active page. For some of them it was a wonderful revelation. Less than ten people in the audience said they knew the keystroke command.

We have been offering computer classes and genealogy classes at the Great Bend Public Library for years. Before people can enroll in my classes about genealogy on the Internet, they have to have had at least one computer class. Computer literacy is a must for any genealogist today.

Getting Acquainted with the Audience

Here are a few points to keep in mind as you prepare to offer instruction to researchers.

1.   Genealogists tend to be smart people and they can bring helpful information to the class.

2. Genealogists are highly motivated to find their ancestors.

3. Genealogists come in all ages—they are not all over 65.

4. Persistence is a common characteristic of genealogists. Who else would spend hours with their head in a microfilm machine?

5. Genealogists are acquainted with failure. They can spend all day in a library and go home with nothing and still come back the next day.

6. Genealogists get excited over the tiniest scrap of information and they will want to share it in the class.

7. Genealogists have very specific information needs. That is why you need to teach research skills and strategies, rather than just finding the information for them.

8. Genealogists like to show off their family trees. If you had spent years compiling a book, wouldn't you want someone to recognize your efforts?

9. Genealogists see every class as an opportunity to ask a specific question about their research, so be prepared to give them answers.

Developing Teaching Techniques

When librarians understand how genealogists think they can develop teaching techniques that will take advantage of their learning styles. Here are a few ideas for librarians who are preparing classes for genealogists.

1. Assess the audience before you begin a presentation. It helps to know the knowledge level of class members and what they expect from the class.

2. Provide for multisensory learning. Not everyone learns by reading. It helps if you have a technology lab for teaching genealogy on the Internet.

3. Build on what they already know. Let those who have experienced what you are teaching share their knowledge with members of the class.

4. Give them something they can do immediately. I tell people who come to my classes that if they don't use at least one idea they learned from the class within the next three days, they probably should have stayed home and watched television.

5. Ask them to come back to the library to show you what they have found. This gives them a chance to show off and reinforce their learning.

6. Give them a handout with lots of white space for their own notes. Their notes are a critical part of the learning process. Notes help them link what they have just learned with what they want to find out.

7. Put something online to which they can refer again, if they need or want to. I put all of my classes on my Web page so students can go there and review the presentation. See the "Online Workshops" page (Available: www.ckls.org/~jswan/WKSHPS.HTM).

8. Show a case study to help them visualize a successful effort. I use lots of examples in my classes, but I know ahead of time the results I will get when I do a search a certain way.

9. Let them tell about themselves at the beginning of your program. I always go around the room and ask participants to introduce themselves and tell one thing they hope to learn from the class.

10. Allow time for individual questions and answers at the end of your program. Without fail, at the end of the class someone will come up with a question or want to share a successful experience.

Planning a Genealogy Workshop

Here are the keys to planning your presentation to a group of genealogists.

1. Identify your class goals before you do anything. What do you want the people to be able to do when the program is over?

2. Select objectives that reinforce the goal. Everything you say should lead back to the main purpose of the class.

3. Decide on learning activities. Carefully select a variety of ways to present the lesson.

4. Determine your method of presentation. For example:

    •   hands on with actual research tools in the classroom;

    •   hands on in a technology lab;

    •   handout with template or examples;

    •   PowerPoint or video presentation; and

    •   online with links (show and tell).

5. Suggest ways they can apply what they have learned. Say, "You can go home and do this."

6. Establish some form of evaluation. You can ask a few class members to tell you one idea they want to try in the next week.

Determining What to Teach

When the whole waterfront of genealogical research stretches before you, it may be hard to narrow down your options. Here are a few examples of topics for genealogy classes.

1. Show off and tell about the resources in your library.

2. Demonstrate how to find resources outside your library.

3. Teach how to use basic genealogical tools.

4. Explain how to use cemetery books as an index for obituaries in newspapers.

5. Demonstrate how to locate other genealogists who share common ancestors.

6. Teach how to write query letters.

7. Show how to find mailing lists and join one of them.

8. Reveal how to do an advanced search in an online search engine.

9. Demonstrate how to download and install a computer genealogy program like Personal Ancestral File.

10. Show how to use the online version of the Family History Library catalog.

11. Teach how to use free genealogy Internet sites.

12. Demonstrate how to access and search online databases.

13. Show how to download/import a GEDCOM file (see Chapter 11).

14. Demonstrate how to export a GEDCOM file.

15. Teach advanced online search techniques.

16. Highlight the differences between various genealogy sites.

17. Teach the genealogical research process.

18. Show how to document sources and take notes.

19. Reveal how to look for clues based on new data.

20. Teach how to create files for organizing genealogy.

21. Teach Library of Congress Subject Headings (e.g., Cemeteries—Missouri—Wayne Co).

22. Teach researchers how to search the online catalogs of other libraries.

These are just a few of the concepts and skills genealogists need to learn to be successful. Prepare handouts containing this information for people who cannot attend the classes you offer.

Using a Variety Presentation Options

Don't feel that you have to do all of this yourself. The thought could be overwhelming. Think about these choices.

1. Develop your own class curriculum. Take your time and do one class at a time. Let the second and third classes flow naturally from the first class.

2. Bring in outside experts. Even if you think you can do it all yourself, bringing someone in from another state will give credibility to your program.

3. Draw on local expert to teach classes. Often local people know more than someone from a thousand miles away.

4. Use online genealogy classes. Brigham Young University offers a free online class to anyone interested in genealogy. Go to http://ce.byu.edu/is/site/index.dhtm and click on "Special Offers." Then click on "Free Family History Tutorials."

5. Use videos to teach research techniques. There are lots of videos on various aspects of genealogical research. You will not want to show all of a two-hour video, but a brief segment from one could enhance your teaching.

Suggestions for Helping Genealogists

1. Hold a hands-on workshop using the resources in the library.
2. Offer technology-training classes for beginners.
3. Offer a class at the library on how to use the Internet for research.
4. Sponsor a professional presenter to do a genealogy workshop in your library.

Summary

If a library provides sources for genealogical research I believe it has a responsibility to offer instruction to researchers. The handouts and printed forms are passive ways to help genealogists. We suggest that a library staff member get up in front of a group of people and teach them how do research in the library.

Bibliography (Ratings Guide explanation follows last citation)

Burroughs, Tony. 2003. *Finding Your Family History in the Attic*. Pleasant Grove, UT: 123 Genealogy. Videocassette.

This video starts at the very beginning with sources in the home. It tells where to look for long-hidden personal documents we need to start our research. It shows us how to authenticate the documents we find with handwriting comparisons, published dates and timelines. It suggests where we can look beyond the obvious places, and teaches us how to archive the documents we find. **LL**

Fleming, Ann Carter. 1997. *Teaching Genealogy: Tips and Techniques for Successful Adult Classes*. Valley Forge, PA: Pennsylvania Cradle of a Nation. Audiocassette.

This audiocassette is designed to help librarians and others learn how to teach genealogy classes. **LLL**

Hill, Mary E. Vassel. 2000. *FamilyRoots Organizer*. Hurricane, UT: The Studio. Videocassette.

Beginning genealogists and seasoned researchers alike need to see this video. Every library should have a copy to loan. It teaches how to organize the information we find in our research. Mary Hill makes to important points for all of us. Genealogy is fun when you can find things you once had and genealogy is frustrating when you can't find what you know you have. This video takes a step-by-step process that, if followed, will ensure that we can find anything we want after we have filed it properly. **PPP**

Lemmon, Stephen. 2001. *Personal Ancestral File 5*. Hurricane, UT: The Studio. Videocassette.

This is a step-by-step training video. It teaches how to use the many functions of the program, including basic navigation, adding information, editing data, importing and exporting files and adding multimedia files to the database. **PPP**

McClure, Rhonda R. 2003. *Using RootsWeb.com*. Hurricane, UT: 123 Genealogy. Videocassette.

This video covers:

- using RootsWeb Meta Search;

- searching RootsWeb Surname List;

- finding individuals in the WorldConnect database;

- locating messages in the mailing list archive.

Good details and solid examples. **LLL**

Ratings Guide

The ratings for each bibliography describe not only what each resource contains, but also how it might fit into the library collection. Some of the materials are more appropriate for larger libraries with substantial budgets, and others belong in collections of any size—even in the personal research collection. To help you identify materials most appropriate for your collection, each resource is marked as either "L" for libraries and "P" for personal. They are ranked from one letter for recommended, two letters for preferred, and three letters for essential.

CHAPTER 7
STAYING CURRENT PROFESSIONALLY

Not all reference librarians work with genealogy researchers all day long. For them, staying professionally current can be especially challenging. Just as computers and the Internet have changed the way we do library reference work, so also will they change the way we do genealogy. All we can do is hope we can keep up.

What to Look for in This Chapter

If librarians expect to stay abreast of what is happening in genealogical research they will have to become proactive in their own continuing education. In this chapter we offer a few suggestions for librarians who want to keep themselves informed. Many of the suggestions also apply to researchers.

Reading Professional Literature

Reading genealogy magazines is one way to learn of new publications for your collection. Another way is to request publishers' catalogs. These two strategies will keep you conversant in the field. Subscribe to several genealogy magazines and read each issue faithfully. Write to genealogy book publishers and ask them to send you their catalogs. You don't have to buy anything, but perusing them regularly will keep you knowledgeable about new publications.

Here is a list of genealogy magazines you may want to consider for your library.

General Genealogical Periodicals

Ancestry Magazine

Ancestry Inc.
360 W 4800 North
Provo, UT 84604

Web site: http://shops.ancestry.com/product.asp?productid=1026062&shopid=0

Informative and authoritative, this genealogical journal consistently provides articles from top-notch researchers and experts in the field. They stay on top of current topics and techniques.

Everton's Family History Magazine

PO Box 70813
Sandy, UT 84070-8130

Web site: www.everton.com/shopper/browse.php?Category=Magazine&Action=Browse

Articles, advertisements, and classified ads help genealogists connect with each other and stay aware of new developments in genealogical research.

FGS Forum (Federation of Genealogical Societies)

PO Box 3385
Salt Lake City, UT 84110

Web site: www.fgs.org/fgs-forum.asp

Has news and information of interest to genealogists and member societies. Includes news about record access and record preservation. Provides notices of important genealogical events, conferences and workshops. Reviews indexing and publication projects in progress or completed. Offers news from genealogical and historical societies and family associations. Features book reviews and notices of many publications.

Genealogical Computing Quarterly

360 W 4800 North
Provo, UT 84604

Web site: http://shops.ancestry.com/product.asp?productid=1026062&shopid=0

This quarterly is a must for those who use computers in their research. It is the only genealogical magazine that offers in-depth coverage of technology issues for genealogists. Unites the newest in computer technology with time-honored pursuit of genealogy. Includes hands-on tips, software reviews, and updates.

Heritage Quest Magazine

PO Box 540193
425 North 400 West, Ste. 1-A
North Salt Lake, UT 84054

E-mail: Editor@HeritageQuestMagazine.com

This is an excellent reference tool for beginners and advanced researchers alike. It keeps up with technology for genealogists. Library news, periodical directory, tips for societies, library research technique articles, books, microforms, and periodical reviews.

National Genealogical Society Quarterly

4527 17th Street North
Arlington, VA 22207-2399

Web site: www.ngsgenealogy.org/pubsquarterly.htm

This is an academic/scholarly publication that features scholarly essays on methodology and resources for family history research. It focuses on readability and practical help in solving genealogical problems. It has well-written, how-to-do-it articles on items of current interest.

New England Historical and Genealogical Register

101 Newbury Street
Boston, MA 02116

Web site: www.newenglandancestors.org/rs1/articles/theregister

This is a quarterly journal of scholarly research that publishes family histories and genealogies of archival quality, with emphasis on New England families and their European origins. Subscription is free with membership in the New England Historical and Genealogical Society (NEHGS). The *Register* is the oldest publication of its kind in the United States.

New York Genealogical and Biographical Record

122 E 58th Street
New York, NY 10022

Web site: www.nygbs.org/info/record.html

The *Record* is the second oldest genealogical journal in the United States, founded in 1870. It has a long history of scholarly articles written on genealogy, biography, and history relating to New York State. They include source material and compiled genealogies for New York State families. Articles usually fall into the following types:

- Compiled genealogies
- Solutions to specific problems
- Immigrant origins
- Source material

Prologue: The Quarterly of the National Archives

NEPS-Room G6
National Archives
Washington, DC 20408

Web site: www.archives.gov/publications/prologue/index.html

For 35 years, *Prologue* has been bringing readers stories of the rich resources and programs of the National Archives and Records Administration from facilities across the nation.

Regional and State Genealogical Periodicals

American Genealogist (TAG)

Box 398
Demorest, GA 30535-0398

Web site: www.americangenealogist.com

This academic/scholarly publication includes documented analyses of genealogical problems. Includes short compiled genealogies, generally in the southeastern United States. It is dedicated to the elevation of genealogical scholarship.

Connecticut Nutmegger

Connecticut Society of Genealogists
PO Box 435
Glastonbury, CT 06033

Web site: www.csginc.org

This is a 180-page quarterly bulleting. It publishes articles of original family research for Connecticut and New England. Includes book reviews, advertisements, Connecticut vital records, queries, Bible records, and unpublished genealogies. It is free to members of the Connecticut Society of Genealgists.

Illinois State Genealogical Society Quarterly

Illinois State Genealogical Society
PO Box 10495
Springfield, IL 62791

This quarterly publishes articles on Illinois settlers, genealogies, Illinois history, research aids and sources, computer genealogy, and offers free queries to members.

North Carolina Genealogical Society Journal

Box 1492
Raleigh, NC 27602

Web site: www.ncgenealogy.org

This is a scholarly publication with articles of general genealogical value, including source data from original documents, and other material from previously unpublished sources.

Magazine of Virginia Genealogy

Virginia Genealogical Society
5001 W Broad Street, Ste. 115
Richmond, VA 23230-3023

Web site: www.vgs.org

Provides primary source material for Virginia genealogy and oral history, with emphasis on eighteenth and nineteenth-century vital statistics, court, and land records.

Subscribing to and reading several national genealogy magazines and one or two state magazines should keep you informed about current trends in genealogy.

Considering All Forms of Publishing

Librarians should keep up with what is being published, not only by major publishers, but also by what is being "self-published." Announcements appear in countless newsletters and journals such as *Everton's Family History Magazine*. Self-published authors usually include their name and address for ordering. Librarians shouldn't hesitate to ask for a free copy of a self-published book that is relevant to their collection. If an author says no, the librarian can then decide whether or not to buy the book. Most authors of self-published genealogies are flattered by the request even if they cannot contribute the book as a donation.

Subscribing to Mailing Lists

Librarians can learn a lot from each other by participating in mailing lists like *Librarians Serving Genealogists* (Available: www.cas.usf.edu/lis/genealib). The exchange of ideas, genealogy education, sharing thoughts, swapping materials, and discussing problems are just a few of the ways *Librarians Serving Genealogists* helps librarians. The Web site features three collection development guidelines for genealogy collections.

They have a mailing list known as GENEALIB, for announcements, discussion, and question-and-answers of interest to genealogy librarians. If you have access to e-mail, join the group. Go to http://mailman.acommp.usf/mailman/listinfo/genealib. Fill out the form and submit it. You will receive an e-mail requesting confirmation, to prevent others from subscribing your name without your knowledge or permission. This is a hidden list, which means that the list of members is available only to the list administrator. The list administrator is Drew Smith.

All messages sent to the list since December 1, 1998 have been archived and can be accessed by going to http://mailman.acomp.usf.edu/pipermail/genealib, and using the search engine to find the discussion you want.

If you want to submit a message to the list, send it to genealib@mailman.acomp.usf.edu. Use a brief but descriptive subject line. All messages posted to GENEALIB have to be of interest to genealogy librarians. If you are new to the list it helps to subscribe and "lurk" (read messages to the list without responding) for a while, just to become familiar with the types of questions other genealogy librarians are asking. A one-time mention of new genealogy products every three months is permissible. The list prohibits other advertising of commercial products and services.

I recommend that librarians join a genealogy mailing for their county. RootsWeb.com (Available: http://lists.rootsweb.com) lists over 27,000 mailing lists. Many of them are surname-based, but there is probably a genealogy mailing list for the county you live in. Go to the Web site click on the state. Then look for the county you live in. Subscribe by clicking on one of the shortcut links. Send the message with the single word "subscribe" in the message subject and body. If you are doing your own genealogy, try one or more surname lists by subscribing in the same way. RootsWeb.com also has links to several special interest genealogy mailing lists.

Conferences with Programs for Librarians Who Serve Genealogists

Librarians can keep up professionally by attending state and national conferences. If you are involved with your state library association, you are probably already involved as a presenter, as well as a participant in state and local genealogy meetings. At the national level the History Section, Genealogy Committee, American Library Association (ALA), Reference and User Services Association (RUSA), is a good place start.

This committee seeks to meet the interests of genealogists and librarians who work with researchers. Members of the committee come from all sizes and types of libraries. The committee plans programs that focus on the needs of librarians in history departments and public libraries.

Federation of Genealogical Societies (FGS)

FGS annually sponsors a national conference for genealogists at all levels of research proficiency. Nationally recognized speakers present programs at the conferences. Regional experts and vendors provide access to genealogical materials and supplies.

National Genealogical Society (NGS)

NGS GENTECH is the conference for genealogists with a focus on technology. NGS annual conferences are the biggest and best of all the conferences for genealogists. They usually have a pre-conference for librarians who help genealogists.

Classes on Genealogy Reference

Graduate schools of library science around the country offer classes on reference of a specific discipline like science, art, or engineering. Some of these schools offer classes on genealogy reference. These reference classes may not be as plentiful as reference classes on the arts, but they are available. Some genealogy classes are offered at the undergraduate level, if the university does not have a library school. BYU offers genealogy classes, some of which are online. This is another way to keep up with the business of helping genealogists.

Looking at Future Trends

I am not a crystal ball gazer, but I have seen some definite trends. Here are some of the advances I expect to see in the way we do genealogical research in the coming years.

- Federal census records will soon be completely indexed with all of the images online.

- Researchers will find digital images of more books, photographs, newspapers, and other documents on the Internet.

- Entrepreneurs will see online genealogy as a profitable venture and take advantage of the opportunity.

- Commercial genealogy sites will become more prevalent.

- Researchers will be willing to pay for access to the information and images on commercial sites.

- E-mail will continue to speed up the way we communicate and share data with each other.

- Researchers will continue to upload their data to the Internet.

- Online services will continue to grow, while CD-ROM technology will wane.

- Publishing on demand will become a viable option for researchers who want to publish their family histories.

- Researchers already spend a lot of time viewing microfilm. They will continue to do so.

- Researchers will still travel to the places where their ancestors lived, not just to find the information they need, but also for the warm feelings they get from being where their forebears lived.

- Books will always be with us—thank goodness.

Here are a few things I do not expect to happen any time soon.

- A beginning researcher will not be able to go to the Internet and download his or her complete genealogy.

- We will never see all of the genealogical resources in libraries and archives on the Internet.

- We will never find an easy way to verify or check the genealogy we find on the Internet.

Suggestions for Librarians

1. Subscribe to and read genealogy periodicals. Recently, I learned about a solid-state computer chip that could be affixed to a headstone and read by a laptop computer. The text could contain biographical information about the deceased and even have a link to a Web page that contained the person's genealogy.

2. Join some mailing lists and learn what you can from other librarians and genealogists.

3. Participate in conferences and workshops that will enhance your skills as a librarian who helps genealogists.

143

Summary

Opportunities abound to help genealogy librarians keep up professionally. The trick is to find the time to meet all of the other demands on our time. You usually have a stack of professional reading that you can't see over, and you could be attending professional conferences every month if you could afford it. Thank goodness for technology that helps us speed up communications and makes it possible to stay in touch with our colleagues. This chapter discusses ways librarians can maintain their genealogical reference skills. I hope you select and try one or two of the suggestions. Staying current takes constant intentional effort and an attitude of always looking for ways to help others.

PART II

THE LIBRARIAN'S GUIDE TO GENEALOGICAL RESEARCH

CHAPTER 8
STARTING AN ORGANIZED SEARCH

Genealogical research starts with the individual who is doing the research and goes back to his or her parents, then grandparents, great-grandparents, and so on back in history—one generation, one individual at a time. That is why it is important to gather personal information first and record the facts from the documents you have in your possession.

What to Look for in This Chapter

In this chapter for researchers you learn about the step-by-step process of genealogical research and how it will help you find every scrap of evidence you need to flesh out your family tree.

These are the steps:

1. Write down what you know about yourself, your relatives, and your ancestors.

2. Gather, organize, and extract genealogical information from personal documents.

3. Identify and contact family members for information

4. Focus your research on one ancestor.

5. Discover if someone else has already researched the ancestor you have selected.

6. Examine compiled sources for your ancestor.

7. Identify the resources that are most likely to have the information you seek.

8. Acquire access to the document and search it.

9. Extract any valuable information you find.

10. Record the source in the research log.

11. Add the information to the genealogical record form or the computer database.

12. Evaluate the data and look for clues obtained from your most recent find.

Look for examples and how they illustrate the main points in this chapter.

Genealogy is a step-by-step process, in which some steps are repeated every time we find a new piece of information or a new ancestor. If we miss one of the steps we create the chance for error and the potential to take a wrong turn in our research.

Ancestor Interview Form

Question	Answer	Verified	Approximate	Next Step
Name	_____			_____
Birth date	_____	☐	☐	_____
Birth place	_____	☐	☐	_____
Marriage date	_____	☐	☐	_____
Marriage place	_____	☐	☐	_____
Death date	_____	☐	☐	_____
Death place	_____	☐	☐	_____
Cause / death	_____	☐	☐	_____
Spouse	_____	☐	☐	_____
Father	_____	☐	☐	_____
Mother	_____	☐	☐	_____
Children	_____	☐	☐	_____
Occupation	_____	☐	☐	_____
Religion	_____	☐	☐	_____
School	_____	☐	☐	_____
Places lived	_____	☐	☐	_____
Other	_____	☐	☐	_____
Other	_____	☐	☐	_____

Figure 8.1 Ancestor Interview Form

1. Write down what you know about yourself, your relatives, and your ancestors.

You start with what you already know or what think is correct. You try to verify what you think you know and fill in the blank where you are missing data (see Figure 8.1, Ancestor Interview Form; also available as Tool 3.1 in Part III). If you know your grandfather's death date and place, but you don't know where or when he was born, finding that information is a logical step in discovering information about his parents. Identifying the documents that will most likely have that information and obtaining the record is essential to the process.

Genealogy is sort of like police work. When detectives investigate a crime they start with the crime scene and look for clues. Then they interview family members, neighbors, and associates. As they interview people they learn things about the victim and the perpetrator. Discrepancies in stories uncover clues for further investigation. Solving the case requires filing the missing pieces and connecting the dots. Genealogical research involves the same process, except we can't interview dead people. We have to use documents.

2. Gather, organize, and extract genealogical information from personal documents.

Since genealogical research is all about uncovering clues and checking out leads, it is important that we organize and record our efforts. If I were just starting on my genealogy I would make a copy of the Checklist of Personal Genealogical Sources (Figure 8.2, also in Part III as Tool 3.2) and go around my home gathering together in one box all of the documents I could find. Check at home for these items.

Gathering the documents on this checklist will inevitably take some time, because remembering where you put some documents will take time. Don't try to do it all in one afternoon. But I wouldn't put off finding a box or getting started on other phases of research because the first step isn't complete. In fact, you may find some of these documents years from now in places you never dreamed they would be.

Next you should sit down with all of the stuff you have gathered and sort it into three piles—one for yourself, one for your parents, and one for the rest of your ancestors. Then take out the pedigree chart and fill it in as completely as you can, starting with yourself in position number one. This will be a worksheet, because you will add information to it as you find it, and eventually want to put all of your genealogy on the computer.

This chapter includes four forms to use as worksheets—the Ancestor Interview Form (Figure 8.1), a Pedigree Chart (Figure 8.3, available as Tool 3.3 in Part III), a Family Group Sheet (Figure 8.4, also Tool 3.4 in Part III), and a Research Log (Figure 8.5, also Tool 4.1 in Part III). Each of these forms is designed to help you organize your research and be a guide to the next step.

The Pedigree Chart takes a broad view of your research. On it you record only your direct ancestors. It starts with the individual who is doing the research and works back one generation at a time. Put your own name in position number one. The Pedigree Chart is a skeletal summary of the research you have completed. It can also provide a road map for where you want your research to go. You can see from your Pedigree Chart which ancestral lines are the shortest.

Checklist of Personal Genealogical Sources

___ Abstracts of title
___ Administrations of wills
___ Annulment decrees
___ Automobile insurance
___ Bankruptcy filings
___ Birth announcements
___ Burial reports
___ Cemetery records
___ Church membership lists
___ Church transfers
___ Club membership records
___ Contracts
___ Court judgments
___ Criminal convictions
___ Deeds
___ Drivers license
___ Employment applications
___ Family Bible
___ Family histories
___ Fire insurance policies
___ Funeral home receipts
___ Guardianship documents
___ Honor roll recognition
___ Hunting license
___ Income tax records
___ Job transfers
___ Land grants
___ Letters
___ Loan applications
___ Marriage applications
___ Medical checkups
___ Military disability papers
___ Military pension
___ Military service medals
___ Minister's records
___ Motor vehicle registration
___ Newspaper clippings
___ Passenger lists
___ Pension applications
___ Personal property tax records
___ Probate records
___ Property settlements
___ Real estate tax records
___ Scholarship applications
___ Scrapbooks
___ Service awards
___ Tax notices
___ Union dues book
___ Water rights
___ X-rays

___ Accident reports
___ Adoption papers
___ Apprenticeship diplomas
___ Awards
___ Baptism certificate
___ Blessing certificates
___ Business license
___ Charitable donations
___ Church minutes
___ Citizenship papers
___ College applications
___ Correspondence
___ Court minutes
___ Customs records
___ Diplomas
___ Economic records
___ Employment termination
___ Family group sheets
___ Family records
___ Firearm registration
___ Genealogical records
___ Health records
___ Hospital receipts
___ Immigrant records
___ Institutional records
___ Journals, diaries
___ Land patents
___ Library cards
___ Marine insurance
___ Marriage certificates
___ Medical records
___ Military discharge
___ Military records
___ Military service record
___ Mission reports
___ National Guard records
___ Obituaries
___ Passports
___ Personal interviews
___ Personnel records
___ Professional certificates
___ Property surveys
___ Report cards
___ School tax records
___ Secondary school registration
___ Sextons records
___ Tombstone rubbings
___ Vaccination records
___ Wedding books
___ Yearbooks

___ Achievements
___ Anniversary announcements
___ Auction receipts
___ Baby books
___ Biographies
___ Bonds
___ Case files
___ Christening certificate
___ Church records
___ Club dues
___ Confirmation certificates
___ Court dockets
___ Court subpoenas
___ Death certificates
___ Divorce documents
___ Elementary school registration
___ Engagement announcements
___ Family heirlooms
___ Farm records
___ Funeral programs
___ Graduation programs
___ Historical society membership
___ Hospital records
___ Immunization certificates
___ Insurance papers
___ Judicial summons
___ Legal papers
___ Life insurance
___ Marriage announcements
___ Marriage licenses
___ Military citations
___ Military firearms
___ Military separation papers
___ Military uniform
___ Mortgages
___ Naturalization logbooks
___ Ordination certificates
___ Pedigrees charts
___ Personal papers
___ Probate inventories
___ Property leases
___ Publications
___ Retirement applications
___ School transcripts
___ Selective service cards
___ Social security card
___ Traffic tickets
___ Visas
___ Wills

Figure 8.2 Checklist of Personal Genealogical Sources

Using my Pedigree Chart to help me decide where to focus my research, I have been able to identify all of my great-great-grandparents and all but four of my great-great-great-grandparents. When it comes to extending the ends of other lines, it helps to start with the next person back from the ancestor at the end of the Pedigree Chart. Even though you might have the name of the person at the end of the line you don't have enough information to find him or her. The Pedigree Chart is one tool you will want to have beside you when you are checking the Internet to find out what information other researchers have found on your ancestors.

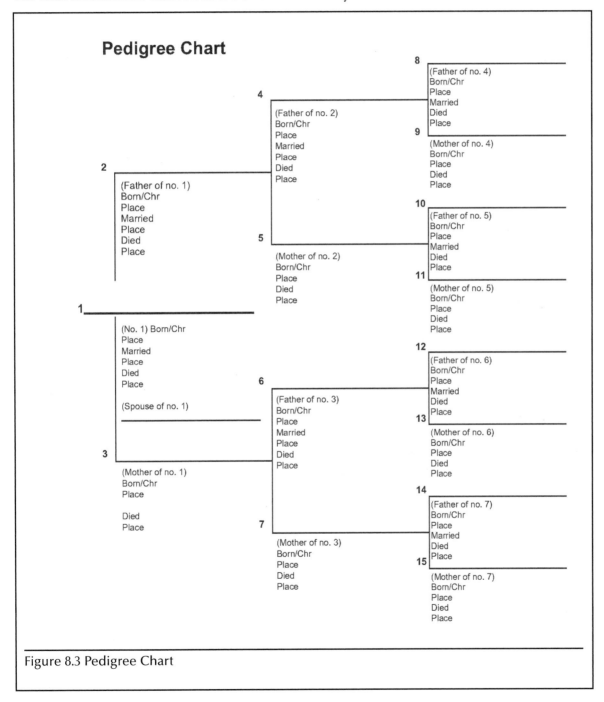

Figure 8.3 Pedigree Chart

The Family Group Sheet is used to organize individuals into families. Certain pieces of vital information are recorded for each individual. It is obvious that you can't record all of the information gleaned from the Ancestor Interview Form on this sheet, but the facts from one individual may lead to clues or assumptions to check out later. For example, if you know the birth order of the children and the date of birth for one of the children, you can predict that other siblings were born about two years apart. Creating a family group sheet will give you a snapshot of a single family and is an integral part of our genealogy. When you use a computer program you add children to the family one at a time and print out the family group report, as needed.

Family Group Sheet

HUSBAND'S NAME _____

Born (Date) _____ (Place) _____
Married (Date) _____ (Place) _____
Died (Date) _____ (Place) _____   Your Name & Address

Father of Husband _____
Born (Date) _____ (Place) _____
Married (Date) _____ (Place) _____
Died (Date) _____ (Place) _____   Sources, Notes, Etc.

Mother of Husband _____
Born (Date) _____ (Place) _____
Married (Date) _____ (Place) _____
Died (Date) _____ (Place) _____

WIFE'S NAME _____
Born (Date) _____ (Place) _____
Died (Date) _____ (Place) _____

Father of Wife _____
Born (Date) _____ (Place) _____
Married (Date) _____ (Place) _____
Died (Date) _____ (Place) _____

Mother of Wife _____
Born (Date) _____ (Place) _____
Died (Date) _____ (Place) _____

CHILDREN	BORN Date Place	DIED Date Place	MARRIED To whom Date
1 M F			
2 M F			
· 3 M F			
4 M F			
5 M F			
6 M F			
7 M F			
8 M F			
9 M F			

Figure 8.4 Family Group Sheet

I created the Ancestor Interview Form (Figure 8.1) to help genealogists visualize what they know and what they don't know concerning the ancestor about whom they want to learn more. You don't need to fill one out for yourself or your siblings. You could use this form for any other person in your family tree, including living parents, grandparents, and great-grandparents. Being thorough at this point in the process will pay big dividends later. You may no get another chance to interview a living grandparent or elderly relative. Using the same thinking, extract all of the pertinent information you can when you have a genealogically rich document in your possession. The opportunity to search it again may slip away.

The Research Log (Figure 8.5, Tool 4.1, in Part III) is a tool that has been used for years. It helps us keep track of the documents we have searched and when. It keeps us from wasting time reviewing documents we have already viewed. It also tells us where we have found the good stuff. Experienced genealogists have many notebooks full of research logs. So, research logs need to be organized by name as well as date. Otherwise it could take us more time to find the right research log than to search the document over again.

Research logs work for static documents like books and rolls of microfilm. They don't work very well at all for dynamic sources of information like the Internet. In fact you really need to recheck Internet sources about every six months to a year, because they change all of the time.

Research Log

Ancestor's Name _____

Objective		Approximate Date	Locality	
Date of Search Number	Location/ Call Numbers	Description of Source (Author, title, year, pages)	Comments/Results (Purpose of search, years, names)	Document

Additional notes:

Figure 8.5 Research Log

3. Identify and contact family members for information.

The next step in the step-by-step process is to contact family members for information on your family tree. Start by contacting the relatives you know, like your parents, grandparents, and aunts and uncles. Call them or send an e-mail, and ask if they have any organized genealogy. If they say yes, go visit them. I know people who ended up with boxes of information. Their relatives were just waiting to give them the material. Ask them for copies of other documents like family photos, birth certificates, death certificates, family Bibles, and anything else of value. You could go down the Checklist of Personal Genealogical Sources with them.

Once you have tapped the relatives you know, ask them if they know other relatives that might have some information of genealogical value. Contact these relatives and ask them the same questions. Remember to thank every person you contact whether or not they give you anything. Don't expect them to go out and make copies of everything they have; that could be a lot of work.

Once you have contacted the circle of relatives you know and the relatives they know it is time to contact relatives you don't know. Here are a few techniques I have tried.

Look in the telephone directories of places you know that your ancestors lived. Call the people with the same last name as your ancestor and tell them that you are looking for relatives of your ancestor. If they are not relatives they might know someone who is and tell you to call him or her. Unless there are two pages of people with your surname, you have a good chance of finding someone within five to ten calls.

Switchboard (Available: www.switchboard.com) is the online version of thousands of telephone books. Do a search on the surname only, the city, and state. The result will be a list of people with that surname along with their addresses and telephone numbers. If the list isn't too long you could call each person on the list and ask if they know of someone who is related to your ancestor and is working on genealogy.

For example, my father Walter Swan lived in two places most of his life—Bisbee, Arizona, and Stockton, California. I did a Switchboard search for the surname Swan in each of these towns. I got less than five hits per each search. One of the hits was my brother and three were first cousins. Any of them could have told another Swan researcher to contact me.

Another way to find living relatives that you don't know is to do a search on one of the family genealogy databases like Ancestry.com or FamilySearch.org. If you find a match to your family data, you can contact the submitter and find out what else they know.

RootsWeb Surname List, http://rsl.rootsweb.com, is another way to find cousins. The search engine will search a list of surnames by state and return a listing of active researchers who are actively researching that name. If you get a match you have probably found a cousin you can contact for more information.

You might find other family researchers by doing a search on a general search engine like Google and AltaVista. If someone has put his or her genealogy on the Internet you can trace the information to the source and contact the person who posted it.

Another way to share information is to let other family researchers find you. Put your genealogy on the Internet and researchers will contact you. Who knows, they may have some information you don't have.

4. Focus your research on one ancestor.

Focusing your research on only one ancestor is absolutely essential to your success. Most people cannot keep multiple sets of facts in mind at the same time. You can select any ancestor you want, but limit yourself to just one. You might use the pedigree chart and select the shortest line. You might want to do a quick Internet survey of the names at the end of your pedigree chart to find out how much information has already been compiled. To start with, pick an ancestor that is not too difficult to research. Don't start with someone whose name is all you have to go on. Start with an ancestor with dates, places, and relatives connected to his or her name.

Conducting genealogical research is a learning process and we learn as we do it. I attended a genealogy class once entitled, "When all you have is a name." It was interesting to follow the logic and discovery skills of the teacher, but the process is difficult. I believe that as we commit the facts about an ancestor to memory, we turn over to our subconscious the task of bringing to our minds the places and sources we need to search for additional information.

5. Discover if someone else has already researched the ancestor you have selected.

With one caveat, the easiest way to do your genealogy is to find research on your lines and copy it. The caution is to make sure it is correct before you add the information to your records and base further research on it. Thousands of researchers have spent countless hours on their own genealogies and have published them in one form or another. They have published their genealogies in books and journals. They have published them electronically, over the Internet or on CD-ROM. At this point in your research, you have to remember that someone has to publish the information somewhere before you can access it.

The chances of someone else submitting genealogical data for this site increases with every generation you can go back. Assuming a family size of five children per family, here is a chart that shows the number of cousins you could have from just one ancestor. Here is a little chart that explains why it is important to go back as far as you can before checking compiled sources.

The number of relatives who could have made the compiled data available increases exponentially with each generation.

6. Examine compiled sources for your ancestor.

If I were just getting started on my genealogy I would get on the Internet and go to FamilySearch.org (Available: www.familysearch.org). The main compiled databases are the

Cousins	Number	Generation	Birth
First cousins	25	Same grandparents	1900
Second cousins	625	Same great-grandparents	1870
Third cousins	3,125	Same great-great-grandparents	1840
Fourth cousins	15,625	Same great-great-great-grandparents	1810
Fifth cousins	78,125	Same great-great-great-great-grandparents	1780
Sixth cousins	390,625	Same great-great-great-great-great-grandparents	1740
Seventh cousins	1,953,125	Same great-great-great-great-great-great-grandparents	1710

Figure 8.6 Potential Cousins Generation-by-Generation

155

Ancestral File, the International Genealogical Index, and the Pedigree Resource File. The single search engine can search all databases at one time and return a list of possible matches in each of the database. See Chapter 10 for an expanded description of these databases.

Searching these databases takes skill and proficiency. You have to learn how much data to include or not included to maximize the potential of the search engine. You can waste time checking each possibility when you have too many hits. You could miss information that is in the databases, but not displayed if you refine your search parameters too tightly.

Source or submitter information is included with each record. This feature makes it easier to verify the data, but don't be surprised if the contact information is out of date. When it comes to verifying the information you find, you might find Kathy Rippel's Genealogical Verification Tools helpful (Available: www.ckls.org/~kdr/ill/genverif.html). It has links to tools you can use to verify research that has been done by others.

From FamilySearch.org you can also download a GEDCOM file if you find something you want to import into your own database. Check Chapter 11 for a complete explanation of GEDCOM.

The next place to look is Ancestry.com (Available: www.ancestry.com). Even though they charge for access to their databases, they do have some information available at no charge. Gale Research markets the library version of this service, AncestryPlus. Check with your local library to see if it has library subscription. (See Chapter 11 for more information on Ancestry.com.)

I have a personal membership with Ancestry.com, and it is well worth the expense. Images of Civil War Pension Application Index cards and images of census records are two of the best values. I also found some relatives I didn't know who were also working on the Swan line at Ancestry.com.

Look next at HeritageQuest Online (Available: www.heritagequestonline.com). This database is marketed only to libraries, but it is very affordable. Check with your local library to see if they have licensed it for their customers. They have a growing list of indexed federal census images and the images of over 25,000 family and county histories.

Next, go to a general search engine like Google (Available: www.google.com), or AltaVista (Available: www.altavista.com), and search for the ancestors on your pedigree chart. This shotgun approach can produce mixed results depending how far back you can start. See Figure 8.6, Potential Cousins Generation-by-Generation, for a way to approach this search.

Searching compiled sources is a way to get to the good stuff right away. Your success will depend on how genealogically minded your relatives have been. Nevertheless, it is always exciting to find out that one of your ancestral lines has already been traced back several generations. The information may or may not be accurate. You need to check it out—verify it from other sources if you can. The clues for future research are the best thing about compiled genealogies. Compiled research will help you place one ancestor in a single place at a given time. This is where real genealogical research begins.

7. Identify the resources that are most likely to have the information you seek.

When I was a child I used to go with my family to pick peaches. We would start by picking the fruit we could reach by standing on the ground. Eventually though, we had to get ladders and climb them to get the rest of the peaches. Genealogical research is a similar process. We find the easy stuff on the Internet, but sooner or later we have to put on our thinking caps to look for clues and look for documents that have recorded the events of our ancestor's lives.

Your public library is the first place to look for documents that may contain the information you need. Public libraries are good for having copies of old newspapers and census records on microfilm. Histories of local families are also often found in public libraries. The Family History Library Catalog is the next most convenient resource locator. The online catalogs of other libraries will lead you to their resources. (See Chapter 5)

Sometime you will have to go to local courthouses or request copies of documents they have preserved. Statewide birth, death, and marriage indexes will be the keys to accessing these documents.

Checklist for Evaluating a Genealogical Record

1. Did the person who created the record have personal knowledge of the event being recorded? A mother reporting a birth record is probably accurate.

2. How long after the event was it recorded? Even though family Bible records are primary documents, the records may have been made months or years after the events took place. The more time that elapses between the event and the recording of the event, the greater the possibility for error.

3. Why was the record made? Some records have only incidental value, but they may be the only records we have for that place at that time.

4. Does the book or register have an index?

5. Indexes make the work easier, but don't ignore a book just because it doesn't have an index. A key caution to keep in mind: don't rely solely on the index. Some census indexes have a fifteen to twenty percent error rate.

6. What is the potential for error?

7. Any time human eyes and hands come between the original writing of the document and the document you are reading, errors can occur. Even a microfilm copy or a photocopied page can result in errors.

8. Can you read the document?

9. It may be in a foreign language. The handwriting may be illegible. The copy may be blurred, too light, or too dark.

10. Can the information be verified?

11. If sources are included, you can check the sources, but don't disqualify a piece of information just because you can't check it. Use it as a clue to find corroborating evidence.

12. What is the possibility that the person who gave the information was not telling the truth? Many spouses who were older than their husband may not want that information to be known, so they could lie about their age.

Deciding Where to Look First

If you want to know the date of a person's marriage you wouldn't look in a land record first, though it might be the only place you will find a clue. Genealogists always want to know where they are most likely to find the information they want. With all of the possibilities, it is not easy to give a standard answer that will take them to the best place first. It is important not to discount a particular type of record just because it doesn't have a name, date, place, or event connected to it. Remember, we are detectives looking for the clues to our ancestry. With that caution, the list that follows provides good starting places for these types of information.

Print off the checklists on the CD-ROM with this book for the checklists of first places to look and use them to organize your search.

Where to Look First for Genealogical Data	
Adoption	Try guardianship (court) records, adoption agencies, compiled genealogies, and census records.
Age of a Person	Look in census records, birth, death or marriage records, and cemetery records, military records.
Birth Date	Look in birth records, church records, Bibles, and family records, obituaries, cemeteries, and funeral home records.
Birthplace	The first place to look is birth records, followed by census records, church records, family records, and obituaries.
Birthplace (Foreign City)	Try church records, genealogies, naturalization and citizenship first.
Birthplace (Foreign Country)	Look in census records, emigration and immigration records, naturalization and citizenship records, and church records.
Children	First, try census records, birth records, church records, probate records, wills, Bibles and obituaries.
County of Origin	Look in county histories, compiled genealogies.
Death of a Person	Start with death and cemetery records, obituaries, mortuary records, professional directories (e.g., physicians), wills, and probate records.
Ethnicity of an Ancestor	First try journals, tribal enrollment for American Indians, and slave rolls (census) for African Americans.
Immigration Date	Emigration and immigration records, and naturalization and citizenship records are the first places to try.
Living Relatives	Search compiled genealogies, Internet directories, Internet mailing lists, county heritage books, and surname search engines like Roots-L Surname List.
Marriage	First try marriage and church records, Bibles, newspapers, photographs, wills, land, and court records.
Parents	First try census records, birth and church records, probate records, oral histories, and obituaries.
Photos	Contact all living relatives and check county histories, county and state archives, and family Bibles.
Physical Description	Check military records, military draft registration, court records, and biographies.
Religion	The obvious place to check is church or synagogue records, followed by family and cemetery records, and biographies. Also try Bibles, and genealogies.

Figure 8.7 Where to Look First for Genealogical Data

Recognizing Primary and Secondary Sources

Up to this point we have not discussed the differences between primary and secondary sources. These differences are critical to serious researchers. *Primary records* are documents created at the time of the event by someone who witnessed the event. Even within this category of records there are gradations of quality. Primary records like church and vital records, which provide names, dates, and family relationships, are the type of records every genealogist hopes to find. Other records like immigration/emigration, probate, military records, tax lists, school, and pension records are still primary sources, but they often lack the names, birth and death dates, and relationships needed to add to the family record. *Secondary records* are sources created from primary records, or by people who were not present when the event occurred. Compiled records are secondary records. A will is a primary source. So is a death certificate, but only to the fact of the place and date of death. The other types of the information on a death certificate (birth date, birthplace, parents, and so forth) are secondary records. A county history or a family group sheet are secondary sources, because they are more than likely created from more than one source by someone who was not there when all of the events occurred. These distinctions are important when it comes to resolving conflicts between two different records. The primary source will usually take precedence over other sources.

Primary Sources

We really need to rank records based on the quality of the information they contain when we consider the immense historic fabric that must be examined for the few threads of useful data. When dealing with historic records, most historians and genealogists begin by classifying records as either primary or secondary documents.

Here is a list of generally accepted primary sources:

1. Birth records

2. Marriage records

3. Death records

4. Census records

5. Probate records

6. Land records

7. Tax records

8. Military records

9. Church records

10. Cemetery records

11. Mortuary records

12. Burial permits

13. Court records

14. Naturalization records

Someone in an official or governmental position will have recorded most of these sources.

Secondary Records

Secondary sources have not been created be a government official. Contrast the nature of primary sources to the secondary sources in this list.

1. Obituaries

2. Newspaper

3. Published Family Histories/Genealogies

4. County Histories

5. City/County Directories

6. Tombstone Inscriptions

Ranking Records for Reliability

While it is essential to recognize whether we are working with a primary or secondary document, other ways of labeling sources may be more helpful. Consider the following as a ranking of reliability.

1 Original records

2 Copies of original records (including photocopies and microfilm)

3 Extracted records (including typewritten copies of original records)

4 Compiled records with documentation

5 Compiled records without documentation

Caution to Researchers

I must caution that these lists should not be considered absolute. A researcher may find an original record, but the document may be unreadable. I have seen writing on deteriorated paper where the ink had faded so much that no one could read it. Some census microfilms are so light they can't be read, and the handwriting on some wills is so bad that it takes special skill and a lot of time to read them. Some old handwriting may be illegible, not because of poor penmanship, but because the way people formed their letters hundreds of years ago is not recognizable today. Microfilm copies of original documents may be unreadable, because they are too dark, and extracted documents may carry human or typographical errors. With these possible problems in mind, the foregoing list still can be very useful to researchers in comparing the relative value of information they find in various types of records.

Follow the suggestions in this list.

- Always look for an additional source to corroborate the data you find.
- Verify every piece of information you receive from other people.
- Do not trust secondary or compiled sources.

- Do not trust published family histories.
- Do not believe everything you find on the Internet.

If you find an extracted record, check out data in the original document.

Using Research Outlines

Another way to learn where to go first is to use the Research Outlines prepared by the Family History Library. In 52 pages or less, these outlines introduce strategies and describe content, uses and availability of major records for specific topics, states, or regions (see Chapter 2). Even the smallest libraries should have a copy of the Research Outline for their state.

8. Acquire access to the document and search it.

Not all of these documents will exist for every individual, but the events of every individual will have been documented in some of these. The task of a researcher is to find the documents that relate to the lives of his or her ancestors and search them to find out if they have the information he or she needs.

The Internet has made it possible for us to search census indexes online and view the images of census records from our home computers. How much easier can genealogy get? Yet much of genealogical research is a lot more difficult and time consuming. We might have to send requests and pay for copies of documents that are only available from governmental agencies. We might have to request and pay for microfilms and search them. We might even have to go to the places where our ancestors lived to find the information we need. The key to finding these records will be the catalogs and indexes of the agencies that hold them (see Chapters 4 and 5). If we are lucky the full text of the document we seek will be available online, but usually we will have to rent or borrow the material, or hire a researcher in the area to look up the information for us.

This step of genealogical research is repeated every time we look for another source. Indeed the essence of this book is how to acquire access to documents of genealogical research value.

Courthouses and state offices of vital statistics are some of the best places to look for documents. Also, the Family History Library has microfilmed many of the records in courthouses across the country and these records are available on microfilm through local Family History Centers.

Looking at an Example

When I started my research on Joseph Ridgeway all I knew was that he was the husband of "Poley" and the father of Florence Ridgeway, who died in childbirth in Wisconsin about 1871. I found a death index for Wisconsin, which gave his name, death date and place. This was enough to send for a death certificate, which cost me $7.00. The following is a transcription of the death certificate.

Many research documents will not be as rich in genealogical data as was this death certificate. In fact most death certificates have much less information.

9. Extract any valuable information you find.

Genealogical research is about filling in the details of the lives of our ancestors. It is wise to keep copies of these certificates and revisit them later to see if you can glean additional information from them.

REGISTRATION OF DEATH	
Information requested	**Information given**
1. Full name of deceased	Joseph Ridgeway
2. Maiden name (if wife or widow)	
3. Color	White
4. Sex	Male
5. Race	
6. Occupation of deceased	File Manufacturer
7. Age, (years, months and days)	67 yr. 5 mo. 26 days
8. Name of father	Wm Ridgeway
9. Birthplace of father	England
10. Name of mother	Elizabeth (Ashton) Ridgeway
11. Birthplace of mother	England
12. Birthplace of deceased	England
13. Name of wife of deceased	Mary Jane (Stinson) Ridgeway
14. Name of husband of deceased	
15. Date of birth of deceased	August 1st 1831
16. Condition (single, married, or widowed)	Married
17. Date of death	January 27th 1899
18. Residence at time of death	114 W Division Street, Fond du Lac, WI
19. Cause of death Primary	Carcinoma of the liver
20. Place of death	114 W Division Street Fond du Lac, WI
21. Duration of disease	
22. Was the deceased ever a Soldier or Sailor in the Service of the United States?	
23. Place of burial	Rienzi
24. Name of undertaker	D. W. McLain
25. Date of certificate	
26. No. burial permit	140
27. Date of burial permit	Jan. 27, 1899
28. Other important facts not related to death	Only seen by me once before death. T. F. Mayham, MD (Physician)
State of Wisconsin	
County of Fond du Lac	

Figure 8.8 Example of Registration of Death

Different documents for the same event will often corroborate the information found in other documents or lead to other records with additional information. Sometimes a death certificate will include the names and places of birth of the decedent's parents. Sometimes it will barely have the name of the person and his or her date and place of death and his or her age. An obituary, if one is available might tell you how long the person lived in the area or who the surviving family members are. Probate records will often have the names and places of residence of the surviving children. All of this information needs to be extracted and made part of your family history.

Information Extracted from Death Certificate

Joseph Ridgeway was a file manufacturer.

He was 67 yr. 5 mo. 26 days when he died.

His father was Wm [William] Ridgeway.

William was born in England.

His mother's maiden name was Elizabeth Ashton.

Elizabeth was born in England.

Joseph was born in England.

Joseph's wife's maiden name was Mary Jane Stinson.

Joseph Ridgeway was born August 1, 1831.

He was married.

Joseph died January 27, 1899 of carcinoma of the liver.

He was living at 114 W Division Street, Fond du Lac, Wisconsin where he died.

Joseph was buried at Rienzi Cemetery.

The undertaker was D. W. McLain.

The attending physician was T. F. Mayham, MD (Physician).

10. Record the source in the research log.

Earlier in this chapter is a research log (Figure 8.5). You need to enter the source of the data and a brief summary of the information you found. The ancestor's name is at the top of the Research Log. The entry could be as simple as: "Death certificate for Joseph Ridgeway obtained from Fond du Lac County, Wisconsin. Copy in file folder for Joseph Ridgeway."

If the same information had been obtained from a microfilm borrowed from the Family History Library, you would want to include the film number and the description of the title in the Family History Library Catalog.

11. Add the information to the genealogical record form or the computer database.

You will want to make a copy of the death certificate for the paper file of documents of your ancestor and enter the data to you genealogical computer program, and make a note for the person that includes the information on the death certificate and the source of the document. See Chapter 11 for adding data to a software program on your computer.

12. Evaluate the data and look for clues obtained from your most recent find.

Once we have extracted the data from the record it is time to look for clues or leads to the next possibilities. Let me illustrate with a personal example from my research.

As we check other sources to verify the information on the death certificate we may run into dead ends, but some of the clues will provide corroboration to information on the death certificate and provide clues to additional sources to check. Following up on the clues is the heart and soul of genealogical research.

Figure 8.9 shows how one piece of information can lead to other records and other searches.

Clues for Additional Research

Event: Death of Joseph Ridgeway

Document	Event	Data found	Clue to search	Corroboration
Marriage license	Marriage of Florence Ridgeway	Father of bride: Joseph Ridgeway	Fond du Lac, Wisconsin	
Death index	Death of Joseph Ridgeway	27 January 1899, Fond du Lac, Wisconsin	Death certificate	Location of marriage of daughter.
Death certificate	Death of Joseph Ridgeway	Death date and location	Obituary	Death index
Obituary	Death of Joseph Ridgeway	Lived in Fond du Lac for more than 30 years	1870 census	Death certificate
1870 census	Family enumeration	Names and ages of individuals in family and places of birth	International Genealogical Index for England	Age of Joseph Ridgeway, obituary, wife's name
International Genealogical Index	Christening of Joseph Ridgeway	Date of Christening location, parent's names	Date of parent's marriage in IGI	Age of Joseph Ridgeway, census, obituary
Death certificate	Death of Joseph Ridgeway	Death date and location	Probate record	Death index
Probate Record	Death of Joseph Ridgeway	Heirs of Joseph and Mary Jane Ridgeway	San Francisco city directory for children	Census record
Death certificate	Death of Joseph Ridgeway	Name of wife	International Genealogical Index	Death index

Figure 8.9 Clues for Additional Research

As soon as I received the death certificate in the mail I checked the International Genealogical Index and hit a gold mine of information. I found records that had been extracted from parish records of the Church of England. I checked microfilms of the actual records, but found nothing new. The death certificate gave me the maiden name of Joseph Ridgeway's wife—Mary Jane Stinson, which opened up a new vane of research that took my research back several generations in New England.

Learn how to deduce potential clues from newly acquired information and you will become a skilled genealogical researcher. Every new piece of information will lead you to a new source. Many genealogists will not add a new fact to their database until they have found the same information in another source. The second source will often lead you to additional clues for further research.

Checking Out the New Clues

Once you have worked your way through the research process a few times, it will become as natural as breathing. As you discover new facts about your ancestors, new clues for where to look next will come into your mind. It will become difficult to take you time to be thorough and verify the data in other sources. You will begin to feel the enthusiasm felt by so many who have taken up genealogical research.

Once I had the death certificate for Joseph Ridgeway I was able to get a copy of his obituary. I got a copy of his probate record from the district court. I found his family in the 1870 census by browsing through a microfilm. He is not listed in the 1870 census index. I found a record of his marriage to Mary Jane Stinson in Lowell, Massachusetts on Ancestry.com. I found his sons and a grandson in the San Francisco city directory for several years in a row. They were all in the file-making business. Each of these documents led me to other documents and additional information about the family of Joseph Ridgeway.

Adding Up the Expenses of Conducting Research

These discoveries took time and money to uncover. Though I could have done the research using a variety of methods and incurring some expense, this is how I obtained the documents and information just mentioned. I called the Fond du Lac (Wisconsin) Public Library and gave them the exact death date and they sent me a copy of his obituary. They sent me a bill for $2.83 with the obituary. (Public libraries are still the best bargain in the world.) I sent an e-mail to the clerk of the district court to get a copy of the probate records. It cost me $4.00 to have her look for the record and $4.00 to get copies of the genealogically significant documents. I found the 1870 census record at the NARA Regional Archives in Kansas City, Missouri. The trip cost me over $150.00, but I also went to Independence, Missouri to check out the Mid-Continent Public Library. All of the copies I made that day cost me less than $5.00. My membership to Ancestry.com costs me about $180.00 per year, but I use the Web site all the time and find lots of good information. I went to the Sutro Library in San Francisco, California while I was at an ALA conference. All of this research took time and money to accomplish—a reality of the business of finding my ancestors. Sometimes we have to take advantage of opportunities that present themselves to us and other times we have create opportunities on our own.

Implementing the Research Process

If I were a beginning genealogist, just getting started with research, the first thing I would do would be to find a large box and put it on my kitchen table and label it with GENEALOGY DOCUMENTS—on all four sides. My new project would never get far from my mind. Every glance would plant a seed in my subconscious, where my mind would go to work on the problem and bring me ideas of where to look for genealogy documents. As I found them I would put them in the box. The more valuable ones I would make copies of and put them away for safekeeping. Here are some other things I would do, as I got started—maybe not in this order, but I would do them early in the process.

Work with the Living First.

I would:

- Get my birth certificate, make a copy of it, and put the copy in the box. Return the original to its place of safekeeping.
- Do the same thing with the certificates of my parents' birth—and their marriage.
- Go talk to my mother. She is still alive and will have copies of all kinds of genealogical documents.
- Use the Internet and Switchboard.com to find other living relatives who might be able to help me.
- Download a free copy of Personal Ancestral File, a genealogy program for my computer. Anyone who is just getting started with his or her genealogy should have a computer with Internet service. Let your computer help you with your genealogy (see Chapter 11).

Begin Researching the Dead.

I would:

- Start gathering information about the ones who are no longer alive after contacting all of the living relatives I could find.
- Check the catalog of my local public library to see if it has genealogical materials that might have information I could use.
- Check the Family History Library Catalog and the online catalogs of other research facilities for microfilms of document you can borrow.
- Order a film and search it for the information that I have a good chance of finding.
- Check the Social Security Death Index to see if it lists the ancestor I am looking for.
- Send for a copy of the ancestor's Social Security Card Application. (See Chapters 9 and 10)
- Use AltaVista or Google on the Internet to see if anyone has posted anything about my ancestor (see Chapter 12). (My father died in 1994. In 2004 I can still find articles about him on the Internet.)
- Search for the selected ancestor on FamilySearch.org. I wouldn't bother to search for people who are still living or recently deceased. They won't be there. You will be lucky to find deceased grandparents on any of the genealogy search sites.
- Check RootsWeb.com. This free site has millions of names and thousands of pedigrees linked together. Just remember that someone has to put it up on the Internet before you can take it down.
- Obtain copies of death certificates for recently deceased ancestors. (See Chapter 9 for how to do this.)
- Write down or make a copy of pertinent information you find. Add this information to the database and look for the clues to the next line of research.
- Search online census records. I would start with the most recent census my ancestor could appear in. Fill out the census chronology and move backwards.
- Repeat the process as I work my way back. Remember that not all attempts at finding information will produce results, but sometimes no results only means that you have tried another source that did not have the information you are looking for.

Suggestions for Researchers

1. Get a copy of the Research Outline for each of the states in which you are doing research. At FamilySearch.org Look for Order/Download Products Family History Research Products Locality Research Papers, then select the individual item.

2. Use the *Handybook for Genealogists* to find out what records are available in the county where your ancestors lived.

3. Do a place search in the Family *History Library Catalog* www.familysearch.org/Eng /Library/FHLC/frameset_fhlc.asp.

4. Look for new clues as you find new information.

5. Open your thinking to the fact that you will probably have to spend some money to get the information you want. It costs money to pursue genealogical research just like any other hobby or business.

6. Thank people who help you and be willing to share what you find.

Summary

Researchers never know if they will find the mother lode of their research just around the next corner. That is what makes genealogical research exciting. As we find new information and new clues, we have to turn our research problems over to our subconscious and let it bring opportunities. If we are in the right place at the right time it will happen.

In the next chapter we will take a look at a long list of potential sources for information about our ancestors. Keep your mind open to the possibility that you could find some information in any of the resources listed. You are just as likely to find an ancestor in a poor farm record, as you are to find one in a million dollar probate.

Bibliography (Ratings Guide explanation follows last citation)

Baggett, Joan J. 1998. *Genealogical Research for the Beginner: Why, Where, How*. Tampa, FL: J&P Genealogical Research.

The book for beginners has some good insights on how to find the sources genealogists need to move their research forward. **P**

Best, Laura. 2003. *Genealogy for the First Time: Research Your Family History*. New York: Sterling Publishing.

Genealogy for the First Time is a great book for beginners. This comprehensive guide will help the novice get a jump-start with his or her research. This inspiring guide explores the basics of getting started and outlines some of the fundamental investigation techniques. **PP**

Carmack, Sharon DeBartolo. 2003. *You Can Write Your Family History*. Cincinnati, OH: Betterway Books.

Your family history doesn't have to be boring. In fact it can be fascinating, lively, and inspirational—according to Sharon Carmack—the author of this book. She draws on her vast writing experience to show genealogists how to make their genealogy stories fun to read. This book is the like having your own personal writing coach at your side. **PPP**

Coletta, John Philip. 2003. *Finding Your Italian Roots: the Complete Guide for Americans*. Baltimore, MD: Genealogical Publishing Company.

This revised and expanded edition of the book, first published in 1993, helps researchers locate information about their Italian ancestors. In short this is a bigger and better book and well worth having if your roots go back to Italy. **L**

Croom, Emily Anne. 2000. *The Sleuth Book for Genealogists: Strategies for More Successful Family History Research*. Cincinnati, OH: Betterway Books.

This is a strategy book for genealogy detectives—a delight for mystery fans who also happen to be genealogists. This is a good tool with a different slant on genealogical research. **PPP**

Croom, Emily Anne. 2003. *The Genealogist's Companion and Sourcebook*. Cincinnati, OH: Betterway Books.

This classic work on genealogical sources has been completely revised and updated. It introduces researchers to the many varieties of public sources. The real-life research examples show readers how to interpret different tools. The author shows the reader how to use clues from one source to branch to another. **PPP**

Eakle, Arlene H., and Linda E. Brinkerhoff. 2002. *Family History for Fun and Profit: The Genealogy Research Process*. Tremonton, UT: The Genealogical Institute.

The research system promulgated in this book guarantees a 96 percent success rate. The jurisdiction approach keeps the researcher focused on the locations of the major events in a person's life. The process leads researchers to the records they need. More than 3,526 sources are described in detail in this book.
Family History for Fun and Profit belongs in the personal collection of every serious genealogist. **PPP**

Hinckley, Kathleen W. 1999. *Locating Lost Family Members and Friends: Modern Genealogical Research Techniques for Locating the People of Your Past and Present*. Cincinnati, OH: Betterway Books.

The best way to do your genealogical research is to find a living relative, who has already done it and ask him or her to share information with you. This book breaks the process down into bite-size pieces. It tells the reader where to look and how to do it. It covers the obvious and the obscure including directories, birth certificates, marriage and divorce records, death records. It covers 100 resources to search for lost relatives. This book can also be used to find long-lost military buddies, school friends, or close family members who have lost contact with the family. The illustrations make the text come alive. *Locating Lost Family Members and Friends* is essential for any library and worthwhile for a personal collection. **PPP**

Jones, Henry Z. 1993. *Psychic Roots: Serendipity and Intuition in Genealogy.* Baltimore, MD: Genealogical Publishing Company.

Psychic Roots is all about the influence of coincidence and serendipity on genealogical research, the chance combination of events, over which the researcher has no control, but which nevertheless, guides him or her to a fortuitous discovery. Certainly chance or dumb luck sometimes leads us straight to a record kept in an improbable place, to an ancestor's second wife we didn't know anything about, and so on. **P**

Lennon, Rachal Mills. 2002. *Tracing Ancestors Among the Five Civilized Tribes: Southeastern Indians Prior to Removal.* Baltimore, MD: Genealogical Publishing Company.

The five civilized tribes of the Southeast are the Choctaw, Cherokee, Creek, Seminole, and Chickasaw. Researching the ancestry of someone from one of these tribes is difficult, to say the least. It requires identifying and gaining access to some very obscure, but available records, like the records of missionaries to the Indians, U.S. archives, and slave-related materials for those of African-Indian descent. This is a "must read" for anyone engaged in ancestor research of the five civilized tribes of the Southeast. **LL**

McClure, Rhonda. 2003. *Finding Your Famous And Infamous Ancestors: Uncover the Celebrities, Rogues, and Royals in Your Family Tree.* Cincinnati, OH: Betterway Books.

This one-of-a-kind book will help researchers find out if they are related to someone famous. Beginners to professional will find this guidebook as a refreshing enjoyable read. **LL**

Melnyk, Marcia Yannizze. 2002. *The Genealogist's Question and Answer Book: Solutions and Advice for Maximizing Your Research Results.* Cincinnati, OH: Betterway Books.

Beginning genealogists sometimes miss important clues or waste research time, because they don't know how to interpret the data they see. This handy question and answer format makes it easier for them to pick up obscure details they might otherwise miss. **PPP**

Nevius, Erin. 2003. *The Family Guide Book to Europe: Your Passport to Tracing Your Genealogy Across Europe.* Cincinnati, OH: Betterway Books.

When researchers are ready to cross the Atlantic Ocean to find their ancestors they face unfamiliar ways of gathering and preserving records. This user-friendly guidebook demystifies the different ways researchers need to overcome if they are going to get the information they need. This is also a good travel guide to Europe. **PP**

Quillen, W. Daniel. 2003. *Secrets of Tracing Your Ancestors.* Cold Spring Harbor, NY: Cold Spring.

In this beginner's guide to genealogy, professional genealogists share their tricks and techniques of genealogical research. They also suggest how to write a lively family history that will be treasured by generation of descendants. **PP**

Renick, Barbara. 2003. *Genealogy 101: How to Trace Your Family's History and Heritage*. Nashville: Rutledge Hill Press.

I wish I had written this book, because it says everything I would say to the beginning researcher. It deals with the essentials, such as how to use libraries, the Internet, and other places for research. The author emphasizes that just because genealogical data gets published in a book or on the Internet doesn't mean it is correct. Researchers constantly need to verify the information they find. **PPP**

Rice, Donal, and Anne Collins. 2000. *How to Trace Your Family History: A Brief Guide to Sources of Genealogical Research for Beginners*. Dublin, Ireland: Dublin Corporation Public Libraries.

This hands-on guide for beginners includes valuable suggestions, including how to begin, where to go for help, and how to organize your findings. It offers guidance in gleaning information from local, state, and government sources. **PP**

Rose, James M., and Alice Eichloz. 2003. *Black Genesis: A Resource Book for African-American Genealogy*. Baltimore, MD: Genealogical Publishing Company. P

Schmal, John P., and Donna S. Morales. 2002. *Mexican-American Genealogical Research: Following the Paper Trail to Mexico*. Bowie, MD: Heritage Press.

If you can find the town of your ancestor in Mexico, you will probably be able to trace your roots back several generations, which is typical of research in any other part of the world. The authors talk about using birth and death certificates, obituaries, naturalization records, and church records, which are amazingly complete in Mexico. This is a "must have" book for anyone whose roots lead to Mexico. **LL**

Smith, Franklin Carter, and Emily Anne Croom. 2003. *A Genealogist's Guide to Discovering Your African-American Ancestors: How to Find and Record Your Unique Heritage*. Cincinnati, OH: Betterway Books.

Genealogical research for African Americans poses some unique and challenging opportunities. This book discusses the main resources, including census records, family and oral histories, manumission records, tax and land records, bank records, and slave holding families. This is a good place to start for anyone who is beginning his or her research in African American genealogy. **PPP**

Smolenyak, Megan. 2002. Honoring Our Ancestors: Inspiring Stories of the Quest for Our Roots. Orem, UT: Ancestry Publishing.

This book is about sharing the stories of our ancestors with others. In a fun-to-read manner the author shows us how other researchers have shared the fruits of their research with their families and friends. *Honoring Our Ancestors* takes us to the next level of enthusiasm after we have learned about our ancestors. **PP**

This new edition has 100 more pages and a new format to make it easier to find resources related to slaves and free African Americans in the United States. This guide discusses how to gain access to archives, census records, cemetery records, newspapers, manuscripts, and church records.

Most importantly it refers to original research materials that can be found at all levels of government. **PPP**

Woodtor, Dee Palmer. 1999. *Finding a Place Called Home: A Guide to African-American Genealogy and Historical Identity.* New York: Bantam Books.

This is an easy-to-understand book for anyone who is searching for African American ancestors. It set researchers on the right path for finding their roots. While readers will have to check out other sources to find their ancestors, this book tells them where to look. **PPP**

Ratings Guide

The ratings for each bibliography describe not only what each resource contains, but also how it might fit into the library collection. Some of the materials are more appropriate for larger libraries with substantial budgets, and others belong in collections of any size—even in the personal research collection. To help you identify materials most appropriate for your collection, each resource is marked as either "L" for libraries and "P" for personal. They are ranked from one letter for recommended, two letters for preferred, and three letters for essential.

CHAPTER 9

FINDING GENEALOGICALLY SIGNIFICANT SOURCES

Every year thousands of people everywhere begin searching for their ancestors. For many, this search will eventually bring them to a library. How librarians see this opportunity will make a tremendous difference to their customers. Through the library door genealogists can have access not only to local information and collections, but also to the vast and sometimes very specialized holdings of resource centers around the world.

What to Look for in This Chapter

This chapter reviews the various types of reference sources researchers use to find their ancestors. We examine sources, explain why they are important to genealogists, and suggest where to find them.

Non-Genealogical Sources

Many valuable reference tools were not created with a genealogical purpose in mind. Census records cannot be expected to offer generations of family records in a page or two, but the information they do provide serves as a clue to more productive sources. Land records are another good example. A father and mother may deed a piece of land to a son or daughter. That deed may be the only record available to prove the parent/child relationship.

Sometime a record may appear to lack words identifying a single individual. I know of a genealogist who had a photograph that had been handed down to him. The photo was of a man and a woman who appeared to be in their early twenties. There were no names on the back, only a faint stamp of the photographic studio on the face of the photograph. On very careful examination the researcher could see a year and the city of the studio. When he searched the county records for the year and the city he found a marriage record for his great-great-grandparents. The photo didn't have an index or any names, but it was a very valuable clue to finding additional genealogical evidence.

Important Genealogical Sources and Where to Find Them

In solving the puzzles of family history, you will find yourself using sources that are close at hand and those that are in remote libraries and archives. The list that follows is designed to identify the most important sources and their possible locations.

Personal and Family Sources

While it is not likely that individuals will have many of the types of records listed, it is possible that they will have some of them. It is highly likely that families will have records like a family Bible, birth, death and marriage records, as well as documentation for events that might have influenced a life of an ancestor. Immigration, naturalization, name changes, divorces, baptismal certificates and adoption decrees are very likely to be found among personal possessions.

Local Libraries

The genealogical holdings of local libraries can vary widely in their quality. It is reasonable to expect that a public library will have at least those materials published about local citizens.

Other Local Agencies

Included here are county courthouses, local museums, mortuaries, cemeteries, and historical and genealogical associations. They will have records created by their agency in the past.

State Archives

These agencies are sometimes part of the state library and sometimes they are separate. They are generally open to the public and often have newspapers on microfilm and original vital records not housed at county courthouses.

National Libraries/Archives

These facilities have a global perspective. They were established with very specific goals and have significant resources. Although they were not created with genealogist's needs in mind, their large collections are well indexed and access is usually very good.

Family History Library

This library is in a class all by itself, not because it is the largest library of its kind in the world, but because of its vast network of branch libraries or Family History Centers—one of which may be near to your home. The Family History Library has a tremendous variety of record types. It is safe to assume that the Family History Library Catalog will include records for each topic or type of record listed in this chapter.

The Internet

In the past ten years the Internet has given researchers access to hundreds of millions records that were only available to the few who had the time and could travel wherever they wanted. Searching census records used to require hours, even days, to find a family. Now we can sit in our homes and view census images on our computers. Some researchers have even been able to use the Internet to purchase photos, diaries, or wills of their ancestors.

Review of Potential Genealogical Sources (Arranged Alphabetically)

The following list gives a brief description of the source, how to use it and the most likely place to find it. These sources offer high potential for finding usable data.

Account Books

In the days before credit cards many retail stores counted on credit accounts for much of their business. Especially in rural communities, merchants would run adds in the local newspaper after harvest that said, "Please settle up your account, so we can run you again next year." These records may have information about individuals and families that could lead to other types of records. If nothing more, account books could be the only document to place a person in a specific place at a given time.

Adoption Records

Looking for a child or a birthparent is a form of genealogical research. Genealogists want to locate relatives and discover their family roots. Adoption court records are made at the time of the adoption. Availability of records varies from state to state, but most adoption records before 1930 are open to the public. Since then, stricter right-to-privacy laws have made it more difficult to access these records. Researchers generally have to prove a relationship and contact the state agency in charge of the records directly. In some states, adoption information is limited to adoptees only.

Ahnentafel Charts

Ahnentafel means "ancestor table." It shows all known ancestors of an individual. It lists ancestors generation by generation. It is like a pedigree chart in a linear table. Each name has a designated number. The first half of the numbered persons is on the paternal side, and the second half are on the maternal side. All even numbers are assigned to males and all odd numbers are for females. Spouses are consecutively numbered pairs, with the husband having the lower number of the two numbers. Missing numbers are for unknown individuals.

Many genealogists have put their Ahnentafel charts on the Internet and can be accessed by using a search engine like Google or AltaVista. Search terms might look like this: "Ahnentafel chart" [name or surname of individual]. If a researcher finds an Ahnentafel chart associated with a name of an ancestor, there is a high probability of finding a match.

Alien Registration Cards

From 1802 to 1828 immigrants (aliens) were required to register with local courts. Some of these records are preserved at the National Archives and others are indexed in *Passenger and Immigration Lists Index*. We now have some valuable data for individuals who immigrated after 1800, because the law was enforced during the War of 1812.

In 1929 the Alien Registration Act was created. Aliens had to register with the federal government. Information included their residence and place of employment. In order to be considered legal aliens, they had to carry one of these identification cards with them. Any alien without a card could be deported without a hearing. Researchers are more likely to find these cards among home sources.

Anniversaries

Sometimes anniversaries are celebrated in a public way and often a record is made of the event. Invitations may be sent to family and friends, but the most common record of anniversary celebrations occur in newspapers. In the 1800s local newspapers thrived on news of families and the events of their lives. If family members came to help a couple celebrate their anniversary, the news article often carried the names of the visitors and where they were from. Generally, researchers have to use microfilms of newspapers found in local libraries.

Annulment Records

Sometimes marriages are nullified by action of a court. The reasons for an annulment include: lack of parental consent if one of the parties is under age; lack of understanding by one of the parties; fraud by either of the parties, and so forth. Annulment records are court records and need to be secured from the jurisdiction where the records were created. Family members may have personal copies of their own annulment. The records often contain the names of the individuals, possibly their ages and names of family members.

Apprenticeship Records

Apprenticeship records are contracts between a tradesman and the father of the boy who is to serve the apprenticeship. The apprentice was indentured to the tradesman for a specific period of time. The tradesman was obligated to teach the apprentice his trade in exchange for money from the father. Also the tradesman had free access to the labor of the apprentice for the period of the apprenticeship. In the 1600s most apprentices were boys in their teens. Apprentices were usually bound until they were twenty-one, so the length of the indenture specified in the document gives an excellent indication of a boy's age. If a boy was indentured to the tradesman for eight years, for example, he was probably about 13 years old when the contract was signed.

Genealogical information often found in apprenticeship contracts include:

- the date the contract was signed;
- the name and age of the apprentice;
- the name of the parents and place of residence; and
- the tradesman, his trade, and his place of residence.

These records are found in historic court records, and books are available to help researchers find them.

Archives

The purpose of all archives is to preserve records that are important to the people. The National Archives and Records Administration sees itself as the keeper of the nation's records. Its mission is to ensure ready access to the essential documents that record the rights of American citizens, the actions of Federal officials, and the national experience. The National Archives (NARA) has the backing of the federal government and a constitutional mandate to preserve the records of our country. Its broad powers and vast resources have allowed it to build a network of research facilities and amass a collection that is second to none.

National Libraries and Archives

These facilities have a global perspective. They were established with very specific goals and have significant resources. Although they were not created with genealogist's needs in mind, their large collections are well indexed and access is usually very good.

State Archives

These agencies are sometimes part of the state library and sometimes they are separate. They are generally open to the public and often have newspapers on microfilm and original vital records not housed at county courthouses. Many state archives have the personal papers of an individual that can be accessed through their catalogs.

City Archives

New York City Municipal Archives and Department of Health has birth, death, marriage, and passenger lists. These collections have been indexed to make them readily accessible to researchers. Some records are available on microfilm through the National Archives.

Church Archives

Most church records are available at the church where they were created. Sometimes Catholic Dioceses have archives with church records that span many years.

The most important thing about using any archive is to learn how they are organized. Researchers can hit a "gold mine" in an archive or they can waste a lot of time if they don't understand the indexing system.

Atlases

Genealogists can resolve some research problems by using maps, atlases and gazetteers. An atlas is a collection of maps and is a valuable tool of every family researcher. Not only is a plat atlas good for locating the family homestead, it can also include biographical sketches and photographs. Plat maps of a county are especially helpful, because they indicate the size of the property and the owner's name. This information is a lead to land records. Even though the family may have moved on and the family home no longer exists, a detailed township/plat atlas can lead a family member to the old homestead, which could be the site of a family cemetery. Public libraries and county courthouses are good places to find a plat atlas.

Auction Records

Families have held auctions to liquidate assets whether the items are part of an estate or the property of someone who needs to sell his or her property to pay debts. An estate auction will often list the items in the auction, the amount they sold for, and the person who bought them.

The date of the auction could be a clue to the death date of the last survivor. Using the date of the auction might help a researcher bracket the date for a probate record. The possessions of a family can speak volumes about their life style and what was important to them. Auction records could also produce the names of children in the family, as well as other relatives.

Bankruptcy Records

Bankruptcy laws have provided relief to individuals and helped businesses pull through excessive financial hardship. Those who found themselves in such conditions could seek protection in court. Most bankruptcy records generally lack the vital statistics genealogists are looking for, but they can provide worthwhile insights into the lifestyle of an ancestor. Bankruptcy records usually have a schedule of assets and liabilities, and they may have extensive accounts of real and personal property. Sometimes they will have photographs or maps.

It is not easy to find bankruptcy records, but some can be accessed through major indexes, but most likely it will require a trip to the county courthouse or one of the regional National Archives. The researcher needs to have the name of the petitioner and the county of residence, and the date when the filing was made. A beginning point may be to look for public notices of the filing for bankruptcy in local newspapers.

Baptismal Records

These are church records. Since baptism is considered a scared ordinance or sacrament by many religious faiths, these records will often provide valuable vital statistics. Baptismal records will usually give the name of the individual, the person's date of birth, the names of both parents, and often the names of the grandparents.

Beliefs about baptism vary between religious faiths. The baptismal record of older individuals will usually include the birth date. Knowing the religious preference of an ancestor will help researchers narrow the scope of their search for baptismal records.

Bible Records

Individuals recorded the births, deaths and marriages of their family members in the family Bible, to make a record they hope will be preserved. Generally a person who was present at the event recorded it in the Bible soon after it happened. Sometimes several entries are made at once after accumulating over a period of months or years, opening the record to inaccuracies. Despite the generally high level of accuracy of Bible records, there are instances when the actual marriage date or birth of the first child may be altered to hide an out-of-wedlock birth or an underage marriage. The DAR will not accept a Bible record as proof of lineage unless the petitioner can prove who has the Bible.

Copies of family Bibles are available on microfilm or microfiche. The Periodical Source Index (PERSI) is a good place to look (see Chapter 10). Also, you can check Bible Records Online (Available: www.biblerecords.com).

Biographical Sources

Biographical Dictionaries

These reference works were created to document the accomplishments of individuals, who usually shared a common discipline or field. But, your ancestors do not have to be persons of prominence in a profession or occupation to be included in a biographical dictionary. Entries usually contain birth, marriage, family, and death information and often a long list of achievements, which can lead to additional research. Information is usually well researched and accurate, though sometimes incomplete. If they are in print, these dictionaries are readily available from the publishers. If not, look for a reprint or a microfilm copy.

Three of the most important collective biographies are: the *Dictionary of American Biography*; the *National Cyclopedia of American Biography*; and *Who's Who in America*. Many of these dictionaries are indexed in *Biography and Genealogy Master Index*.

Biographical Directories

These research tools are often a good place to start, because they help narrow the scope of the search. They tend to be organized either by surname or by geography. Some of the more important directories include: *Directory of Family Associations* (Bentley, 2001) and *Directory Of Genealogical And Historical Societies in the U.S. and Canada* (Carson, 2002).

Biographies

Biographies focus on, or tell the story of a person's life. They usually, but not always, include essential genealogical information on the subject. Sometimes they include details about family members. Biographies are a secondary source that may have errors, and the genealogical data needs to be verified.

Birth Certificates, Delayed

Birth certificates were not required in many states until 1910 or later. Those whose births were not registered could have applied for a delayed birth certificate to document their age to register for Social Security or apply for a passport, an insurance policy, or other benefits. These people had to prove their age with some other document. Census records were used as well as baptismal certificates, family Bible records, school records, or affidavits swearing to his age. Delayed birth certificate will generally include the person's name, date of birth, and the name, place of birth, and race of the mother and father. The evidence that was presented to obtain the delayed certificate is usually noted on the certificate.

Bonds

Before marriage licenses were required by state or local jurisdictions, the grooms posted marriage bonds with the father or the brother of the bride, to guarantee that the marriage would take place. In the event the marriage did not happen the bond money could be used by the bride's family to hire a lawyer to sue the reneging man. Marriage bonds were important documents because marriage carried with it significant property interests. Once a woman was married she was entitled to her husband's estate or at least half of it if he died.

Bonds were often posted in the bride's home county, the place where the marriage was to take place. In many jurisdictions these bonds are only marriage records available for researchers. Bonds often included the name of the bride's father or brother. The names, ages, and county of residence were included in the bond. In many cases, the actual date of the marriage was added to the record soon after the ceremony, but it didn't always happen. Most marriages took place within a few days of the posting of the bond. Although the missing information could mean that the marriage did not take place, though more often it reflects poor record keeping or failure of the justice or minister to report the marriage to local officials. Marriage bonds can be found in the registers of most churches or the county records.

Bounty Awards

My fifth great-grandfather, Benjamin Robinson, raised a company of Minute Men during the Revolutionary War. From 1776–1778, he fought in the battles of Brandywine and Germantown. For his service in the war, he was granted a land bounty of 3,000 acres in western Virginia (now

Harrison County, West Virginia). This was a common practice during colonial times. It was an attractive reward for previous service or to encourage men to enlist.

The practice was prevalent from 1788 to 1855. Land bounty records are doubly valuable. They can help locate a person in a time and a specific place and they can prove military service, which can lead to other sources. Applications for bounty awards are of the filled with gems of genealogical information.

Burial Registers

Church burial registers often contain information about other family members. They may include information on other family members. Gravesites are most often sold in lots with eight plots or spaces for graves to the lot. A block in a cemetery will have from four to ten lots depending on the layout of the cemetery. Not everyone buried in a family lot will be siblings or children of the owner of the lot. You might find cousins, grandparents, or individuals who have married into the family. The information in a burial register is valuable to the genealogist, but often difficult to find. Church records can be passed down to a university that is affiliated with sect, or passed down to family members of the clerk who originally made the record. They may also be kept in a central church archive or another safe place that has only a remote connection to the church where the records originated. Researchers may have to hunt for them, so be pretty sure your ancestor was buried in the cemetery before you try to find the burial register.

Business Records

Business records can place an ancestor in a time and place, which could lead to a census record. Business records can be used to fill in the details of an individual's life. An account book might reveal that a tradesman provided significant service to a famous person in history. In the absence of a mortuary record the business record of a doctor or a casket maker might reveal details on the death of an ancestor.

These records may be archived in the business if it still survives or with the heirs of the proprietor. Some but not all of these records may have been microfilmed and made more accessible. Otherwise it could take some serious digging to find business records that could help genealogists.

Catalogs

Catalogs may not contain any genealogical data, but they can lead to vast collections to be searched. Genealogy libraries all over the country have produced printed CD-ROM, and online catalogs to help genealogists find out if the records they have might help them in their research. Just to name a few, the Allen County (IN) Public Library and the Mid-Continent (MO) Public Library have made their collections more accessible by creating a catalog to their genealogy collections.

Automation of libraries in the past two decades coupled with Web server software have made online catalogs possible for even small libraries. The Great Bend (KS) Public Library, not known for its strong genealogy collection, serves a population of 15,000. Its online catalog includes genealogical materials.

Cemetery Records

Volunteers usually copy these records from grave markers for genealogical purposes. The records are compiled into books and are often published by local historical or genealogical societies. The records include birth and death dates for individuals, though, sometimes, complete dates (month and day) are not available. They sometimes give the names of other family members and their relationships. Cemetery records are usually reliable for a death date and place. Birth dates may be inaccurate and maiden names for women are rarely given. Local public libraries will often have printed cemetery books. They often go out-of-print soon after they are published and are often not kept up to date.

More and more cemetery records are becoming available as interested individuals are making the effort to create Web pages and put them up on the Internet. We may never see the records of every cemetery in the United States on the Internet, but we will very likely find cemetery records of some little-known graveyards. Check out Cyndi's List (Available: www.cyndislist.com/cemetery.htm).

Cemetery records are valuable links to other genealogical sources like probate records, obituaries, and mortuary records.

Census Records

Agricultural Census

Agricultural census records are often overlooked, but they can be used to fill gaps when land and tax records are missing or incomplete. They can help researchers differentiate between people with the same names, document land holdings of ancestors with suitable follow-up in deeds, mortgages, tax rolls, and probate inventories, and identify others who may not appear in other records. They can be a good source for African American genealogy.

The federal census takers compiled agriculture census from 1840 through 1880. State agricultural census records vary from state to state. In many cases they have a wonderful amount of specific detail that provide clues to additional places to look. Probate inventories can give tons of information about a person's occupation.

Federal Census

Population schedules were taken by the federal government starting in 1790 and by some states in various years. The purpose of the federal census was for apportionment of representation in the national congress, and for potential military recruitment, and taxation. The 1850 Federal Census was the first to record the names of a spouse and the children with living parents. The 1840 Federal Census is good for identifying Revolutionary War pensioners. Birth dates, marriages, and deceased children are missing from these records. The best way to access census records is online at Ancestry.com or HeritageQuest Online. Federal census microfilms are available for rent from the National Archives, and several other agencies. They are also available for sale to the public. In Chapter 10 we take a closer look at federal census records.

State Census

States conducted local census to gather specific information about the needs of communities. They asked questions that reflected the financial needs and strengths of communities. State censuses were often taken in years between the federal censuses. These records can be used to fill in gaps left by missing censuses. For example, state and territorial censuses taken in years between 1885 and 1895 can partially compensate for the missing 1890 census schedules. Some state censuses give considerably more information than was gathered in the federal census for the same time period.

The 1925 Iowa state census is a real gold mine for genealogists. It asked for the names of all inhabitants and their relationship to the head of that household; sex; color or race; age at last birthday; place of birth; marital status: if foreign born; the year naturalized, etc. Some public libraries may have selected state censuses for their state.

Change of Name Records

Individuals can change their names in every state. Regular courts with the power to grant a divorce usually have the authority to approve name changes. Divorces or adoptions make names changes critically important to researchers. It is a good idea to search the indexes for all surnames on your pedigree, and for names that married into your lines.

Christenings

Genealogists have relied on records christenings or the baptism of infants when not civil record of the birth event was made. We are inclined to believe that these records are generally accurate, but many children may never have been christened, and some were christened several years after they were born. Even so, most researchers tend to accept the christening date for a birth date if a birth date cannot be found. After all it is a proof of birth even if the date is a few weeks off. Christenings records often include the name of the father and the mother and the place of the family's residence.

Church Records

Christenings (baptisms), marriages, confirmations, and funerals are sacraments or ordinances in most Christian faiths. In early America, ministers were required to submit their records to civil authorities. Usually accurate, these primary source documents for births, marriages, and deaths can be used in lieu of vital records gathered by the state or county. They often include information on extended families.

Family Books

These are pure treasures if you can find them. Members of the clergy created these records to keep track of families. They list the mother and father and all the children. Genealogists can create a family group sheet, including birth, marriage and death, from a single primary record. They even have information on the extended family, often three generations. The best place to look for church family books is the church where they were created or a national repository.

City Directories

Published city directories may be a good way to locate an ancestor, which can lead to finding the person in the census population schedules. Finding an ancestor in a city directory may lead to a marriage or death record. Occupations are often listed, which can specifically identify a person. The earliest directories were done in the late 1700s. They became more common in the early 1900s. Many city directories are now available in microform.

County Farm (Poor Farm) Records

One of the first organized efforts of local governments to care for the poor and the needy was to establish a "county farm." This movement started in the last decades of the 1800s and continued, in some cases, through the middle of the twentieth century. It was believed that, if given a chance, anyone could work and help grow food, and thereby avoid starvation. If individuals could do any type of work, they did. Receipt books show the farms earning cash by selling the milk, eggs, flour, etc. Conditions in these places were often deplorable and the people who ended up there were not very able to provide for themselves. In the end county farms became more like nursing homes than centers of farm production.

County farm records are a good place to begin a search for individuals that seem to have disappeared. Those in charge generally kept good records. Many of the residents died and were buried on the farm. Though it may be difficult to find individual graves, other documentation is often very good.

There were also births, some with the exact time of birth and date of the birth. The records often list the fathers name along with the mother's maiden name, place of birth, age, and physical and mental condition.

I have seen census records listing individuals who resided at the county farm. So, a census index might be a good starting point if an ancestor seems to have just disappeared.

County Histories

Many county histories were created by entrepreneurial publishers around the turn of the century as well as at other times. They often contain good general information about the county and its more prominent citizens. They have good clues for settlement and migration patterns. Some have good genealogical data on the people they include. Scholars have written some county histories spending many years compiling their data.

Unfortunately many county histories were created by people who were more interested in making money than producing an accurate, well-written record for posterity. Don't count on finding the names of every person who lived in the county in these accounts. If you didn't have the money to be included you were left out.

Court Records

Court records are created as a result of some action in a court of law. Some actions of particular interest to genealogists are adoption, guardianship, probate, divorce or custody. Genealogists are interested in the records of the courts such as docket books, minute books, and case files. Docket books can serve as an index to court records. Researchers can scan the docket for a surname, and then find the records they need. For every action pertaining to a case, the case number is found by scanning the pages of the minute book for every occurrence of the case number found in the docket book. The case file (or packet) contains all the papers filed in connection with the case. Court records on microfilm can be found in county, state, and federal archives.

Courthouse Records

Besides court records these documents include births, deaths, marriages, deeds, land records, probates, guardianships, and naturalizations, as well as county histories, census records, obituary indexes, and cemetery records. Researchers who travel to locations where their ancestors lived should check out the courthouse even if they have already written and asked for information before. I know researchers who came up empty-handed after they wrote to a courthouse, but later they visited the courthouse in person and found the records that they had been told didn't exist.

Customs Records

Customs records can help researchers determine the origin of their ancestors and enable to trace their family trees. Getting across the Atlantic Ocean is often one of the most difficult tasks for genealogical researchers. Depending on when the ancestors came, it can be easy or difficult. Regardless it will be fascinating to learn the stories of how it happened. The answers will come in customs records. The records of the Ellis Island Immigration Station of New York are examples of customs records. These records have been extracted and put online—a powerful tool for those with ancestor who came through Ellis Island.

Deeds

Deeds document the conveyance of property from one person to another. They are usually recorded in the county courthouse and maintained to show a clear title for the current owner. No researcher should ever overlook this resource. Deeds can be used to show relationships, as in a father and mother deeding some property to a son or daughter.

Deeds can be used to find the maiden name of a woman. If a woman in her own right deeds property to another party and without her husband's permission, she is selling her own property—property that was probably deeded to her by her father. Look for the deed from the father to the daughter and you will find the woman's maiden name.

Deeds can also be used to predict a man's age. Under English Common Law, which followed colonists to America, a male had to be 16 years old to receive property.

Diaries

A diary can be a precious possession to a family history researcher. These primary source documents are as valuable as the information they contain. Some may go on for volumes and never mention a useable genealogical fact, but the insight into the writer's personality may be priceless. Diaries or journals may contain detailed descriptions of a marriage or courtship or some particularly difficult times for the individual. They may also be fraught with omissions or a perspective favorable to the writer. Copies of journals or diaries may be found in archives or large libraries.

Directories

Directories contain the names and contact information for individuals and groups. Directories have been published accommodate any special interest imaginable. The following types of directories might have useable information for genealogists:

- School alumni
- Associations
- Business
- Cemeteries

- Churches
- Ethnic organizations
- Occupations
- Passenger ship arrivals
- Farmers
- Fraternal organizations
- Genealogical societies
- Insurance companies
- Libraries
- Military academies
- Morticians
- Newspaper
- Postal
- Railway officials
- Religious organizations
- Schools
- Telephone

While these directories may not have vital records information, they could lead researchers to other more fruitful sources.

Emigration Records

Countries from which immigrants have migrated create emigration records. Several European countries have compiled and indexed emigration records. These records of departure will give name, age, relatives or traveling companion, for each person. They may also contain the last place of residence. These records are usually available from the archives of the countries that created them. Some have been compiled and published in books.

Employment Records

Employment and occupational records include: union membership records professional licenses, employment files, and professional associations. They may be difficult to find, but they can be handy for the genealogical data they may include. Some professional associations keep files on their members. Company histories, worker biographies, published company directories, and almanacs may have information about their members. Some these documents may have been deposited in a corporate library. If you can link your ancestor to a particular trade you may be able to find helpful records with in that business or trade group. You may be able to find records of local companies in your local library. *The Encyclopedia of Associations*, (Detroit: Gale Research) is a good place to start on you quest for employment or occupational records.

Census records from 1850 forward give the occupation of individuals who were working. This information could be a clue to finding occupational records that could include you ancestor.

Family Histories

A family historian who wants to share his or her efforts with other family members could publish a family history. These publications have the potential for lots of good information. They can contain lineages, families, events, dates and places. However, some portions of the families or family skeletons may be omitted because of a family feud or family secrets.

Federal Courts

The United States district courts are the trial courts of the federal court system. The district courts have jurisdiction to hear nearly all categories of federal cases, including both civil and criminal matters, including bankruptcy cases. Court cases involving large estates or complicated probate proceeding may have been heard in a federal court. If the estate of one of your ancestors was adjudicated in a federal court, you may find a gold mine of genealogical information.

Start by locating the jurisdiction where the case may have been heard. This Web site will help you get started (Available: www.law.emory.edu/FEDCTS). Then search for the name or names of your ancestors. Many of these indexes are now online. Do not overlook this potentially rich source of information.

Fire Insurance Maps

The Sanborn Map Company has published comprehensive maps for cities and towns since 1867. Insurance agents used these maps to assess the risks associated with underwriting insurance policies. Individual residents do not appear on the maps by name, although specific addresses are shown. If you can find your ancestor in a census record of city directory, you can establish exactly what house the family lived in. Sandborn maps are available online by subscription. Check this Web site: http://sanborn.umi.com.

The Geography and Map Section of the Library of Congress has prepared a document entitled, "Fire Insurance Maps in the Library of Congress." It lists the maps available for each town and city. Copies of specific maps can be secured from the Library of Congress, Photoduplication Services. Some libraries may also be able to make copies of the maps they have.

Genealogical Directories

Genealogical directories are finding tools for genealogists. They list places, people, or resources that share a common focus, like genealogy libraries or professional researchers. Before the days of the Internet they were all published in printed form, and likely to be out of date before the first issue was sold. Today they are found in hard copy and on the Web. Many printed genealogical directories can be found in libraries or purchase for personal use from genealogical vendors. Beware of online directories. They may not be complete, or they may only push the products or services of those entities that have paid to be listed. The same thing can be true of printed directories.

Genealogical Queries

Queries have been a standard way of requesting genealogical information for years. After researchers had contacted family members and were seemingly at a brick wall, they would put an advertisement (a query) in a genealogy magazine and hope someone with information would see it and respond. Granted this shotgun approach produced disappointing results—most of the time. On occasion genealogical queries have produced the link to take a pedigree back several generations.

Today we can search the Internet and find queries that other people have submitted in hopes that someone will see them and respond. GenForum.com http://genforum.com is a popular site. E-mail speeds up the process and makes it easier to correspond with others who may have information to share. MyFamily.com is another site worth checking out.

Genealogical Societies

Genealogical societies records are an important source of information. When individuals join the society they are often asked to submit copies of their pedigrees and family group sheets. These records are organized into a file or database and made available to other members of the association. The National Genealogical Association is a leader in this type of activity. Genealogical associations also publish and index genealogical research data—generally restricted to the area of their expertise. For more than a hundred years The New England Historical and Genealogical Society has done an excellent job of gathering genealogical research of the New England area and published for its members, and then indexing every article they have published. Among the resources of genealogical associations you could find indexes of local cemetery records, mortuary records, court records, newspapers birth, death, and marriage notices, collection of tombstone inscriptions, and lists of members interested in a particular surname. Their regular publications might include voter registration lists, immigration lists, and censuses for the region.

The Federation of Genealogical Societies (Available: www.fgs.org) is a good place to start to find the genealogical society that matches your interest and area of research.

Genealogies

Compiled genealogies can be a rich source for research. More than just a few online genealogy companies invite people to submit their genealogical records to be uploaded to the Internet. Leading the list is FamilySearch.org who publishes genealogies on the Internet in the form of the Ancestral File. Ancestry.com offers the *Ancestry World Tree*. Members have access to other databases.

Because people create these genealogies, and some people are more careful researchers than others, some data will be inaccurate.

One of my ancestors was supposed to have been named Henry Jackson and his wife was supposed to be Elizabeth or Caroline. This information came from an uncle, whose name was Henry, and he was sure he was named after his great grandfather. The wife's name was based on the name of their daughter. Recent research revealed that none of this was true, and I had spent 30 years looking for the wrong couple. Their real names were James T. Jackson and Mary Murphy. A relative who is also interested in genealogy submitted the incorrect information to Ancestry.com, and now other family researchers are being misled.

Grantee/Grantor Indexes

These are indexes to land or deed records. Seller indexes are also called grantor indexes. Buyer indexes are called grantee indexes. These indexes are essential to researching land records. Land records are some of the largest collections of official records found in any courthouse. And so, researchers grantee/grantor indexes to do their research. Some counties have only grantor indexes and no index for buyers. In these cases researcher have to go through the entire grantor index from A to Z to find the buyers, because the buyers are listed next to the sellers. These deed indexes can be inaccurate. So it is a good idea to check a few of the index entries to see if they match the deeds they claim to reference.

Guardianships

These are court records kept at the county level or in a state archive. The selection of a guardian may have been legally mandated to administer an inheritance left to a minor child or to care for the minor in the event of both parents' deaths. Courts also appointed guardians for adults who were incapable of managing their own resources. In guardianship records researchers have found the names of the minor, the guardian, and the natural parents. They also discovered details of inherited property and the minor's relationship to the benefactor. The age of the minor can be estimated from dates of the documents. Individuals had to be 18 years old to release a guardian.

Families may have original records that pertain specifically to their family members. In some cases guardianship records may be the only place where the natural parents of a child are listed. Check the courthouse where the guardianship hearing was held. The records might have been turned over to a state archive. You may have to prove a relationship to gain access to these records.

Heirlooms

Heirlooms passed down from one generation the next may help us decide where to search next. Heirlooms with provenance document will tell us which family members own the item over a period of time. These names will give us more clues. Even the smallest trinket should not be overlooked. Wedding bands, pocket watches, and other pieces of jewelry often carried inscriptions of names and dates. Fraternal lodge buttons, military buttons and ribbons, uniforms, awards, and trophies can be fruitful leads.

Heirlooms without an inscription or lack a connection to an ancestor should not be overlooked. A well-informed antique dealer may be able to tell you who made the item, when and the region of the country it came from.

Heirlooms are usually passed down from one relative to another. If you have some, consider yourself fortunate. If not try to find some from your ancestor and ask to examine them.

Hospital Records

Hospital records are valuable sources for genealogical information, but because of confidentiality rules, they may be difficult to access, even if you can prove relationship. Hospital records from over 100 years ago may not be quite so difficult to access. Generally, hospital records will include patient's name, age, birthplace, date of entry or admission, reason for hospitalization, and the date of release or death. Death records from hospitals will usually give the deceased's name, death date, and cause of death.

Immigration Records

Ship passenger records are generally referred to as immigration records. They can give evidence that a person came to the United States, coming from a foreign country. The National Archive and Records Administration has immigration records for various ports from 1800 to 1959.

Not until 1820 did the federal government require ship captains to furnish passenger lists to federal officials. Generally, NARA does not have passenger lists of ships arriving before 1820.

They do have Arrivals at New Orleans from 1813 to 1819. The also have arrivals at Philadelphia for the years 1800 through 1819.

It helps to know the full name, a birth or marriage date, a place of origin—hopefully a town or parish, relatives, family traditions, neighbors, religion, ethnicity, and name change information. Knowing the date of departure, place of departure, city of arrival, and the name of the ship, will also help you find your ancestor.

One of the best documents you can use to identify your ancestor is the declaration of intent to become a citizen. The good ones contain lots of personal information. They are even better than the citizenship document. Other sources include family and home sources, research already done by others, local libraries and courthouses. Genealogists who take immigration research seriously need to find books that specialize on this topic.

Here are a few books I consider worth the money.

Shaefer, Christina K. 1997. *Guide to Naturalization Records of the United States*. Baltimore, MD: Genealogical Publishing Company.

Carmack, Sharon DeBartolo. 2000. *A Genealogist's Guide to Discovering Your Immigrant and Ethnic Ancestor: How to Find and Record Your Unique Heritage*. Cincinnati, OH: Betterway Books.

Anderson, Robert Charles. 1999. *The Great Migration: Immigrants to New England, 1634–1635*. Boston: Great Migration Study Project, New England Historic Genealogical Society.

Szucs, Loretto Dennis. 2000. *Ellis Island: Tracing Your Family History Through America's Gateway*. Provo, UT: Ancestry Publishing.

Indentures

Foreigners, who wanted to come to America but could not afford it, would sell their services as servants to someone for a certain amount of time to gain the cost of passage to the United States. These contracts were called indentures. They kept their copy of the contract with them so they would know how much they owed. Other individuals could buy the contract and have the person become their indentured servant.

The contracts were often sworn before a magistrate or some other legal authority. These records are most often found in local court records. For more information refer to Colonists in Bondage: White servitude and convict labor in America, 1607–1776 by Abbot Emerson Smith. The University of North Carolina Press reprinted from the original in 1947 for the Institute of Early American History and Culture at Williamsburg, Virginia. Good information can also be found in: The Bristol Register of Servants Sent to Foreign Plantations, 1654–1686, by Peter Wilson Coldham.

Institutional Records

Don't overlook institutional records. They are some most important sources of genealogical data available. Records from schools, hospitals, mortuaries, coroners, orphanages, and prisons are some of the most fruitful of all institutional records. Since they are records of a special population, they may not be available to just anyone who asks to see them. Older record will be more accessible than more recent ones, which are protected by laws of privacy. Some institutional records have been around for up to 200 years—potentially powerful sources for genealogical researchers.

Earlier records may include priceless genealogical information, so it is important to know the various types of records, what they contain, what makes them special, and how to access them. These records contain a lot of raw data that has not been indexed or compiled into a more useable format for genealogist. Hence the tendency to pass them by when they could contain exactly the information you need.

Land and Property Records

Before there were birth, death, and marriage record, land and property records kept track of the people. When a landowner died, land records reflected the transfer of the land to the heirs. When a child got married, parents would often give him or her a piece of land. If a land record listed the estate of "John Doe" as the owner of the property, there was a good chance that the person had died within the past year.

When the land records were destroyed they were the first document to be reconstructed. Today we use title insurance to guarantee a clear title to property. In earlier times a title search was conducted to prove a clear title. Land records were essential to everyone who owned property. These records were also important to governmental agency because land records were the basis for taxation.

Don't overlook land and property records—especially if you think you are up against a brick wall. Locate the land or property records for the time and location of your ancestor and dig in. You may want to get a book like Locating Your Roots: Discover Your Ancestors Using Land Records, by Patricia Law Hatcher, 2003. Land records will be found in county courthouses.

For researchers whose ancestors might have homesteaded land, the Bureau of Land Management has a great site for finding land patent records (Available: www.glorecords.blm.gov). In just a few minutes I found two land patents of ancestors and was able to view an image of the actual document.

Legal Notices

Legal notices in newspapers can lead to probate proceeding, divorce cases, estate sales, or tax sales. These items may be difficult to find, but they are there for any researcher with the determination to find them. Most public libraries will have local libraries on microfilm, but they won't be indexed. Some of the larger newspapers are being loaded on Ancestry.com, OCLC, and other Web sites. These offerings have limited indexing, and it is like looking for a needle in a haystack. To find anything useful you almost have to know for sure that your ancestor lived in the city of the newspaper you are searching. It still takes persistence to find anything.

Letters

Correspondence with family members can be a treasure trove of genealogical information.
After my father left home he wrote letters to his father in Arizona. My father kept the letters and my mother transcribed them and put them into a book, which she gave to her children as Christmas gifts along with one of the original letters.

I have a letter from my great grandfather to his adult daughter. The letter mentions a second wife and two children I didn't know about.

All of this correspondence is priceless. If we can find it and get copies from our relatives we will be glad we did. Most correspondence will be found with family heirlooms and only rarely found published and on the shelf of a local library.

Licenses

Starting about the turn of the twentieth-century government agencies required businesses and certain professional to have a license to engage in their enterprise. These licenses were required to make sure that the holder possessed the necessary knowledge or expertise to practice a trade or a profession. Business licenses were a form of revenue and as a means of protecting local business from unauthorized peddlers.

License applications of shopkeepers, saloonkeepers, peddlers, and other local business owners requesting permission to operate a business in a particular city may have been microfilmed or archived. These records often include the applicant's age, birthplace, marital status, and residence. Professional organizations often keep records on licensed professionals such as teachers, doctors, pharmacists, or lawyers.

Manumission Certificates

Slaves who purchased their own freedom or were set free by their owners were given a certificate of manumission. Manumissions were also recorded with local courts and have been found in land records that document the sale and ownership of land since slaves were considered personal property. A manumission certificate would be a rare find today, and a priceless possession. Copies manumission documents will be found in county or city records. Do a title search in the catalog of a research library located near where the ancestor may have been freed.

Manuscript Collections

Manuscripts are usually found in state historical archives or national archives. They include: Bible records, letters, genealogical notes and charts, personal papers, local government records, state government records, church records, cemetery records, business records, military records, organization records, maps, and plans. These are not easy to access, but they often contain information not available from any other source. Check with the state historical society or the National Archives. Also check: *National Union Catalog of Manuscript Collections*. Washington: Library of Congress, Annual, –1985. Biennial, 1986/1987–1988/89. Annual, 1990–1993.

Maps

Genealogists can solve many research problems by using maps. Maps show the location and approximate size of a town and neighboring communities. Many local libraries will have atlases covering the entire United States. The Library of Congress and the National Archives and Records Administration have has extensive map collections. Instructions for securing copies of specific maps can be found at their Web sites:

- Library of Congress (Available: www.loc.gov/rr/geogmap)

- National Archives (Available: www.archives.gov)

Marriage Licenses

County officials issue a marriage license before the wedding ceremony is performed. This license is the most common marriage record in the United States. A minister or someone else who has been authorized to perform the ceremony completes the form with dates and proper signatures. The completed license is returned to the county official to be recorded at the county level and sent to the state. Researchers can usually expect to find the full names of the bride and groom, their ages or birth dates, their places of birth, their race, and sometimes the names of their parents, their occupations, and previous marriages. In most states marriage licenses have been required from the 1860s through today.

Copies of marriage license can be obtained from county clerks. Consult *The Handybook for Genealogists* (Everton, 2002) to find out what records are available and where to write for them. Searching fees and copying charges will vary and researchers may have to prove their relationship the couple.

Military Records

Military records can be magnificent sources of information for genealogists. These records will include biographical information including date and place of birth, place of birth, enlistment residence. Military records will tell you where in the armed forces the soldier served, and whether that person was an officer or an enlisted person. Letters, photographs, and discharge papers may be available in family sources. Military records for those who served before World War I are in the National Archives. Go to their Web site (Available: www.archives.gov/global_pages/inquire_form .html) to order copies of the forms to request copies military records. You will need the name of the soldier, the branch of the service he served in, his unit and where he lived when he enlisted, and in which war he served.

From World War I on, the records are archived in the National Personnel Records Center, 9700 Page Boulevard, St. Louis, Missouri, 63132. Also checkout: *Tracing Your Civil War Ancestors*, by Bertram Hawthorne. Winston-Salem, NC: John F. Blair 1995.

If the person has ever been in the military get a copy of Richard Johnson's book, *How to Locate Anyone Who Is or Has Been in the Military: Armed Forces Locator Guide*, 8th ed. Spartanburg, SC: MIE Publishing, 1999. He tells you exactly how to do it.

Military Histories

Sometimes the only way to find an ancestor who served in the military is to read military histories. This could be a tedious task but if think of the thrill when you find your ancestor. Many histories have been published on the Internet—state by state. Check the USGenWeb Project.

Ministers' Records

Ministers kept some of the earliest marriage records we have available today. Some date back to colonial times. Ministers kept the records in a logbook or journal. Before governments began to require marriage licenses, they required ministers to report the marriages they performed to the city or county clerk. These records may still be available in town archives.

Mortality Schedules

These list individuals who died the year before the census was taken. A mortality schedule includes: the individual's name, age, sex, occupation, cause of death, date of death, and place of death by county. If an ancestor died in 1849, 1859, 1869 or 1879, they will likely be listed in a mortality schedule taken the year after the death. These primary source documents will be found with the census records. They are available through the National Archives, the National Archives regional centers and at many libraries.

Mortuary Records

These records are created by local funeral homes at the time of service. They can be a good source of information. Most entries give the date and place of death, place of burial, spouse's name, place of birth, an obituary, and an itemized list of the funeral and burial expenses. Many funeral homes will give out the information over the telephone, but they need the exact date, at least the month and year.

Some mortuary records are available on microfilm. Local libraries often have locally produced indexes. The easiest way to find a funeral home is to use one of the telephone directories on the Internet, such as Switchboard (Available: www.switchboard.com). Select "Funeral Directors" from their list of categories. Then type in the city and state where the person died.

You may also want to try FuneralNet Directory (Available: www.funeralnet.com/search .html). There are over 20,000 U.S. funeral homes listed on this site. You can search by state, county and city. Results will give you name, address, telephone number, and fax (if available). In a town with only a few funeral homes, one or two telephone calls could yield the genealogical information you need.

Name Changes

If you know that an ancestor lived and died in a certain area and you still can't find anything; or if you know that he or she changed his or her name, look for name change records in the county courthouse where he or she resided. Courthouses and archives are the best sources of these records.

National Union Catalog of Manuscript Collections

In 1959 the Library of Congress started preparing meticulous descriptions of manuscript collections held in over 1,000 repositories in the United States. The National Union Catalog of Manuscript Collections is an index with cross-references to these collections. It is accessible through a 27-volume set or online through the Library of Congress Web site (Available: www.loc .gov/coll/nucmc).

Naturalization and Citizenship

These records are primary source documents that were created by the federal agency that provided citizenship service. Naturalization records provide: the place and date of birth, date of arrival into the United States, residence at the time of naturalization, and a description of the individual. The name of the ship that brought the individual to the United States is sometimes listed. For the years 1781 through 1906, naturalization records are available through the National Archives. Records after 1906 are available through the Immigration and Naturalization Service.

Newspapers

Newspapers are some of the most readily available sources of genealogical data. They regularly have articles or short pieces on births, deaths, marriages, obituaries, wedding anniversaries, retirements, visits from relatives and trips to visit relatives. The best place to look for newspapers is in the local public library. The next place is the state archives. Most newspapers are not indexed, which makes it difficult, but it helps to have close approximation of a date as a beginning point.

Ancestry.com is indexing historical newspapers and is making them available online to its subscribers. The search engine highlights the search terms within the body of the text, though moving around page is a little clunky.

Obituaries

Obituaries announce the death of an individual and are a primary source for death date and place. They usually give birth and death dates and marriage information, along with the names of parents and other family members. The birth information they provide is not always reliable. Marriage information may not be reliable either, unless the surviving spouse gave it. Obituaries in newspapers are regularly found in public libraries—even small ones. Some state archives have undertaken extensive microfilming projects to copy every newspaper in the state.

Don't count on every newspaper to have an obituary of people who died in their city. Especially in large cities, most of the deceased did not (and does not—to the present) have obituaries published unless the deceased was a notable or prominent person. The average citizen's death was not noted with an obituary. Many obituaries written around the turn of the twentieth century were especially void of detail. They often gave the name of the deceased and the death date, followed by "He left a large family to mourn his passing."

Oral Histories

These are the stories that living individuals tell about their past, or about the experiences of other people. Family members or serious oral historians usually collect oral histories. Armed with a tape recorder and a set of questions, collectors of oral history visit the homes of people they believe have valuable stories to tell about the past. An oral history was the key to establishing the identity of the father of one of my ancestors whose parents were not married. Oral histories are available at libraries and archives, but many are likely to be kept by families in their home records.

Orphan Agencies

Most orphanages were financed and operated by religious groups or local governments. Children without parents that were not old enough to become apprentices were sent to these institutions.

Orphanage records will usually include a child's name, date of birth, parents' names, birthplaces of parents, information about the next of kin, and an explanation of why they were admitted to and discharged from the orphanage. The completeness of the information will vary depending on the organization that operated the institution. Information from defunct orphanages will most likely be in church archives, state archives, child welfare agencies, and local and university libraries. Orphanages run by an order of the Catholic Church may hold records of orphanages run by their order.

When orphanages in the east became overcrowded someone decided that it would be better for the children to live in the wide-open spaces of the Midwest. So, trains from large eastern cities transported homeless children with guardians to towns and farms in rural areas. Between 1853 and 1930 some 200,000 orphans had been placed in new surroundings. Many of these children were immigrants or children of immigrants. County court records document adoptions and apprenticeship agreements resulting from the relocation.

The Orphan Train Heritage Society of America (OTHSA), P.O. Box 322, Concordia, Kansas, 66901, is a national resource for information about individuals and institutions of the orphan train program. You can e-mail OTHSA at: jhill@usd333.com, or log onto their Web site (Available: www.orphantrainriders.com/othsa11.html). For more on orphan trains, see Marilyn Irvin Holt, *The Orphan Trains: Placing Out in America*. The University of Kansas Library has a great Web site dedicated to orphan trains (Available: www.kancoll.org/articles/orphans/index .html). It is one of the most comprehensive sites on the topic.

Passenger Lists

These lists are important because they help link our immigrant ancestors to their home countries. Sometimes they give us family information that establishes the age, marital status and place of birth of an ancestor. Published passenger lists will appear in books or periodicals. They are often indexed, and many are found in libraries. Unpublished passenger lists may or may not be indexed, and are available primarily from archives.

Passport Applications

The United States started issuing passports in 1795. At first only a few were issued and the applications didn't contain much information of value to genealogists. The only times that passports were mandatory were briefly during the Civil War and again during World War I. The present law went into effect in the late 1920s.

Since the early 1900s passport applications have included the applicant's full name, birth date, birthplace, current residence and dates of departure and destination. Foreign-born applicants needed documented proof of naturalization. Minor children needed the name of the father, his date and place of birth, and proof of the father's naturalization. Physical descriptions were also provided, and many had pictures attached. This could be a good source of information if an ancestor traveled abroad. Passport applications indexes through 1925 are available at the Family History Library. They are also available from the U.S. State Department and a copy can be obtained for $14.00 per applicant. Contact the Passport Office, U.S. State Department, 1425 K Street, NW, Washington, DC 20520.

Patriot Index

The Daughters of the American Revolution have compiled a list exceeding 125,000 who participated in the Revolutionary War. It provides basic descriptive information on these individuals, and the appearance of a name in the index indicates that there has been at least one membership based on this ancestor's service. In most cases researchers can request copies of lineage papers with documentation for the patriot and descendants. Some corrections to this three-volume set have been made since its publication in 2003. This is a wonderful research tool for anyone whose ancestors were in the Revolutionary War. This set is available in most libraries. The DAR will search their database of proven Revolutionary patriots for you free of charge.

Pedigrees

Siblings are the only ones who share the same pedigree. So, individual pedigrees are of only partial value to a researcher. Most people have to go back five to seven generations before they find a connection with someone else's pedigrees. The value of pedigrees is the link to the person who created it.

Before access to the Internet was so widely accessible, people typed their pedigrees and gave them to the Family History Library. These have been microfilmed and are available to patrons. Many other individuals have put their pedigrees on the Internet and they can found by using a regular search engine or using the search engine on Cyndi's List.

Pension Records

Governmental and private pension records include the pensioner's full name, date and place of birth, names of spouse and children, place of residence, and death and beneficiary information. Private employers and governmental bodies often keep records of employees that have received pensions. They may release them if the pensioner is deceased. City archives will probably have police and firefighter pension records.

Railroad pensions started in 1936. The U.S. Railroad Retirement Board should have records railroad retirees. These records include: employee's death certificate and the application for employee annuity under the retirement act. The board charges a fee to search for information on deceased persons. Pension records are normally located in archives, museums, and historical societies.

Civil War pension applications are a rich source for genealogical information. You can find them at the following:

National Archives, Microfilm Publication T288: General Index to Pension Files, 1861–1934 (Available: www.archives.gov/research_room/genealogy/military/pension_index_1861_to_ 1934.html).

Family History Library Catalog (Available: www.familysearch.org/Eng/Library/FHLC/frame-set_fhlc.asp). Conduct a title search on "General index to pension files, 1861–1934." You will find 544 rolls of microfilm organized by last name.

Ancestry.com Civil War Pension Index (Available: www.ancestry.com/search/rectype/military/ cwpi/main.htm). They charge a membership fee to view images of application index cards online. When you find a pension application you want to get a copy you need to get NATF Form 85. It is best to send use your credit card as the form of payment because they don't know what the final charges will be if you ask for a copy of everything they have in the file. Then be prepared to wait six months to get the application material in the mail.

I have copies of pension applications for three of my ancestors. They vary in the amount of genealogical information they supply. One set of papers is several affidavits explaining why the widowed mother should get a pension—only two or three dates of any value. The other two were real treasures. They included marriage certificates, proof of guardianship, declaration for minor children to obtain army pensions, pension claim, original pension of minor children, receipt of pension application, birth certificate, claim for increase of widows pension, and a death certificate.

Personal Papers

Personal paper can contain lots of genealogical data about the individual as well as lots of anecdotal information. We may be surprised at what we will find when we search for personal papers. If you are looking for personal papers of an individual use the search terms "personal papers" +[surname] of your ancestor. Check online catalogs of genealogy collections and state archives.

Photographs

Photos are valuable primary source documents, though they rarely contain any family data. However, they often provide clues for further research. Sometimes a photograph can tell us more about the people in them than any other source available. It is unlikely that a small library will collect and preserve photographs, but they are commonly found in museums, archives and private collections.

Postal Records

These records may include a box number and individual records kept by the U.S. Postal Service. Files may also include records with private mail carriers. These records may help to locate families or individuals when other finding tools fail. They are good "between censuses" finding tools.

Probate Records

Probate records are important to genealogists because they are some of the earliest documents available. They were created to settle their estate of some one who had died. As such, probate records help verify family relationships and dates of death. A will may list the wife and/or husband and all the children by their given names, as well as some grandchildren's names and the married names of daughters and their husbands' names. If a person owned property, and most people did, there has to be a probate record, even if there was no will. These court records can be found in county courthouses or in state archives. If you search long enough and hard enough you can almost always find some court record of a person's death.

Revolutionary War Pension Records

For the time period Revolutionary War Pension applications contain some of the best genealogical data available. They contain affidavits made by the veteran and his neighbors, a synopsis of his service, the soldier's military unit, the dates of service, his date and place of birth, names of heirs, his movements after the war, and information from family Bible records.

I have copies of military records from the Revolutionary War. They are not complete, but they are priceless to me. One of my Revolutionary War ancestors was denied a pension because he deserted. He went home when the war was over but before he was discharged. Another ancestor was denied a pension because he was a Tory.

The following indexes will help researchers locate Revolutionary War Pension applications of their ancestors.

- Index of Revolutionary War Pension Applications in the National Archives by the National Genealogical Society

- *Genealogical Abstracts of Revolutionary War Pension Files* by Virgil D. White (National Historical Publishing, 1990–1992)

- The Pension Lists of 1792–95; With Other Revolutionary War Pension Records by Murtie J. Clark, (Genealogical Publishing Company, 1996)

School Records

Some states have kept school records that can provide family information. These records usually include school districts, student attendance figures, grade taught, length of school year, school finances, names of teachers and condition of schools. The California State Archives (Available: www.ss.ca.gov/archives/level3_genie.htm) has school records from 1862 to 1960. Colorado also has online access to school records (Available: www.archives.state.co.us/school.html). Check the state archives for the holdings of state school records.

Scrapbooks

Many libraries and archives maintain scrapbook collections that can be a major resource for genealogists. Subjects include churches, people, families, events, businesses, etc. Many scrapbooks are accessible through the library's catalog.

Sexton Records

A sexton is the person in charge of a cemetery. These records show every grave in the cemetery, even those that are not marked, and record the name of the person buried there. The sexton records are filed chronologically and usually kept at the cemetery, often with a copy in the office of the church or city hall. These records usually hold the names of parents or nearest of kin, and the name of physician or informant. These records are important for those who want to pinpoint the exact location of someone's grave. If they are not indexed they could be difficult to use.

Slave Schedules

Slaves were enumerated separately in the 1850 and 1860 censuses. Very few personal names were recorded, but these records are useful to corroborate information from other sources. They do give age, gender, color, and the names of the owners. These schedules will be found with other census records.

Social Security Death Index

This is an index of Social Security death records compiled by the Social Security Administration. This index lists about 50 million Americans who died during the period 1962–1990, and whose survivors applied for the Social Security burial benefit. See Chapter 10.

Tax Records

Tax records can be used for genealogical purposes in lieu of land or census records. They document that a person lived at a certain place on a specific date. They provide a record of lands assessed for taxation showing names of resident and nonresident owners, a legal description of land, number of acres, value of real estate established by the assessor and the equalized value of the land, and the amounts of the several taxes levied on each parcel. Sometimes these records are the only records available to document an ancestor's existence and place or residence. These records are available in county courthouses and state archives.

Tombstone Inscriptions

Volunteers from local and state genealogical and historical societies across the United States have walked through thousands of cemeteries, writing down inscriptions they found on tombstones. Some of the inscriptions were barely readable several years ago when they walked the cemeteries. Many of them have since been obliterated by the weather. These volunteers have saved the names, vital records, and biographical data from periods before the registration of vital statistics began. Many libraries have books with compiled tombstone readings gathered by local genealogical societies. Exact death dates found in these records can lead to an obituary in a local newspaper. Check the online catalog of the local library to see if it has tombstone inscriptions—sometimes called cemetery records.

Vital Records

The more recent vital records are the more difficult the may become to acquire because of increasingly more restrictive privacy laws. I know that I cannot get a copy of my father's Arizona birth certificate, even though he is dead, unless I can prove that he is my father. A copy of my birth certificate will do the trick.

Deaths that occurred over 50 years ago are public records in most states. Privacy laws in many states protect deaths that happened less than 50 years ago.

Births

The purpose of registering births was to establish citizenship, proof of age, and property interest, if any, for the person who was born. The registration of births didn't happen in every county or state at the same time. About the mid-1800s counties in some states began civil registration of births and by 1920 most states required it. However, some states have birth records that go back much further. Some states have gathered all of the birth records in the state, archived them, and made them available on microfilm. In other states, counties still hold the records that were created for the county, and the state holds the records sent to the state.

Deaths

Civil registration of deaths somewhat parallels civil registration of births. The main purpose of registering deaths was to establish the basis for a pension from the government and to settle the property interest in an estate. Death certificates are required to claim the benefit of a life insurance policy, to probate a will, or some other Social Security death benefit. Death certificates, like obituaries, are primary sources for the death date and place of the individual. However, they are not entirely reliable regarding birth, marriage and family information. But they do give us clues to other information. Too often, the information you hope will be on a death certificate, like a parent's name or an exact place of birth, is not there.

Death certificates of individuals who died more than 50 years ago are readily available from most states. There is usually a charge of a few dollars. For those who have ancestors who lived and died in Kentucky, the Kentucky Department of Health and Statistics has compiled an index to deaths and mounted it on the Internet. These files contain an index to deaths, which have been registered in Kentucky from January 1, 1911–December 31, 1992. Information in the file includes the name of the deceased, date of death, age at death, and county of death and residence. The Kentucky Department of Health Statistics produced the original file, and it is the official data used to generate the annual Kentucky Vital Statistics Report.

Divorce Records

Sometimes divorce records can serve as proof for marriage. If no marriage record can be found, the divorce record may be used to prove that the couple was married at one time; otherwise why would they need a legal divorce. A published legal notice for divorce will generally provide the names of both partners. Divorce records are county court record and will most likely be found there.

Marriages

Marriage records are some of the earliest vital records available, primarily because of the property interest connected to a marriage. The law of property interest for spouses varies from state to state, but generally a property interest changes when a marriage occurs. On early marriage records the parents' names did not appear in the record, unless the bride or groom were under the age of majority. Marriage records are available from city, county and state archives. Many marriage books have been compiled and published. They are also published on CD-ROM and on the Internet.

Check out this handy Web site, *United States Vital Records Offices by State* (Available: www.ok-history.mus.ok.us/lib/usvital.htm). It lists vital records offices by state, giving the following information: State, Address, City, Zip, Birth, Death, and Telephone.

Voter Registration Records

Some county archives may have voter registration records. These records may include: name, address, age, color, occupation, duration of residence in the county, place of birth, naturalization details, and signatures.

These records, if they exist, in the county where they were created. Some of them have been microfilmed and are available through the Family History Library.

Wills

Wills preserve and distribute the assets of the owner upon his or her death. These primary documents establish the birth and death of the testator. They often establish the names and relationship of heirs. They name a living spouse and living children. Sometimes they name spouses of adult female children. They usually do not name deceased children.

Yearbooks

University, high school, and middle school yearbooks are good places to find pictures of students who once attended the school. Annuals of all types, shapes, sizes, and coverage are important research sources, and they will become considerably more valuable with the passage of time. See Chapter 2.

Suggestions for Helping Genealogists

1. Buy *The Handybook for Genealogists*, 10th ed. Everton Publishers, 2002.

2. Buy the PERSI (Periodical Source Index)® on CD-ROM and put it on a public access computer. It is also available on the Internet.

3. Visit your county courthouse to see what vital records they have and learn how to gain access to them.

Suggestions for Researchers

1. Familiarize yourself with this list of sources and review them from time to time.

2. Try to access some of the sources and see what you can find.

Summary

We can be overwhelmed when we think about all of the sources have a their disposal—most of which were never meant to benefit genealogists. Many of the records were created because money or property were involved. The people who created the records had a financial interest in the transactions. Over the years the events they recorded have proven to be valuable to genealogical researchers. So much so that entrepreneurs are making money by compiling the records and making them available to genealogists.

With so many records available we need finding tools to help us locate and use the sources.

Bibliography (Ratings Guide explanation follows last citation)

Anderson, Robert Charles. 1999. *The Great Migration: Immigrants to New England, 1634–1635*. Boston: Great Migration Study Project, New England Historic Genealogical Society. **LLL**

Bentley, Elizabeth Petty. 2001. *Directory of Family Associations*. Baltimore, MD: Genealogical Publishing Company.
This is the updated and expanded fourth edition of this title. It is a complete and reliable research resource for amateur and professional genealogists alike. It contains basic information on approximately 6,000 family associations across the United States, including contact and Web site addresses. This directory is an excellent first step for consultation references when searching for the history behind a family name. **LLL**

Carmack, Sharon DeBartolo. 2000. *A Genealogist's Guide to Discovering Your Immigrant and Ethnic Ancestors*. Cincinnati, OH: Betterway Books.
This is a book for researchers who are just getting started in their quest to find their immigrant or ethnic ancestors. Most Americans come from varied backgrounds and except for Native

Americans their ancestor came from different part of the world. This book will point them in the right direction as they delve into different heritages that make up their family tree.

This book is very easy to use and belongs in the personal collection of anyone who is searching for immigrant or ethnic ancestors. **PP**

Carmack, Sharon DeBartolo. 2002. *Your Guide to Cemetery Research*. Cincinnati, OH: Betterway Books.

This book gets to the heart of cemetery research. It shows researchers how to read headstones and extrapolate information that may not be there. It also has a glossary of death related terms. **LLL**

Carson, Dina C., ed. 2002. *Directory of Genealogical and Historical Societies in the U.S. and Canada*. Niwot, CO: Iron Gate Publishing.

This is a reference tool for genealogists who want to share their research with other researchers. It lists over 21,000 societies with their address, telephone, fax numbers, and e-mail and Web addresses. **LLL**

Clark, Murtie J. 1996. *The Pension Lists of 1792–95; With Other Revolutionary War Pension Records*. Baltimore, MD: Genealogical Publishing Company.

This book indexes 4,000 who file a claim for a pension as a result of their service in the Revolutionary War. While fires destroyed some of the earliest Revolutionary War pension application records, this book tries to bring together the Pension lists between 1792 and 1795. **LLL**

Daughters of the American Revolution. 2003. *DAR Patriot Index*. Baltimore, MD: Gateway Press; Washington, DC: National Society of the Daughters of the American Revolution.

This three-volume set is an update to the 1994 edition. The *DAR Patriot Index* contains the names of male and female patriots whose Revolutionary service (1774–1783) and lineage have been established by the National Society, Daughters of the American Revolution. **LLL**

Everton Publishers (Staff). 2002. *The Handybook for Genealogists*: *United States of America*. 10th ed. Logan, UT: Everton Publishers.

This is the best and most sought after guidebook available to genealogical researchers. It belongs in every library as a primary tool for anyone who does genealogical research. Many individuals have their own copy because they use it so much. Librarians may want to have additional copies in their circulating collection.

The Handybook includes a current, comprehensive list of archives, genealogical libraries, and societies for each state. The lists of valuable printed sources have also been reviewed and updated for this edition. Information for each state follows the same format, with general information on the state, its history, its records, its genealogical societies, libraries, and valuable publications on genealogy in the state. **LLL**

Holt, Marilyn Irvin. 1994. *The Orphan Trains: Placing Out in America.* Lincoln, NE: University of Nebraska Press.

This is a fascinating book, carefully written very informative. It does not list the names of the children who were placed out from the orphan trains. It does give an excellent explanation what happened. It is a good, scholarly social history—a solid contribution on a little-known phenomenon. **LL**

Johnson, Richard S., and Debra Johnson Knox. 1999. *How to Locate Anyone Who Is or Has Been in the Military: Armed Forces Locator Guide.* 8th ed. Spartanburg, SC: MIE Publishing.

This is the only book available with detailed information for finding someone in the military. It reflects many years of research and experience that will save time and expense. It tells the reader:

- How to obtain the unit of assignment, home address, and telephone number of any member of the Army, Navy, Marine Corps, Air Force, Coast Guard, the Reserve Components and National Guard;

- How to locate people through their driver's license or vehicle registration;

- How to have a letter forwarded to a current, former, or retired member of the Armed Forces, Reserves, or National Guard;

- How to have a letter forwarded to any of 27 million veterans;

- How to locate people through the Social Security Administration, the Internal Revenue Service, U.S. Post Office, and other state and federal agencies;

- How to locate former service men and women through veterans' and military associations; and

- How to find out someone's address and telephone number. **P**

Knox, Debra Johnson. 2003. *WWII Military Records: A Family Historian's Guide.* Spartanburg, SC: MIE Publishing.

Written for beginning and seasoned researchers, this guide tells you how to discover personnel records, draft registrations, burial sites, awards and medals, and unit histories. Best of all it helps family historians find military documents that have the best potential for genealogical data. **PP**

McManus, Stephen, Thomas Churchill, and Donald Thompson. 2003. *Civil War Research Guide: A Guide for Researching Your Civil War Ancestor.* Mechanicsburg, PA: Stackpole Books.

If your ancestor served in Civil War this easy-to-understand book will lead you through the maze to find him. It will tell you where to look to find out what he did, where he served, and what happened to him. This is a practical book with lots of how-to ideas. **LLL**

Pfeiffer, Laura Szucs. 2000. *Hidden Sources: Family History in Unlikely Places*. Orem, UT: Ancestry Publishing.

I like this book a lot. It truly does list many sources that I had never seen or heard of before. It is well written and the illustrations are priceless. Without extra words it leads the reader directly to the sources it reveals. Here are some of the lesser-known sources covered by Hidden Sources: Internal Revenue Service records, Name change records, orphan asylum records, and Works Progress Administration records. **LLL**

Shaefer, Christina K. 1997. *Guide to Naturalization Records of the United States*. Baltimore, MD: Genealogical Publishing Company.

Naturalization papers and records relating to naturalization can be found in an incomprehensible array of courts. This book helps us weave our way through the maize and get to the information we need. Naturalization records are a gold mine of priceless information and include such items as place and date of birth, foreign and current places of residence, marital status, names, ages and places of birth of other family members, and more. **LLL**

Szucs, Loretto Dennis, and Sandra Hargraves Leubking, eds. 1997. *The Source: A Guidebook of American Genealogy*. . Salt Lake City, UT: Ancestry Publishing.

Written by several respected genealogical researchers, this book lists and explains the use of some of the most significant genealogical research tools available in the United States today. The coeditors have produced a superb and scholarly work. The chapter on "Tracking 20th Century Ancestors" summarizes almost a decade of new resources now available to family researchers. This book will continue to be a "must purchase" source for every genealogist. Libraries should have copies in both the circulating collection and the refesrence collection. **LLL**

Szucs, Loretto Dennis. 2000. *Ellis Island: Tracing Your Family History Through America's Gateway*. Provo, UT: Ancestry Publishing.

This book explains how you can find out if your relatives were among the millions who were processed for entry at Ellis Island. The graphics and text of this booklet give you the quick basics of locating your ancestors in the Ellis Island records. **P**

Ratings Guide

   The ratings for each bibliography describe not only what each resource contains, but also how it might fit into the library collection. Some of the materials are more appropriate for larger libraries with substantial budgets, and others belong in collections of any size—even in the personal research collection. To help you identify materials most appropriate for your collection, each resource is marked as either "L" for libraries and "P" for personal. They are ranked from one letter for recommended, two letters for preferred, and three letters for essential.

CHAPTER 10
IDENTIFYING DATABASES AND INDEXES

Some libraries are so small that we can go to the shelves and read the titles on the spines of the book until we find something we want. Eventually, though, we have to have an index to tell us where to look to find an item more quickly. For over a hundred years this index was called the card catalog. Now we have online catalogs and people wonder how we got along without them. So it is with genealogical indexes and databases. We are now able to zero in on the resources we want to check for genealogical data in a fraction of the time it took us in the past.

What to Look for in This Chapter

In this chapter we look at some specific indexes and databases and discuss how to use them. Even though indexes and databases have verifiable data we can use in our research, they are still more like gateways and starting places to the real data we seek.

Using Databases and Indexes

Some databases and indexes have been specifically created to help genealogists. Since they are mostly compiled sources it is wise for researchers to check the original source. For example, the Social Security Death Index is compiled from the records of the Social Security Administration based on death benefit claims or requests to stop Social Security benefits. Individual listings reveal significant amounts information—enough to enter a birth and death date for your ancestor. Request a copy of the Social Security Application form and send for a copy of the original record, (Form SS-).

The titles presented in this chapter are some of the first places to search, because they are more likely to lead to early success. The information will need to be verified, but the clues you find are invaluable.

Major Indexes and Databases

U.S. Federal Census Schedules

It is obvious that census enumerations were not designed for genealogists. If they had been, they would have listed every person by name, with his or her birth date and place, and his or her relationship to the head of the household. Nevertheless, U.S. Federal Census records are among the best of original source records available to family researchers. The best thing they do is to document that a specific person lived in a particular place at one moment in time. This documentation can lead researchers to other sources for more specific information.

The U.S. Constitution calls for the taking of a census ("an enumeration of inhabitants"). How it was to be conducted and what questions should be asked were left up to those charged with the responsibility. In 1790 George Washington signed the law directing that a census be taken every 10 years. Basically, the first census counted people—males and females and slaves. Only Connecticut, Delaware, Georgia, Kentucky, Maine, Maryland, Massachusetts, New Hampshire, New Jersey, New York, North Carolina, Pennsylvania, Rhode Island, South Carolina, Tennessee, Vermont, and Virginia participated in the first census. The British destroyed much of the 1790 Census during the War of 1812. Officials used contemporaneous tax records as an alternate source for names.

Purpose of Gathering Census Records

One of the main purposes of the census was to provide information on men eligible for the military. Males 16 years and older were considered old enough to serve in the military. The 1790 and the 1820 censuses specifically asked questions to determine the number of men eligible to serve in the military. The United States had freshly won its independence from England and the leaders of the day knew it was important to muster a viable military.

To encourage honest answers and accurate information Census records remain confidential for 72 years. It was assumed that most adults who answered census questions would be dead after 72 years. The 1930 census became available in 2002.

Over the years the amount of information gathered by census takers has increased dramatically—increasing the value of the census to genealogical researchers. In the early censuses, individuals in families were recorded by mark in the appropriate category—male or female in the appropriate age range. From the 1850 census forward each individual's name was recorded with the person who was the head of the household.

Questions in Specific Years

Since genealogists are primarily interested in names, dates, locations, and relationships, the censuses that yielded this type of information are considered more valuable. Watershed years for the federal census are 1850, 1880, and 1900. The 1850 census was the first census to list everyone in the household and give a specific age, gender, race, birthplace, and if married within the year. The best addition to the 1880 census was to ask for the birthplace of the mother and father of the individual. The 1900 census asked for the birth month and year of each person listed—the only census to do so.

Specifically, the questions asked in other census years lead to the following:

- 1820—Double counting of men ages 16–26, which could lead to significant research in military records.

- 1820–1930—All have a question asking about the person's occupation, which could be a means to distinguish between two men with the same first and last name.

- 1840—Asked for names of survivors of the Revolutionary War, which could lead to a military pension application and lots of good information.

- 1880—The 1880 census was the first to give the relationship of the person to the head of the household. This information is critical to genealogical researchers.

Using the Census Elements

Each element or question asked by census takers can be potentially valuable to genealogists. Understanding the elements helps us to link their significance to genealogical research.

- Name: The spelling of a person's name can vary from census to census. So, you will need to use other information within the census record to identify your ancestor.

- Age or date of birth: Except for the 1900 census, which asks for the month and year of the person's birth and the instruction to give the age in a fraction if the person was born within the year, age is the only clue to a birth date. Women who were older than their husbands sometimes lied about their age, and the discrepancy may show up from one census to the next. Though a discrepancy in the age of wives with the same name could also indicate the death of the first spouse and a second marriage for the husband.

- Place of birth: Sometimes birthplace is a distinguishing clue. This detail was first available in the 1850 census. It was included on every census thereafter. This information can give us a good clue for where to look next.

- Female maiden name: A place of birth and age can be used to help discover the maiden name of a woman. Let us suppose a woman is listed in Missouri with a husband (we assume) and several young children. The children are all born in Missouri, but the mother is born in North Carolina and the head of the house is born in Tennessee. The technique is to look for other individuals in the adjacent area who were born in North Carolina within five years on either side of the woman's age. There is a good chance that these people could be siblings of the woman. The surname of the men will be a clue to the woman's maiden name. The next step is to check the census for North Carolina for the year that would include these people. Look under the surname with family members that match the age and gender of the people in Missouri.

- Date of marriage: The censuses from 1850 through 1880 asked if the person had been married within the year. We can assume that those who answered the question "yes" were most likely married in the year of the census or the year before. Starting in 1880 and through 1930 the census asked for marital status. The number of years married was asked for in the

1900 and 1910 censuses. These two censuses also asked for the number of times married. In 1930 the census asked for the age at the first marriage. The age of the oldest child can be used to estimate the date of the marriage—generally one year before the birth of the child.

- Number of children: The number of children in a family can be used to verify other family data. Before 1850, the number of children was indicated by a numeral on the matrix. The 1900 and 1910 censuses asked for the number of children born to each female and the number of children still living. This data can help the genealogist verify family information.

- Death date: Researcher can estimate the date of death within 10 years by comparing family records from one census to the next. If a person is 69 with a spouse who is 65 in the 1860 census, it is reasonable to assume death between 1860 and 1870 if only one of the spouses shows up in the next census. Mortality schedules list individuals who died during the previous year.

- Relationship to head of household: Though it is often assumed that the head of the household was husband and father to the rest of the people listed in the household, it wasn't until the 1880 census that a specific question asked for the relationship to the head of the household. Stepchildren are not always carefully identified, but if they are their last names could be a clue to the mother's previous marriage. Boarders were often relatives like nieces, cousins, or in-laws.

- Citizenship, immigration and naturalization: It is assumed that if U.S. citizenship was not checked, the individual is of foreign birth. The censuses from 1900 through 1930 asked the year of immigration to the United States. This information gives us a clue pertaining to immigration records that we need to search. The dates need to be bracketed by five years each direction, because some people lied about when they came to the United States. The 1870 census asks males over 21 if they are citizens. All of this information can give us clues about where to look for naturalization records.

- Occupation: This piece of information can be used to track an individual from one census to the next. One of my ancestors was a file maker from Manchester England. His father was a file maker; his sons and grandsons were also file makers. This can be traced from one census to the next, and used as a verification point for family continuity.

- Migration: Families with children born in a foreign country and in the United States we can probably estimate the date of their migration. We can do the same if they moved from one state to another in the United States. The places of birth for the older children will be a clue for finding the family in an earlier census.

- Neighbors: Families tended to stay together. There is a good chance that the families on either side of a household will be related. Parents gave their children pieces of their land. If they migrated to a new state, family members would settle on land that abutted each other. It is always wise to record the information about the ten families above and below the family of your ancestors. Often they will be related to each other.

- Real estate: If a person owned property there a good chance of finding land records and possibly probate records, which could provide additional information on the family.

- Education and literacy: Some schools kept good records and they can be very helpful. If the census record for a family indicated that a person attended school or could read, there is a good chance that school records will give us some good information.

- Military service: The 1840 census asked if the person was a survivor of the Revolutionary War. Then not until 1880 did the census ask if the person had served in the military. Pension records for those who served in the military are some of the best records we can find.

- Paupers convicts: County court records could contain good information on individuals who where wards of the court.

Defects in Federal Census Records

The 1790 Federal Census was the first one conducted in the United States—we have no federal censuses before that. The drawbacks to this census are as follows:

- The 1790 census only asked 7 questions—very limited information.

- We are missing parts of the censuses, because they were lost or destroyed.

- The records lack consistency in handwriting and accuracy, because census takers were not trained well.

- Families were sometimes left off the census, because they were not home the day the census taker came.

- Some census takers didn't ask or answer all of the questions—leaving out essential information.

- People who didn't understand English answered questions incorrectly, because they didn't understand the question.

- Handwriting varies from census taker to census taker—from extremely legible to illegible.

- Some copies of the microfilm are too light or too dark to read or make a legible copy.

Overcoming the Obstacles of Reading Census Records

Some census records are not very legible or are difficult to read. Here are a few suggestions that might help researchers overcome legibility problems.

1. Build your own deciphering code. Use tracing paper to form various letters the way the census taker wrote them, and then assign the letter you believe it is.

2. Make a list of common names for the area and use that list to guess the names when you cannot read them; match length of name to space available.

3. Write the entry from the microfilm the way you see it.

209

4. Eventually you may be able to translate the word correctly.

Availability of Census Microfilm

One of the reasons census records are so valuable is that they are readily available in many places. Until recently microfilm was the most common format for the census.

Here are some of the places where you can find microfilmed census records:

• Public and university libraries

• State Archives

• Genealogical societies or libraries

• Family History Library or through Family History Centers

• The Federal Archives and Record Centers

In the past few years, companies that have produced products for genealogists have created indexes and digital images of individual census enumeration pages and put them on the Internet. Check Ancestry.com and HeritageQuest Online to find out which census indexes and images they have added recently to their online databases. Check with your public library to see if it subscribes to either of these databases. Personal memberships are priced within the range of most genealogists.

Before beginning census research it might be helpful for researchers to know the types of information that can be gleaned from these records. The tables that follow give the information requested by the census taker when he or she visited individual homes. From 1790 to 1840 the heads of households were the only ones to have their names written out. Other family members were indicated by a hash mark in the appropriate square that indicated gender and age.

In 1850 census takers started reporting the names of everyone in the family, their ages, sex, color, occupation, value of real estate, place of birth and if married within the year. Additional questions cropped up in succeeding censuses. The 1880 census was the first to ask the birthplace of the parents of the individual listed. The 1930 census even asked if the family owned a radio.

The tables that follow cover the census years from 1850 through 1930.

The Federal Census Chronology (Figures 10.3 and 10.4) is a tool for researchers. It is used to track an ancestor through time.

1880 United States Census and National Index

FamilySearch.org has the 1880 census transcribed and it is free. This database contains some 50 million individuals and was created from extracted federal census records. As with all extracted records, there is a possibility for errors and I have found a few. The online version is available at www.familysearch.org. The CD-ROM version, available for sale, has two sections—the National Index and the census records, which are divided into seven regional sets. The index displays a list of possible matches, and indicates which state to load.

Census Questions	1790	1800	1810	1820	1830	1840
Name of head of house	X	X	X	X	X	X
Address		X				
Free white males under 16 years	X					
Free white males 16 years and up	X					
Free white females under 16 years	X					
Free white females 16 years and up	X					
Slaves	X	X	X			
Free white males under 10 years		X	X	X		
Free white males 10 and under 16		X	X	X		
Free white males 16 and under 26		X	X	X		
Free white males 26 and under 45		X	X	X		
Free white males 45 and up		X	X	X		
Free white females under 10 years		X	X	X		
Free white females 10 and under 16		X	X	X		
Free white females 16 and under 26		X	X	X		
Free white females 26 and under 45		X	X	X		
Free white females 45 and up		X	X	X		
Free white males between 16 and 18				X		
Male slaves under 14 years				X		
Male slaves 14 to 26				X		
Male slaves 26 to 45				X		
Male slaves 45 and up				X		
Female slaves under 14 years				X		
Female slaves 14 to 26				X		
Female slaves 26 to 45				X		
Female slaves 45 and up				X		
Free male colored persons under 14 years				X		
Free male colored persons 14 to 26				X		
Free male colored persons 26 to 45				X		
Free male colored persons 45 and up				X		
Free female colored persons under 14 years				X		
Free female colored persons 14 to 26				X		
Free female colored persons 26 to 45				X		
Free female colored persons 45 and up				X		
All other persons except Indians not taxed		X	X	X		
Occupation				X	X	X

Figure 10.1 Federal Census Questions at a Glance 1790–1840

211

Census Questions	1790	1800	1810	1820	1830	1840
Free white males under 5 years					X	X
Free white males 5 and under 10					X	X
Free white males 10 and under 15					X	X
Free white males 15 and under 20					X	X
Free white males 20 and under 30					X	X
Free white males 30 and under 40					X	X
Free white males 40 and under 50					X	X
Free white males 50 and under 60					X	X
Free white males 60 and under 70					X	X
Free white males 70 and under 80					X	X
Free white males 80 and under 90					X	X
Free white males 90 and under 100					X	X
Free white males 100 and up					X	X
Free white females under 5 years					X	X
Free white females 5 and under 10					X	X
Free white females 10 and under 15					X	X
Free white females 15 and under 20					X	X
Free white females 20 and under 30					X	X
Free white females 30 and under 40					X	X
Free white females 40 and under 50					X	X
Free white females 50 and under 60					X	X
Free white females 60 and under 70					X	X
Free white females 70 and under 80					X	X
Free white females 80 and under 90					X	X
Free white females 90 and under 100					X	X
Free white females 100 and up					X	X
Male slaves under 10 years					X	X
Male slaves 10 to 24					X	X
Male slaves 24 to 36					X	X
Male slaves 36 to 55					X	X
Male slaves 55 to 100					X	X
Male slaves ages 100 and up					X	X
Female slaves under 10 years					X	X
Female slaves 10 to 24					X	X
Female slaves 24 to 36					X	X
Female slaves 36 to 55					X	X
Female slaves 55 to 100					X	X
Female slaves ages 100 and up					X	X
White persons deaf and dumb under 14					X	
White persons deaf and dumb 14 under 25					X	
White persons deaf and dumb 25 and up					X	
White persons who are blind					X	
White persons foreigners not naturalized				X	X	X
Name and age of Revolutionary War pensioner						X

Figure 10.1 Federal Census Questions at a Glance 1790–1840

Census Questions	1850	1860	1870	1880	1890	1900	1910	1920	1930
Address						X	X	X	X
Name of head of household	X	X	X	X		X	X	X	X
Names of other persons in home	X	X	X	X		X	X	X	X
Relationship to household head				X		X	X	X	X
Age	X	X	X	X		X	X	X	X
Date of birth, month and year						X			
Month born if under one year			X	X					
Sex	X	X	X	X		X	X	X	X
Single				X		X	X	X	X
Married				X		X	X	X	X
Widowed/divorced				X		X	X	X	X
Number of years married						X	X		
Mother of how many children						X	X		
Number of children living						X	X		
Color (Race)	X						X	X	X
Color (White, Black, Mulatto)		X	X						
Color (White, Black, Mulatto, Chinese, Indian)				X		X			
Occupation	X	X	X	X		X	X	X	X
Number of weeks/months not employed				X		X	X		X
Sick or disabled on day enumerators visit				X					
Value of real estate owned	X	X	X						X
Value of personal property		X	X						
Own or rent home						X	X	X	X
Own home free of mortgage						X	X	X	
Does this family live on a farm?						X	X	X	X
Place of birth of this person	X	X	X	X		X	X	X	X
Place of birth of father				X		X	X	X	X

Figure 10.2 Federal Census Questions at a Glance 1850–1930

Census Questions	1850	1860	1870	1880	1890	1900	1910	1920	1930
Place of birth of mother				X		X	X	X	X
Father foreign born			X						
Mother foreign born			X						
Native tongue of this person								X	X
Native tongue of this person's parents								X	X
Married within the year	X	X	X	X		X			
Age at first marriage									X
In school within the year	X	X	X	X			X	X	X
Over 21 and unable to read/write	X	X	X						
Cannot read			X	X					
Cannot write			X	X					
Can read						X	X	X	
Can write						X	X	X	
Can speak English						X	X	X	X
Deaf, dumb, blind, insane, idiotic, pauper, or convict	X	X	X	X			X		
Males eligible to vote			X						
Males not eligible to vote			X						
Year of immigration to U.S.						X	X	X	X
Number of years in U.S.						X			
Naturalization						X	X	X	X
Year of naturalization								X	
Survivor of Union/Confederate Army/Navy							X		
Veteran of U.S. Military and expedition									X
Own a radio set									X

Figure 10.2 Federal Census Questions at a Glance 1850–1930

Name: _____

Date of birth: _____   Date of death: _____

In household of:	Males		Females	Males						Females				
Indicate age group of this person	To 16	16 and up	Females	0-10	10-16	16-18	16-26	26-45	45 & up	0-10	10-16	16-26	26-45	45 & up
1790-County State Name:														
1800-County State Name:														
1810-County State Name:														
1820-County State Name:														

In household of:	Males												Females											Aliens	S. Rev. W.
Indicate age group of this person	0-5	5-10	10-15	15-20	20-30	30-40	40-50	50-60	60-70	70-80	80-90	90-100	100 & up	0-5	5-10	10-15	15-20	20-30	30-40	40-50	50-60	60-70	70-80	80-90	90-100	100 & up
1830-County State Name:																										
1840-County State Name:																										

Dwelling #	Family #	Head of Family	Age	Sex	Color	Occupation	Value of real estate	Value of personal estate	Place of Birth	Married this year	School this year	Can't read/write	Deaf, blind, insane, etc.
1850 – County:			State:			Post Office:							
1860 – County:			State:			Post Office:							

Figure 10.3 Federal Census Chronology 1790–1860

Dwelling #	Family #	Name of each person whose place of abode on June 1, 1870 was in this family	Age	Sex	Color	Occupation	Value of real estate	Value of personal estate	Place of birth	Father foreign	Mother foreign	Month if b. yr.	Month if m. yr.	School this year	Can't read/write	Deaf, blind, etc.	Male Citizen	Can't vote

1870 – County: State: Post Office:

Dwelling #	Family #	Name of each person whose place of abode on June 1, 1880 was in this family	Age	Sex	Color	Relationship to head o this family	Occupation	Mos. unemployed	Deaf, blind etc.	Attended school	Can't read/write	Place of birth of this person	Place of birth of father	Place of birth of mother

1880 – County: State: Post Office:

Dwelling #	Family #	Name of each person whose place of abode on June 1, 1900 was in this family	Relation to head of household	Color	Sex	Month of birth	Year of birth	Age	Marital status	# of yrs. married	M. of # of children	# of living children	Place of birth of this person	Place of birth of father	Place of birth of mother	Immigration Year	# yrs. in U.S.	Naturalization	Occupation

1900 – County: State: Post Office:

Figure 10.4 Federal Census Chronology 1870–1900

The following information is displayed:

- Name

- Birth year

- Birthplace

- Age

- Occupation

- Marital status

- Race

- Head of household

- Relationship to head of household

- Father's birthplace

- Mother's birthplace

The online search engine will search the 1880 U.S. Census, the 1881 British Isles Census, and the 1881 Canadian Census at the same time requires a first name and a last name. Researchers can narrow the search by:

- Identifying a specific census

- Including a birth place

- Giving a birth year and range

- Providing race or ethnic origin

- Filling in the census state, province, or county

1881 British Isles Census and National Index

The 1881 British Census is similar to the 1880 U.S. Census. It was extracted by volunteers and is available online or on CD-ROM. Researchers can narrow the search by:

- identifying a specific census (e.g., 1881 British Census),

- including a birth place country and county,

- giving a birth year and range, or

- filling in the census country, county, or city.

I was able to positively identify one of my ancestors because of his occupation. He was file maker. So were his son and his grandsons.

1881 Canadian Census and National Index

This extracted census is like the 1881 British Census. It gives the name, marital status, gender, ethnic origin, birthplace, occupation and religion.

Researchers can narrow the search by:

• identifying a specific census (e.g., 1881 Canadian.),

• including a birth place country,

• giving a birth year and range,

• providing race or ethnic origin, or

• filling in the census state, province, county/district.

Ancestral File

This database was created by the Family History Library from records submitted by individuals as a tool for genealogical research. It includes information about 35 million individuals linked together in families with ancestors and descendants. The Ancestral File information includes names, along with dates and places of birth, marriage, and death. The Ancestral File protects the privacy rights of people that are still alive by using the word "living" instead of giving details of living people. This designation is for people born less than 95 years ago who do not have a death date listed.

Since the Ancestral File relies on information contributed by individuals and genealogical organizations, the accuracy varies as a result. Conflicting information for one individual is a common occurrence. Even so, it is a very useful resource that allows genealogists to access research done by others. Ancestral File source information provides researchers with contact information of contributors. Contacting submitters is a good place to start when you want to verify the information you find. Unfortunately, many of the addresses are so outdated that they are useless.

An individual record includes a line for submitters. The hyperlink, "Details" takes you to a list of submitters with their names and addresses. This page also provides a microfilm number and a submission number, which can lead a researcher to the original sources.

The Individual Record page includes hyperlinks for parents' names, if available, marriages, family and pedigree. Clicking on "Family" brings up a page with the names of the couple's children with their birth and death dates and places. Clicking on "Pedigree" will bring up the pedigree, if any, for the individual. This information can be downloaded onto a GEDCOM file. Researchers can use the CD-ROM version to create a descendancy chart.

The Submission Number gives you a hint as to the age of submitter's address. Submission "AF83-119444," was probably submitted in 1983. The chances of finding someone at the same address after 20 years are not very good.

The Family Group Record Archives

This is a major collection of microfilmed family group records submitted by members of The Church of Jesus Christ of Latter-day Saints and found in the Family History Library. The collection includes over 8 million family group sheets, mainly from New England and England.

Microfilms are available through Family History Centers. They are in alphabetical order by the husband's last name followed by his given name(s). The legal-size sheets were once kept in post binders so workers could take out the pages and make photocopies of pages for researchers. I used this collection to begin work on my family tree. This collection is particularly useful for families from England and New England. Search the Family History Library Catalog under the title: Family Group Record Archives. The set that lists 1942 to 1969 is the main collection the rest are supplements that were added after 1969.

The Periodical Source Index (PERSI)

The Allen County Public Library in Ft. Wayne, Indiana, created PERSI and updates it annually. The library has licensed it for exclusive online access to HeritageQuest (Available: www.heritage-questonlinecom). Individuals can purchase the CD-ROM version of PERSI from several vendors. This index is the largest and most widely used index of articles from genealogy and history periodicals in the world. The index covers almost 6,000 different periodicals, listing every article according to locality, family (surname), and/or research method. It is a key to genealogical information in periodicals in the United States and Canada.

It indexes publications with considerable local and family history data, such as:

- ethnic society publications,

- family/surname society publications,

- genealogical society publications,

- historical society publications,

- online publications, and

- special interest group publications.

The types of articles indexed are:

- ancestor charts,

- Bible records,

- book reviews,

- family group sheets,

- lists of upcoming local, regional, and national conferences and seminars,

- research tips,

- reviews of new publications,

- source materials, and

- unique and forgotten sources of information.

You can find the order form to the Allen County Public Library at their Web site (Available: www.acpl.lib.in.us/database/graphics/order_form.html).

International Genealogical Index (IGI)

This database is available online at FamilySearch.org, and on CD-ROM at Family History Centers. The IGI was created by the Family History Library from records submitted by individuals to LDS temples for proxy ordinances. (See the Preface for an explanation.) They have birth and marriage information for deceased individuals. The IGI has about 300 million entries. It is a finding aid for deceased ancestors, but it should always be checked against the records it refers to, as it is nowhere near accurate.

The IGI is an index. It is primarily made up of two types of records:

1.   Records submitted by LDS Church members for temple work;

2.   Records extracted directly from original vital or church records. Researchers tend to trust the latter entries, because they were extracted independently by two or more individuals and reviewed by a third. It is also fairly simple to check out the original source.

For example, the online version of the IGI has a record for the marriage of Isaac Stinson and Harriet Wardwell, two of my ancestors. The record for this marriage indicates a "Source Call Number" with a hyperlink. Clicking on the hyperlink takes me to an entry in the Family History Library Catalog, which gives the title of the original document with another hyperlink. Clicking on this title takes me to the page with title details. When I click on the button that says, "View Film Notes," I reach a page that gives me the film number. I can click another hyperlink to reach a printable page. I can print out this page and take it to the local Family History Center and order a microfilm copy of the actual marriage record.

The coverage of extracted records in the IGI is not complete. Extracted vital records are mainly from New England states and represent only a small portion of vital records available on microfilm. Some churches did not allow their records to be filmed, and not all church records that were filmed have been extracted. It should also be remembered that the I.G.I. is only an Index and is neither complete nor totally accurate.

Pedigree Resource File

This is a relatively new database in CD-ROM format produced by FamilySearch.org. The database consists of lineage-linked pedigrees presented by individuals to the Family History Library. Data from each submitter is kept in a separate file, so researchers can compare differences in data found in each file. The online version found at FamilySearch.org is an index to the CD-ROM version.

You can only download GEDCOM files from the CDs. The database includes notes and sources. Researchers can print and download charts and reports from the Pedigree Resource File. The submitter's name and contact information are found at the bottom of each page. Researchers can view additional sources and notes supplied by the submitter.

Social Security Death Index

This database provides vital information on more than 64 million people. Their deaths were reported to the U.S. Social Security Administration. Almost all of the data in this index is about individuals who died between 1962 and the present. The Social Security Administration started using computers in 1962 to record death information—hence the lack of death information on the database before that date. Still there are some records dating back to 1937, but most of the earlier records have not been added to the computerized database. Records for about 400,000 railroad workers are also included in the index.

Information in the Social Security Death Index will include: last name, first name, birth date, death date, Social Security Number, the state of residence when the Social Security number was issued, the last known residence of the deceased, and the location where the last benefit was paid. What makes this index such a valuable tool for genealogists is that researchers can write to the SSA for a copy of the Social Security Card Application. The current fee is $27.00.

When searching the index it is best to start with a few facts like the first and last name and date of birth. I found my father's record by entering his first and last name and his birth date.

You can find the SSDI online at FamilySearch.org, Ancestry.com, RootsWeb.com, and Genealogy.com.

Applicants to the Social Security program had to fill out an SS-5 form. It requested the following information:

- Full name

- Full name at birth including maiden name

- Present mailing address

- Age at last birthday

- Date of birth

- Place of birth—city, county, state

- Father's full name

- Mother's full name, including maiden name

- Sex

- Race

- Whether the applicant had ever applied for Social Security or Railroad Retirement before

- Current employers name and address

- Date signed

- Applicant's Signature

If the person is deceased, the SSA will send a copy of the SS-5 form to anyone who asks for it. Send the deceased person's name, Social Security Number, and evidence of death to:

Social Security Administration
OEO FOIA Workgroup
300 N Greene Street
PO Box 33022
Baltimore, MD 21290-3022

Mark the envelope and the letter with: "Freedom of Information Request." Send $27.00 and wait for 6–8 weeks. If you do not know the person's Social Security Number send $29.00 and the person's full name, date and place of birth, and names of parents.

World War I Draft Registrations

In 1917–1918 men who were born between 1873 and 1900 were required to fill out a draft registration card. Approximately 24 million men completed these cards. The cards requested the following information:

- Full name

- Signature

- Address

- Birth date

- Birthplace

- Citizenship

- Occupation

- Employer

- Family

- Marital status

- Children under 12

- Previous military experience

- Physical description

This database will be extremely valuable to researchers looking for male ancestors born in the last quarter of the nineteenth century. Images of these registration cards are available at Ancestry.com.

Online Searchable Death Indexes for the U.S.A.

This wonderful site is a guide for genealogists and other researchers (Available: http://home.att.net/~wee-monster/deathrecords.html). It has links to death indexes, state by state. It could help you locate the death date and place of an ancestor and lead to securing a death certificate. Some of the links are to fee based services. Others are free.

Civil War Soldiers and Sailors System

Accessible through the Web (Available: www.itd.nps.gov/cwss), this National Park System database has a powerful search engine that will help researchers locate ancestors who served in the Civil War. It gives the National Archives film number where more information can be found.

Suggestions for Librarians

1. To give patrons access to the federal census online, subscribe to Ancestry and HeritageQuest for the library, or encourage the state library to do it for the entire state.
2. Buy microfilm copies of all available years of the federal census for your part of the state.
3. Buy a CD-ROM copy of the Periodical Source Index (PERSI) for the library and make it available on one of the public access computers.
4. Create a brochure to promote genealogy sources in the library.
5. Use some of the information about the census records to create a handout for patrons.
6. Encourage patrons to use the Federal Census Chronology form (see Figures 10.3 and 10.4; also presented in Tool 6.3).
7. Locate and take a tour of the Family History Center nearest to your library.

Suggestions for Researchers

1. Purchase your own subscription to Ancestry.com.
2. Purchase your own copy of the 1880 Federal Census and National Index—especially if you don't have access to the online database.
3. Locate the nearest Family History Center and order at least one film to help you with your research.

Summary

Indexes and databases take the randomness out of our research and give us a place to start. Without them genealogical research would be nearly impossible. It would be too difficult for everyone except the very dedicated. Manual indexes of the past have given way to online databases of today—making it possible for anyone to do his or her genealogy.

Bibliography (Ratings Guide explanation follows last citation)

Family Chronicle (Staff), ed. 2003. *500 Brickwall Solutions to Genealogy Problems, 2003.* Toronto: Mooreshead Magazines.

This is a compilation of "brick wall solutions" submitted by the readers of Family Chronicle. Using traditional techniques and the latest technology they share how they persevered and overcame research brick walls. **PP**

Hinckley, Kathleen W. 2002. *Your Guide to the Federal Census for Genealogists, Researchers, and Family Historians.* Cincinnati, OH: Betterway Books.

In the first census, census takers merely counted the population and placed individuals into age categories by head of household. Every census since then has had more questions to gather statistics for military pension expenses, housing needs, and economic predictors. Some of those who responded to census questions may have resisted the personal nature of the questions, but the result is a record group that is a singularly significant source for American genealogical research.

This book is a detailed guide to the information available in the U.S. Federal Census records and how to use them. With so many of the census records now available online this guide is a must for every genealogist. **LLL**

Thorndale, William, and William Dollarhide. 2000. *Map Guide to the U.S. Federal Censuses 1790–1920*. Baltimore, MD: Genealogical Publishing Company.

This shows United States county boundary maps for the census decades superimposed on modern county boundaries. It gives background information on each census, including census availability for each county. **PP**

Ratings Guide

The ratings for each bibliography describe not only what each resource contains, but also how it might fit into the library collection. Some of the materials are more appropriate for larger libraries with substantial budgets, and others belong in collections of any size—even in the personal research collection. To help you identify materials most appropriate for your collection, each resource is marked as either "L" for libraries and "P" for personal. They are ranked from one letter for recommended, two letters for preferred, and three letters for essential.

CHAPTER 11

FACILITATING RESEARCH WITH COMPUTERS

Not long after I bought my first home computer in 1990, I installed Personal Ancestral File 2.0. Right away, I went to the local Family History Center and downloaded a GEDCOM file that had one of my ancestral lines on it. I came home and imported it to my computer. I was hooked! Today I have over 20,000 names on my family database and I am still hooked on genealogy.

What to Look for in This Chapter

It is quite possible for a genealogist to sit at a computer that is connected to the Internet and do serious genealogical research. I know because I have done it. In this chapter we look at some of the genealogy software programs and describe their capabilities. We will look at the Internet and other technologies to discover how they work together to enhance genealogical research and make easier. Looking at the tools that integrate all of these tasks, I have focused this chapter on the genealogy software currently available to help organize, record, retrieve, copy, and share genealogical research.

I won't go as far as to say that researchers can do everything from a computer, but computers have made genealogical research much easier.

Using Computers for Genealogical Research

Computers and genealogists are meant for each other. Doing what they do so well, computers stockpile and retrieve data, display it, and print it in lots of useful ways. As in solving a jigsaw puzzle, genealogists gather bits of data one fact at a time. Sometimes the pieces fit and sometimes they don't. A computer with a good genealogy program helps the genealogist organize and store the data in a way that will help him or her bring similar pieces of the puzzle together for comparison. A computer connected to the Internet can lead to clues for additional research or even facts genealogists can add to their databases. Once the genealogists has gathered sufficient date to share with family and friends he or she can let the computer program write a book—or at least a report that looks like a book. It still may need some careful editing before being published, but at least the computer has spared the genealogist considerable effort.

Over the years personal computers have become powerful and reliable, as their cost steadily falls. Now, the power of the Internet also makes it easy for genealogists to share the data. This sharing of information and the commercialization of genealogy data has created an explosion in genealogy activity. Family historians can get on the Internet to look for ancestors. When they find a name of someone they think might be a match, they can send an e-mail query to the person who put up the information and pursue the lead further.

GEDCOM and Creating a Standard for Genealogy Software

In the early history of personal computers some genealogists and computer programmers began exploring ways to enter genealogical data, organize it, display it and print it out in traditional genealogical formats. As often is the case in the infancy of technology development, there was no standard and every developer had his or her own way of organizing data into fields. At this time, the Personal Ancestral File (PAF) was developed by the Family History Library, and soon became a leader in the field.

Leland Mietzler, executive editor of *Heritage Quest Magazine*, recalls developers of various genealogy software products coming together in Salt Lake City in 1987. Working for The Church of Jesus Christ of Latter-day Saints, the developers of the Personal Ancestral File proposed development of a standard protocol for the exchange of genealogical data and GEDCOM (Genealogical Data Communication) was born. As more genealogy software developers started using it, GEDCOM became a standard way of transferring genealogical data between different genealogy programs. It remains the standard in the industry today. Any producer of a genealogy software product that wants to compete in the market must include GEDCOM compatibility, and it was considered essential for any software mentioned in this chapter.

Selecting Genealogy Software

Buying a software package to manage your genealogy is not quite like buying a new car, but still, if you make an ill-advised choice, hours of data entry may be wasted on a program you decide to drop. If the replacement program isn't compatible with the old one, you may not be able to transfer the data. That is why GEDCOM is absolutely essential.

There isn't enough space in this chapter to list all of the features every program offers. The best a prospective buyer can do is to learn as much as possible about the major programs, and then make an informed decision. Some vendors will let you have a copy of their program on a 30-free trial. You can try it out and then decide if you want to pay for the program or uninstall it. Some librarians have bought and loaded several genealogy programs on a public access computer to let patrons try them out.

Innovations and new releases are coming out all the time, so the best place to obtain current information on genealogy software is through the Internet. Where available, I have provided a current Web address for each of the software programs listed in Figure 11.1.

Software Selection Checklist (Arranged Alphabetically)

Adding Individuals

Is it easy to enter new individuals, parents, children, or spouses from a single screen or to toggle quickly from screen to screen? After the initial entry that transfers your genealogy from paper copy to the computer, data input is rarely linear. You need the flexibility of moving easily from one individual or family to another.

Backup

Does the program offer easy-to-use backup procedures, or reminders to backup the data? You should backup your data every time you add something to the database. If the process is cumbersome, or if you are not reminded to do it, you might skip it, and some day lose valuable data.

Biography

Does the software offer expanded capacity for biographical information? If you are creating a family record, as well as collecting genealogical data, you will want to have plenty of room for biographical and anecdotal material.

Browse

Can you browse up and down the pedigree chart or the entire database? Many times you may find a name or other piece of data that may apply to your research. The name may not be exact, but other pieces of information fit. You will want to browse the list for other bits of information that will help you make the connection, such as parents, marriage date, spouse, birth date, and death date.

Calculator

Does the program include a calculator that computes dates, ages, and life expectancy? This is a useful little tool. Not essential, but nice to have.

Cut/Paste

Does the program support quick and easy cut and paste between entry fields and note fields? Windows software supports this feature. This is an important time saver. For example, if you find a source that lists several members of a family with their birth dates, you will want to record the source in the notes field for each individual. It is a lot easier to copy and paste that information than retype it for each person.

Database Capacity

Does the program support multiple databases? If you import a database from a source, and want to verify content before adding the data to your main database, make sure the program supports multiple databases.

Date Format

Is the input format for dates standardized (i.e., 04 July 1776) or does the program allow the user to select the date format? This is a personal preference issue. I like the format that forces all dates to follow dd/mmm/yyyy. It does avoid confusion. Others may want to select their own style.

Documentation

Does the program provide space to document every piece of information gathered and prompts the user to add notes? This is critical to good genealogical research. Don't buy a program without it.

Ease of Use

Is the program easy to learn and easy to use (user friendly) with onscreen helps? Don't buy a piece of software that isn't easy to use. If you accidentally buy a program you don't like, buy another one you do like. Don't spend years of aggravation on a piece of software just because you don't want to discard it.

Editing

Is it easy to edit information and notes about individuals and families? Genealogists spend a lot of time editing their databases. If editing is difficult or cumbersome, try another program.

Errors

How does the program deal with potential errors in data? Does it flag possible problems, or does it give you a list when you ask for one? A good program will help identify possible data entry errors by telling you if a person died before she was born, or if she was ten when the first child was born.

Evidence

Does the program help you weigh each piece of evidence for credibility and reliability? This is a useful feature, especially if you are very particular about the data that gets added to the database.

Family Order

Is it easy to rearrange order of children? If you add new children to a family record you often have to rearrange their order. This is a worthwhile feature, but not at the top of the list.

Fields

Does the program provide for user-defined fields or dedicated fields for other data such as religion, nationality, languages spoken, Social Security Number, common name, and aliases? This is an interesting feature, and it may be nice to have it. But, it may not be essential. Are the fields flexible enough to support aliases, nicknames, long names, nationality, and interest-level in various fields? It is sometimes frustrating to be limited to a few spaces to record a name like "de Roquefort-Reynolds."

Files

Are the data files interchangeable with other programs? You might want this if you use more than one program or think you might want to change to another software program in the future.

GEDCOM

Is the program GEDCOM compatible? The GEDCOM feature allows you to share information with others using files in GEDCOM format. It allows you to copy all or part of your data for exchange. This feature has to be at the top of everyone's list.

Graphics

Will it store video and audio recordings, pictures, drawings and scanned images? Computers are now able to deal with graphics fairly easily. It may be nice to have your grandfather's picture on his family group sheet. This is a nice feature that is commonly available, but it is not essential.

Import/Export

Does the software allow for the importing and exporting of data from or to another program? This is absolutely essential. If you can't import data you will have to rekey everything you get from someone else. (See GEDCOM)

Internet

Does the program support direct Internet access back and forth between the program and the Internet? This is a great feature if you are connected to the Internet. If you are not connected today, you probably will be some day. When I work on my genealogy I like to open up Personal Ancestral File and several genealogy search sites on the Internet, then move from one to another as I conduct searches.

LDS TempleReady

Is the program compatible with LDS TempleReady®, and have LDS temple ordinance fields as an option? TempleReady helps researchers determine if temple work has already been completed for the names they are planning to submit. If you are a member of The Church of Jesus Christ of Latter-day Saints and you are going to submit names for temple work, this feature is absolutely essential. For others it is optional.

Match/Merge

Does the program include automatic, semiautomatic, and manual match and merge? This feature allows you to bring up records for two individuals and compare them side-by-side to determine if they are the same person. The software should permit you to merge them into one record if they match. This is an essential function for any program, if you plan to import any records and link them to the database. Automatic match/merge is a real time-saver, if you use only a name and an identification number. Semi-automatic match and merging give the genealogist the choice of whether or not to merge two records for two individuals into one.

Notes

What features does the program have for creating, organizing, storing and manipulating notes? Since notes are an essential part of documenting research, the ease for creating and repeating notes is important.

Parents

Does the program allow for multiple sets of parents? Sometimes researchers do not agree on the parentage of a person. It is a good idea to record all possibilities until you can determine the correct information.

Photos

Does the program allow for photos in standard digital formats to be linked to the database? Some programs also include movies and sound. It is nice to put photos on printed family group sheets (see Graphics criteria above).

Printing

What do the printouts look like? This is an important consideration. No matter how sophisticated the program may be, if you don't like the way the printouts look, you will not be happy with it.

Prompts

Are there screen prompts to remind the user to link individuals, create notes, add notes to the research log, and correct spelling, at the point of data entry? Standardizing entry for dates, places, and events will eliminate errors.

Publishing

What book publishing capabilities does the program include? Researchers who spend thousands of hours gathering data about their family often want to share it with others. Publishing a book is a good possibility.

I have published two family history books using my genealogy program. I save the book to my hard drive. Then I open up Microsoft Word and edit the book from there. I can import pictures and also create an index of names.

Reports

What reports can the software generate? Reports should include at least the following: ancestor, descendant, pedigree, family group sheets, possible problems, and some custom lists. Some programs have report wizards that help create reports.

Two important reports are an Ahnentafel (ancestor table) and a modified register (descendancy). These reports help researchers create a book or parts of a book in a readable format. The Ahnentafel chart starts with a primary individual and goes back one generation at a time. The modified register lists all of the descendants included in the database of a given ancestor. This report creates complete sentences that read like a book. The reports can be save to a file and edited in a word processing program.

Search

What are the search capabilities of the program? Does the search feature include browsing capabilities? When you search for an individual in a large database, you need to be able to browse a list of names for other clues that might help identify the object of the search.

Sources

How are sources identified, managed, and recorded? It is nice to be able to link a note to a source with a single word and attach the full reference to the note without having to retype the entire bibliographic record.

Spell Checker

Does the program include a spell checker? This is a nice feature if you plan to publish your genealogy in a book or on the Internet, but don't reject the program if it otherwise meets your needs. If you are going to publish your genealogy, you will probably put it into a more powerful word processor and check the spelling there.

Web Page Creator

Does the program provide for the creation of a Web page in Hyper Text Markup Language (HTML) format? This is a very nice feature if you plan to publish your genealogy on the Internet, but there are separate programs that will do the same thing, maybe better.

Word Processing

Can you export a report to a word processor? This is a good feature to have if you plan to publish your genealogy.

I know this is a long list, but at least it gives you several important points to consider before buying software.

Software Selection

If I were a beginning genealogist with a new computer recently connected to the Internet, I would install the Personal Ancestral File as a genealogy program. First of all, it is a free download from FamilySearch.org. Secondly, it is a fully functional program that works well. As you become more experienced and develop preferences, you can purchase other programs and load them on your computers and compare the features.

If you want to explore other software programs, look for online links to various genealogy programs. Two good places to start are Louis Kessler's Genealogy Software Links (Available: www.lkessler.com/gplinks.shtml#jg1), and the Genealogy Software Springboard (Available: www.gensoftsbcom). This latter site was created in 1996 specifically to help genealogists and family history researchers evaluate genealogy programs. Many genealogists have turned to this Web site to weigh the pros and cons of genealogy programs, and to determine which genealogy program might work best for them. The site's Pros and Cons section consists of input submitted by the users of the programs. These personal views give us a better evaluation of the programs and their functions than the promotional information supplied by software companies.

While a careful study and comparison is important, any genealogy software is so much better than keeping records the old way that most people really like whatever they select. It is much better than keeping their genealogy manually. There is little chance of making a mistake that can't be remedied by buying another program. Data from most programs can be imported into the new one. Remember that cheap isn't always bad and costly isn't always best.

Right now I have five genealogy computer programs on my computer. They are *Personal Ancestral File, Legacy, Ancestry Family Tree, Generations Suite 8.0*, and *Family Tree Maker 6.0*. Some of these were free downloads and the others cost me about $50.00 each. I have used them all and they all work about the same way. The screens vary somewhat, and I prefer the family view screen from *Personal Ancestral File*. *Legacy* generates nicer looking printouts than the others. *Ancestry*

Family Tree links to Ancestry.com on the Internet and finds possible matches to the names in your database. With one mouse click you can go to Ancestry.com and find out if they have a match for the person in your genealogy. Also, *Legacy* has some nice match and merge features that make that process much easier.

Genealogy Program Comparison Table			
Program	**Description/Features**	**Cost**	**Demo version**
Ages!	This is an easy-to-use, full-featured genealogy software. It has an intuitive user interface, allows for multiple parents, any number of generations, integrated note-manager, flexible date format, is GEDCOM compatible, and offers multiple printout options. Web site: www.daubnet.com/english/ages.html	$35.00	Shareware version allows up to 50 individuals.
Ancestral Quest	This program is for anyone engaged in genealogy research. Data entry is easy; keyboard shortcuts, and super-fast mouse navigation make data entry a snap. The program is compatible with PAF database and is GEDCOM compatible. Web site: www.ancquest.com/aqindex.htm	$29.95	Demo version allows up to 120 names.
Ancestry Family Tree	Automatically searches about 2 billion names at Ancestry.com to find the best matches in a person's family tree. Lets users publish a family tree online. Accommodates photos and multimedia. GEDCOM compatible. http://aft.ancestrycom	$19.95	Free for seven days.
Brothers Keeper 6	The database can hold up to 10 million names. The program can attach sources to events and pictures to people. The print preview is a nice feature. Printing includes ancestor charts, descendant box charts, timelines, birthday and anniversary lists, family group sheets with pictures, and it can print a book with an index. GEDCOM import/export compatible. Web site: www.bkwin.org.	$45.00 to register software	Shareware. Try it before you buy it.
Cumberland Family Tree	This is a versatile and easy-to-use program that features a variety of reports, GEDCOM import/export, and HTML publishing. Focuses on creating a family history book and customizing individual reports. Web site: www.cf-softwarecom.	$45.00	Shareware for 45-day free trial.
Figure 11.1 Genealogy Program Comparison Table			

Program	Description/Features	Cost	Demo version
DoroTree	This is the family tree software for Jewish genealogists. It is easy-to-use with complete bilingual capability—English and Hebrew. It includes direct Internet access to Jewish genealogy sites. Special features include Yahrzeit reports, Holocaust commemoration, and Hebrew-Gregorian date conversion. Users can create Web pages and store multimedia. Web site: www.dorotree.com/features.html	$59.00	None
Family Tree Legends	This is a powerful and easy-to-use program. Features include a smart matching interface that allows users to collaborate with other researchers, GEDCOM merge and find duplicates, and spell checking. Web site: www.familytreelegends.com.	$39.95	None
Family Tree Maker	This is one of the most popular genealogy programs available. The data entry wizard makes it easy to add information. Store any number of facts for each individual. Add photos, sound, video, and text. Display a wide array of trees, printouts, and formats. Web site: www.genealogy.com/soft_ftm.html	$24.00 to $49.00 Amazon.com has the best price	None
Gene Macintosh Software	User can store family data and notes, draw and print family trees and pedigree charts, create web pages from the database, and exchange GEDCOM data with users of other genealogy programs. Gene is capable of handling complicated databases with thousands of names, multiple marriages and divorces, adoptions, illegitimate children, and intermarriage between relatives. www1.ics.uci.edu/~eppstein/gene	$15.00 (single user); site license $300.00	Shareware
Generations Family Tree	Engaging tutorials make it easy to get started. Fill in the blanks for uncomplicated data entry. Stores facts for every individual in the database. Includes a 350-million name database. Program has SnapShot Express, a photo restoration and enhancement software. Web site: www.broderbund.com/Product.asp?OID=4147943	$9.99 to $29.99	None

Figure 11.1 Genealogy Program Comparison Table continued

Program	Description/Features	Cost	Demo version
GenoPro	Users can draw a complete family tree, add pictures, generate and print family reports, and analyze compiled data. GEDCOM compatible. Gold (paid) version eliminates advertising. Web site: www.genoprogoldcom.	Free to $24.00	Gold version Free download version includes advertising.
Great Family	This program makes it fast and easy to create and edit a family tree. It is also great for generating Web pages with pictures and extra text. Navigation is easy and intuitive. Imports/exports GEDCOM files. Includes family tree organizing tools. Web site: www.greatprogs.com/greatfamily	$29.93	30-day free trial.
Legacy Family Tree	Multifunctional, multi-featured program, that lets users see up to eight families at a time, and have two family files open at the same time. Drag and drop features make it easy to copy from one file to another. Pop-up lists make it easy to select the next view. GEDCOM compatible. One of the most comprehensive genealogy programs available. Web site: www.legacyfamilytree.com/Features.asp	$19.95 to $49.95 depending on version	Standard version is available as a free download.
Mac Family Tree	This program for Macintosh computers helps users document, store, and display information about their families. They can draw and print family trees, lists, cards, and heritage charts. Data is exported as html documents to build a Web page. GEDCOM 5.5 is the native file format. Web site: www.onlymac.de/html/macfamilytree.html	$29.95	Free demo download.
The Master Genealogist	Used by professional researchers and beginning genealogist alike, this is one of the most powerful family history programs available. Users can manage volumes of research, organize research trips, keep track of correspondence, or publish a book. Most data fields have no limits. Genealogists can include photographs, sources, events, multiple names per person, relationships, and user-defined events and flags. The program can generate a wide variety of displays, reports, and printouts. Web site: www.whollygenes.com/tmg5.htm	$79.00	Download for a 30-day free trial.

Figure 11.1 Genealogy Program Comparison Table continued

Program	Description/Features	Cost	Demo version
Personal Ancestral File	PAF helps users put in order their family history records. It produces on-screen and printed copies of pedigree charts, family group records, and other reports. The program can accommodate a variety of naming conventions. Accommodates multimedia and GEDCOM imports/exports. Easiest of all programs to use. It has online lessons for beginners. Web site: www.familysearch.org/eng/paf	$6.00 for CD-ROM version	Free download of fully functioning program.
Reunion	Reunion is a genealogy software program for Macintosh computers. Reunion lets users publish family tree information with elegant graphics. It makes creating Web pages a snap. Reunion creates large, high-resolution, graphic charts that allow for easy editing of boxes, lines fonts, and colors. Wall charts are a specialty. GEDCOM compatible. Web site: www.leisterpro.com/index.shtml	$99.00	Download free demo version, which allows up to 35 people.
RootsMagic	Comprehensive yet easy-to-use, this is a new full-featured genealogy program. User can have multiple databases open at the same time and drag and drop data from one program to another. Integrated backup and restore helps safeguard data. Web site: www.rootsmagiccom.	$29.95	Download free demo version, which allows up to 50 people.

Figure 11.1 Genealogy Program Comparison Table continued

Getting Started with a Genealogy Program

I have taught genealogy classes to groups all over Kansas and around the United States. I have discovered that many beginning, as well as seasoned, genealogists do not know how to load or use a genealogy program on the computer. To remedy that situation, I provide the basics here. I want you to be able to have access to and operate genealogy software after you read these instructions.

Downloading and Installing Personal Ancestral File 5.2

1. Go to www.familysearch.org.
2. Click on "Order/Download Products."
3. Click on "Software Downloads—Free."
4. At Personal Ancestral File 5.2.18.0—Multi Language (9.7 MB minimum), click on DOWNLOAD button.

5.   Click on CONTINUE.

6.   Fill in registration information and click on SEND.

7.   At "PAF 5.2 Download Instructions and Options" page, click on DOWNLOAD ENG-LISH button.

8.   When asked, "What would you like to do with this file?" Answer: Save this program to disk. Press OK.

9.   Dialog box will ask where you want to save this file. Desktop is good enough. Click on SAVE.

10.   Download Complete. Click OK.

11.   Locate program icon on desktop. Double click on it to start the installation wizard.

12.   Follow instructions to FINISH and click to restart your computer.

Loading and Utilizing Personal Ancestral File

Personal Ancestral File has now been copied to the hard drive on your computer. The program still needs to be set up for operation before you can enter data and use it. *Personal Ancestral File* provides an installation wizard, which automates the installation process; it is quite easy to follow. Double click on the blue icon "PAF 5 English" and follow the screen prompts. At the end click on "FINISH." You are now ready to begin using PAF.

To begin using the Personal Ancestral File program:

1.   Double click on P.A.F. 5 icon. It should be on the desktop.

2.   To get started pull down the file menu and click on NEW to create a new file.

3.   Give the file a name (e.g., SmithGenealogy and click on SAVE).

4.   Dialog box asks: "Would you like the Enter key always to move to the next field?" Click YES.

5.   Preferences box. Fill in the data about yourself. Leave AFN blank. Press SAVE AS DEFAULT. Then click OK.

6.   Click on ADD individual.

7.   Use yourself or one of your children as the first individual. Fill in the blanks with as much information as you have at this time. Then Click to SAVE.

8.   To add a spouse, parents, or children double click in the blank box indicated and add the individual information. Or pull down on the ADD menu to add a child, spouse, father, or mother for the selected person.

9.   If you make a mistake (for example, if you add a child to the wrong family), select the person who has been entered incorrectly and pull down on the EDIT menu and select DELETE. This will delete the person from the database. You may also select UNLINK. This will unlink the person from the family, but leave him or her in the database.

10.   The ADD command gives you the option of adding a new individual or selecting an existing individual. Since the unlinked individual is still in the database, you may add him or her to the correct family.

11.   Click on "?" for help, or go to PAF 5 README file in PAF folder for more detailed instructions on how to use PAF 5.1.

12. For free lessons on how to use PAF, first make sure your computer is connected to the Internet, then pull down on the help menu and select LESSONS. This command will take the learner to the Internet site: www.familysearch.org/eng/paf/lessons/PAF5.html. Acquaint yourself with the features of the program by pulling down on the menu item or clicking on the task bar. The view bar will let you see the family view, the pedigree view, or view a list of individuals.

Backing Up the Data

Once you have entered data to the program you will want to back it up. To create a backup, insert the proper storage device in the appropriate drive (floppy disks usually go in the A drive, Zip disks go in the Zip; drive, and read-write CDs and DVDs go in the CD or DVD drive). Pull down on the FILE menu and select BACKUP. You may have to point the program to the Floppy disk you have inserted in the A drive. Click on SAVE and the program will automatically save the data.

Importing and Exporting GEDCOM Files

One of the nicest features of a genealogy program is the ability to share files with other researchers. I recently found some well-researched and well-documented information on one of my ancestral lines. I sent an e-mail message to the person who had the data I wanted and asked him for a GEDCOM file. He could not break out the specific part I needed, so he sent his entire database as an attachment to an e-mail message. He asked for the data I had on our common relative. We sent the files back and forth over the Internet in a matter of a few minutes. You can also find and download GEDCOM files from a Web site. Go to PAF 5 README file in PAF folder for instructions on how to import and export GEDCOM files.

Creating Reports

Most genealogy programs give us lots of options for creating reports. From the FILE menu select Print Reports. This will bring up a dialog box that provides several options. The report types include the following:

- Pedigree Chart
- Family Group
- Ancestry
- Descendants
- Books
- Individual Summary
- Scrapbook
- Custom
- Lists

A cascading pedigree chart will print out linked pedigree charts for as many generations as are selected. Selecting the book option gives you a choice between an Ahnentafel Chart (Ancestry table) and a Modified Register (Descendancy table). The Ahnentafel chart starts with an individual and reports his or her ancestors in a table. The modified register starts with a distant ancestor and creates a report that reads like a book, giving all of the descendants of this person that are in the database. You can print the reports to a file and edit them as a word processing document before printing them.

I have included instructions for using some of the more popular features of PAF here, because so many people are intimidated when they try to do some of the basic functions of the program. If you need more help with the program I suggest clicking on the question mark on the task bar of the program to purchase the most current user's guide from the online LDS catalog (Available: www.ldscatalogcom), or buy the video hosted by Stephen Lemmon, which explains how to download, install, and utilize the PAF software (Lemmon, 2001): *Personal Ancestral File 5*. Address: The Studio, 39 S Main Street, Hurricane, Utah 84737; phone: 435-635-8474 (Available: www.pafvideo.com).

Exploiting Mailing Lists

Before we move on to the Internet, we need to discuss mailing lists. Mailing lists, sometimes called discussion lists, are for people who share a common interest. Genealogy mailing lists generally focus on a family name or a locality. Researchers subscribe to a mailing list by sending their name and e-mail address to the server for the list. Enrollment happens automatically. The server also automatically sends you a welcome letter that tells you how to post your messages to the list and how to unsubscribe from the list, which is a different address than the one to which you send messages. Some beginners get on a list and want to get off, but don't know how to do it. They get frustrated when they send a message to the list to remove their name from the list and all they get is the message to the list. They need to go to the welcome message to find out how to unsubscribe. Most of the mailing lists I belong to have a message at the end that tell me how to leave the list. For example, "To unsubscribe, send a blank e-mail message to: leave-genealib-4581@lists.acomp.usf.edu." (Note: This is just a fictitious example. It won't work.)

Advantages of Mailing Lists

By joining a genealogy mailing list, you put yourself in contact with other researchers, who share your interest in a surname or a locality. When you send a message to the list, everyone on the list gets a copy of your message including you. If you don't get a copy of your message you can assume that no one else on the list got your message either. It is all right to join a list ask a few questions and then unsubscribe after you get whatever information comes back.

The advantages of joining a surname list are:
1. If your name is unique you are probably related to many of the people on the list and they will be able to help you.
2. You probably won't get a lot of messages that don't pertain to your research.

The advantages of joining a locality (county) list are:
1. You might find someone who is working on one of your collateral lines.
2. You might find someone who lives in the county who is willing to look up some local information for you.

Once you have subscribed to the list you can just read the e-mails that are sent to the list (lurk) for a while, or you can jump right in and send a query. For example, I just joined the Talmage list and sent the following query:

"I am looking for the ancestor of Anna Talmage, b. 13 Feb 1793 in Connecticut, d. 29 Oct 1832 in McDonough, Chenango, New York. She md. Stephen A. Curtis 3 Jan 1811. I have reason to believe that Anna is related to James Talmage because he was one of the first settlers in Chenango County."

Writing a Successful E-mail Query

- Limit your query to one person and put his or her name on the subject line.

- In the body of the message state the person's name again and be specific about the information you want. e. g., parents, spouse, or children.

- Give the pertinent information you have on the individual (e.g., birth date and place, death date and place, and marriage date and place).

- Give the data you already have and where you found it.

- Say thank you and close with your name and e-mail address.

Other Tips

- Use the most permanent e-mail address you have—preferably the one supplied by your Internet service provider.

- Post your query where it has the best chance of being seen by someone who has the information you seek.

- Respond with thank you notes to anyone who responds to your query, whether or not he or she had information you could use.

- Use capital letters for surnames (i.e., SWAN).

- Check other online sources before sending out a query. Someone may have already posted a family tree for the information you need.

- Use abbreviations sparingly. It is all right to use b. for birth, d. death, and md. for married.

The two best places to find mailing lists to join are John Fuller's Genealogy Resources on the Internet (Available: www.rootsweb.com/~jfuller/gen_mail.html), and RootsWeb.com Mailing Lists (Available: http://lists.rootswebcom).

Using the Internet

For a nice overview of how far genealogy on the Internet has come, see the article by Jan McClintock, Internet Genealogy: What You Can and Cannot Do (Available:

www.leisterpro.com/doc/Articles/IntGen/InternetGenealogy.html). This article lists links to many sites that will point you in the right direction. You might even find a clue, a name, or a date of one of your ancestors.

Immediacy of access is a major advantage of having so much genealogical information on the Internet. I used to think that genealogy was for older people, because they were the only ones with enough patience to spend hours looking at rolls of microfilm or waiting for months to get a response in the mail. The Internet eliminates this delay. Databases, online services, online card catalogs, and e-mail have changed the way we get information. Instead of waiting weeks, we can send messages back and forth several times in one day. Genealogists who faced frustrating challenges in the past are now online, helping others.

I still believe that every serious genealogist should have a fairly new computer with Internet access. To stay with the methods and technology we used through the 1970s is to work hard and not smart. If a researcher can travel a thousand miles to do genealogical research, he or she can afford a computer. Learning how to use a computer could be daunting to some, but it is not impossible. Public libraries and community colleges offer classes to teach people how to use computers.

Types of Genealogy Web Sites

Many genealogy Web sites serve more than one function. To understand the various functions of genealogy Web sites, it helps to classify them into the following:

Gateway Sites

Gateway sites provide researchers with the links they need to get to the good stuff. They contain well-organized lists of links, or have a well-developed, comprehensive search engine. They are better than general search engines, because they can filter out everything that does not relate to genealogy.

Cyndi's List (Available: www.cyndislistcom). This is a mammoth portal site that indexes over 200,000 genealogy Web pages. It is constantly updated and the links are categorized and cross-referenced. Cyndi has put a lot of work into making this site user-friendly. It is perfect for the beginning genealogist and anyone else who uses the Internet to do research. The powerful index helps researchers locate even the most obscure information. Just go to the site and type in a search term and press enter. Cyndi's List can take you to thousands of genealogy places.

AccessGenealogy.com (Available: www.accessgenealogy.com). This site provides links to online genealogy in the United State and several foreign countries. Native American researchers will want to check out this site, because of its links to the 1880 Cherokee census, the final enrollment of the Five Civilized Tribes, and lots of other Native American documents. Even though Access Genealogy is not as extensive as Cyndi's List, it is well worth the effort. Who knows, it might have something no other site has.

Genealogy Resources on the Internet (Available: www.rootsweb.com/~jfuller/internet.html). Not all genealogy on the Internet can be found on the World Wide Web. John Fuller and Chris Gaunt introduce researchers to newsgroups, telnet and Gopher technologies. Even though this site doesn't use a search engine it nevertheless, easy to use and has links to plenty of good information.

Online Catalogs

These sites provide bibliographic data to the genealogical holdings of the library they correspond to. Researchers have to go through additional steps to access materials they represent. Researchers who use online catalogs hope the collection represented by the catalog will be available through interlibrary loan. They are often disappointed, because many libraries do not lend genealogical materials.

WorldCat on OCLC

The WorldCat, available through OCLC, is the best online catalog for genealogy in the world, except possibly the Family History Library Catalog. It contains bibliographic records of more historic newspapers, church histories, wills, manuscripts, and maps than any other catalog in the world. In fact the Godfrey Memorial Library in Middletown, Connecticut catalogs individual obituaries on OCLC as a way to defray OCLC charges to the library. Many other libraries do the same thing (see Chapter 5).

WorldCat is a cooperatively created catalog of materials held by thousands of libraries around the world. WorldCat contains the holdings, including digitized local materials, of these libraries and repositories. You can use their search engine find an ancestor and then have your library request the information from the library that holds the information.

Individuals can access WorldCat through their local or state library. Check with your local library to find out if it offers patron access, or if the state library does. Check out the OCLC Web site for more information (Available: www.oclc.org/worldcat/genealogy).

General Search Engines

Researchers can use general search engines like Google, AltaVista, or Yahoo to find information about their ancestors. Genealogists are adding their family trees to the Internet all of the time. While these search engines contain no data of their own, they use software to search the Internet for names and information. The key to using search engines is learning how to conduct a search. Using double quotes ("_") around first and last name (e.g., "Ben Franklin") will cause the search engine to search for the two words as a single phrase. Using all capital letters will help narrow the search to mostly genealogy sites because genealogist have a long-standing tradition of putting surnames in all capitals. Using the words "family" or "genealogy" will also produce better quality hits for genealogy purposes. You can also put a minus sign "-" before any word you specifically want to exclude.

A researcher can sit down at a computer and search all of the names on his or her pedigree chart in a few hours, unless he or she finds some information that warrants following up. It pays to redo the searches about every year, because researchers put up new pages all of the time.

It has been several years since I did a search on my Widger line using AltaVista. To verify the information, in this section of the book, I performed the search for Eli Widger again, and found well-researched, documented information that I did not have on his wife, Marilla Curtis. The Web site that AltaVista found for me took me back five generations beyond what I already had.

Connecting with Cousins or Other Researchers

One of the easiest ways if not the best way to do genealogy is to find someone who has already done the research and ask him or her to share. The idea is to find a clue—a name, date, and location that matches a name, date, and location in your research, and contact the researcher had put it on the Internet. Any Web site that has genealogical data should also have contact information for the person who submitted the data. I have had some really good luck with this technique, though the older the contact information is, the better the chance of it being out of date and worthless.

RootsWeb.com Surname List was one of the first Internet sites to do this, and is still one of my favorites. Genealogists submit surnames they are actively researching, and usually include their e-mail address. Researchers use the search engine by typing the surname in one space and the two-letter code for the state in another space.

I found a third cousin in Colorado using this tool. I submitted information to this Web site using my ancestor's surname, PAGE. This is what my entry looked like:

Page 1800   1995   VT>IL>FtMadison,IA>CA,USA jswan

Here is his entry:

Page c1800   1883   VT>FtMadison,IA,USA campbellr

The key to this match is "Ft. Madison, IA." Imagine my excitement when I saw Robert Campbell's entry. I sent an e-mail query that gave him information about my ancestral Page family that lived in Ft. Madison, Iowa. About 20 minutes later I received a response.

It started, "Hi Cousin." As it turned out his great grandmother and my great grandfather were sister and brother. He gave me some information I had been seeking for years, and I was able to share some research on the family that he didn't have.

Ancestry.com's *Ancestry World Tree* consists of individual databases that have been submitted by researchers. Not all of the data is accurate but the submitter's e-mail address is prominently presented on the first page of their data.

Data Compiled by Individuals and Organizations

Finding clues to check out is the best thing about data compiled by others. Accuracy of the information is the main problem with compiled data. You could waste countless hours following inaccurate leads put forward by someone who wasn't sure of the data he or she had submitted. So, it is wise to check out the sources the submitter gives for the data he or she has offered.

Web sites of this type generally consist of two types. (1) Web sites created and maintained by the individual who has done the research. (2) Web sites maintained by a commercial or not-for-profit organization. Both are likely to have some inaccurate information.

A few years ago I created my own Web site and included a section that contains some of my genealogy. I have pedigree charts that go back 10 generations on some lines. I also list the descendants of some of my longer ancestral lines. When I created the pages I hoped that researchers with connections to my line would contact me and have information to share. At least once a week I receive an e-mail from someone asking a question about one of my ancestors they found on my Web site. Sometimes they have information to share. Sometimes they have corrections to the data I have put up. I make the corrections as soon as I can.

GenServ.com is one of my favorite sites. Created by Cliff Manis, it is strictly a site of compiled genealogies. I like it because I have found so much good information on it and the membership fee is only $12.00 per year ($6.00 if you are over sixty). Member researchers submit a GEDCOM file and pay the annual fee and GenServ loads your data on their site. Finding data takes a two-step process. You use a search engine to identify the person you want, and then you go to another screen to request a report using the database number and the individual's number. Each report gives the database number and the researcher's name and address plus a hyperlink to his or her e-mail address.

One of my best successes came from this Web site. I was looking for Polly Hunting. I had her birth date, marriage date, and death date and location. I did a search on just the surname Hunting and found Don Weymouth, who had thousands of ancestors with that last name. I should have been able to find Polly in this huge database. Unfortunately, there was no Polly Hunting in his data. I sent a query to Don Weymouth, the owner of the database, and asked him if he had a Polly Hunting who was not listed in the database. He replied that he did not, but would forward my query to his Hunting mailing list.

About two months later I received a message from Ed Spaeth, someone I did not know. He said, "Jim, I think I have found your Polly Hunting. Her real name is Mary Jane Hunting and her father's name is Joseph and his father's name is Joseph." His information matched the data I had. With a father's name I was able to search Don Weymouth's database and take my Hunting line back another nine generations.

GenServ submitters maintain ownership of their own database. The only way a researcher can get a GEDCOM file is to write to the owner and ask for it. Notes and documentation are included with the text of the report. You have to retype the information you want to use into your database, unless you can get a GEDCOM file from the submitter. Complete contact information about the owner of each database is included on each report. Members are encouraged to update their databases at least every two years.

Extracted Official Records

Some of the best official records available to genealogical researchers are extracted records. They are transcriptions of records that were created by governmental officials. For years individuals have been extracting birth records, marriage records, death records, cemetery records, and census records to help other genealogists with the hope of making a little money for their efforts. Many of these extracted records are found on county sites of the USGenWeb Project.

The Ellis Island Project (Available: www.ellisisland.org) is another example of extracted official records. Researchers are asked to register before using the site. Then they can search the site by first and last name. They can view extracted records or images of original records. For a fee the Ellis Island Project will send you a copy of the ship's manifest.

Several states have extracted vital records and have created searchable databases. The Illinois State Archive has one of the best marriage databases (Available: www.cyberdriveillinois.com /GenealogyMWeb/marrsrch.html). Illinois also has a Public Domain Land Tract Sales Database (Available: www.sos.state.il.us/GenealogyMWeb/landsrch.html).

Kentucky Vital Records Index (Available: http://ukcc.uky.edu/~vitalrec) extracts data acquired from Kentucky's State Office of Vital Statistics for noncommercial use only. Files contain an index to deaths, which have been registered in Kentucky from 1 January 1911 to 31 December 1992. Information includes the name of the deceased, date of death, age at death, and county of death and of residence. This is an excellent search engine for Kentucky deaths. Indexes for marriages and divorces are also available at this site.

Researchers can find Louisiana confederate soldiers pension applications at the Louisiana state archives Web site (Available: www.sec.state.la.us/archives/gen/cpa-index.htm).

Census Online (Available: www.census-online.com/links) provides a state-by-state index of locally extracted census records. It is not complete but worth a try.

Images of Historical Documents

Making of America (Available: moa.umdl.umich.edu and moa.cit.cornell.edu/moa) is a wonderful site that is split between the University of Michigan and Cornell University. (Researchers have to search each site separately.) Together these two sites cover thousands of books and journal articles, including the Official Records of the U.S. Navy during the Civil War. The index is user friendly and takes you right to the person in history you are seeking.

The National Archives has a searchable database that goes by the acronym ARC (Available: www.archives.gov/research_room/arc), with more than 124,000 images of historical value. ARC lets you execute keyword for digitized images. You can search by organization, person, or topic using the advanced search feature. I found an image of a Revolutionary War Land bounty certificate photos of individuals.

The Library of Congress also has a collection of prints and photographs with online images (Available: http://lcweb2.loc.gov/pp/pphome.html). If your ancestors were famous enough to have their pictures taken, the images may be on this site.

Multifunction Sites

Many genealogy sites on the Internet are multifunctional. They include online catalogs to their collection of genealogical resources, data compiled and submitted by researchers, extracted and indexed official records, images of documents and published works, links to the Web sites of individuals, and access to mailing lists. In essence, these sites appear to be one-stop-shops. Fortunately for genealogists, none of them have everything. This leaves room for competition for the commercial sites and the opportunity for researchers to pick and choose the sites that best meet their needs. The list of annotated Web addresses that follows represent some of the most helpful sites I have used. To find other sites I recommend *Virtual Roots 2.0 A Guide to Genealogy and Local History on the World Wide Web*, by Thomas Jay Kemp (Kemp, 2003; see bibliography in Chapter 4) and *Genealogical Research on the Web*, by Diane K Kovacs (Kovacs, 2002). Genealogy periodicals regularly publish articles about genealogy on the Web. One of the best articles I have ever seen is written by David A. Fryxell (Fryxell, 2003).

Largest Sites

Ancestry.com (Available: www.ancestry.com)

My personal membership to this site costs about $180.00 per year. Ancestry.com markets it in segments—basic membership, historical newspapers, census images and indexes, and records from the United Kingdom and Ireland. You can add on different segments, as you need access to them. A companion product—Ancestry Plus it marketed to libraries by the Gale Group (Available: www.galegroup.com). A two-user license costs $1,500.00 a year.

After you log into the site you see a search screen that asks for an ancestor's name and where he or she lived. The search engine checks all of the databases on the site and returns a list of hits.

You click on the hyperlink to check a specific database. The databases include Ancestry World Tree, Social Security Death Index, federal census indexes, Civil War service records, Civil War Pension Index, vital records, historical newspapers, and court records. Sometimes you get to see an image or an extraction of the actual record, which is great. Some indexes point you to the document, which you have to find and view yourself.

Of all the genealogy sites on the Web, Ancestry.com probably comes the closest to being the "one-stop-shop" every genealogists hopes for. You can find the "good stuff" here—and all from your home computer. My most exciting success came when I found a Civil War Pension Application for an ancestor about whom I had very little information. From the image of the pension application I was able to write for a copy of papers in the pension file and fill in lots of blanks.

This Web site adds new data everyday, so it can only get better. If you can't afford a personal membership, you can still use parts of the site for free. They do not charge for access to their Ancestry World Tree or message boards.

FamilySearch (Available: www.familysearch.org)

This absolutely free site has no pop-up commercials and is loaded with the largest collection of the best information on the Web.

A key feature of the user-submitted databases is the ability to download a GEDCOM file. Rather than printing out what you find here you can electronically export data from this site and import it into your computer at home. It saves a lot of keystrokes and possible errors inherent with that process. Again, readers should verify all data before making it a permanent part of their databases.

Genealogy.com (Available: www.genealogy.com)

This commercial Web site is an outgrowth of Web pages for users of Family Tree Maker software. User Web pages make this site unique among the larger multifunctional Web sites. Genealogy.com is the home for GenForum (Available: genforum.genealogy.com), probably the most extensive message board system for genealogists on the Web. You can type in a surname and be connected with other researchers who are working on the same name.

Genealogy.com has become an indispensable site for all researchers. It has census images, digitized books, family and local histories, passenger lists and records, and user Web Pages. Basic annual membership is $70.00 per year; deluxe premier membership levels cost more and add additional access. They do have some free offerings, too.

RootsWeb (Available: www.rootsweb.com)

RootsWeb is one of the oldest online services for genealogists. It started as a volunteer effort and has undergone some changes. Although still free, when accessing this site you have to fight off a lot of pop-up advertising. It continues to serve an essential segment of those pursuing online genealogy. It does things no other site does. Researchers need to use several different search engines to access user submitted databases. Categories listed on their main page include the following:

- Getting started

- Search engines and databases

- trees

- Mailing lists

- Message Boards

- Research Templates

- Web sites

- Other tools and resources

- Hosted volunteer projects

- Contributing to Roots Web

- Help

The guides to getting started in genealogy are especially good for beginners. Their compilation of mailing lists is unparalleled any place on the Web. The civilian registration for the draft during World War I is worth checking out (Available: http://userdb.rootsweb.com/ww1/draft/search.cgi). Overall, RootsWeb does a great job of bringing together and organizing tons of disparate genealogical data and making it available free to its users.

USGenWeb (Available: www.usgenweb.com)

This site is a county-by-county network of links, user-transcribed data and queries for the United States. Researchers start with a map of the United States and click on the state in which they want to conduct research. At this point, continuity ends and the pages for each state and each county are as different in content and appearance as a group of volunteers can make them. You will find pages for individual counties. Some have search engines; some do not. You can search the USGenWeb archives by state or all at once. Census transcriptions and tombstones top the list of unique features at this site. I found a marriage record for my grandparents on the Cochise County, Arizona page.

Family History Network (Available: www.everton.com)

This membership site may lack some of the pizzazz of some of the commercial sites, but it doesn't cost as much either. It includes a network of professional genealogists, who will suggest resources to check when you send them a query. The Family History Network also provides access to member-submitted genealogies.

OneGreatFamily.com (Available: www.onegreatfamily.com)

OneGreatFamily.com is another commercial site that uses compiled research of others. Individuals pay their membership fee and send them a GEDCOM file. Their search engine automatically searches all of the other databases and sends a message that they have found a number of possible ancestors.

Everyone who searches these Web sites has to evaluate the data they find. Sometimes the submitter does an excellent job of documenting the information and there is no reason to mistrust the family history they contain. Other times the information is so sketchy that all researchers will want to verify every detail, and the information is little more than a plausible lead for future exploration. Web sites that use the compiled data of other researchers usually provide the submitter's contact information. This is the right place to begin when you want to verify the information they have provided to the Internet.

Getting Started Using the Internet

How to Start Your Family History (Available: www.familysearch.org/Eng/Home/Welcome/frameset_information.asp)

This Web site introduces users to the six basic steps to starting family history research. The steps are:
1. Remember your ancestors.
2. Use sources in your home.
3. Ask relatives for information.
4. Choose a family or ancestor you want to learn more about.
5. See if someone else has already found the information.
6. Search records for your ancestor.

Family Tree Maker How-to Guide (Available: http://familytreemaker.genealogy.com/mainmenu.html?Welcome=1061086127)

This is a great way to begin family research. It has addresses and information about archives and libraries that all researchers will find helpful. It includes step-by-step instructions for locating family information and forms to facilitate research.

The Genealogy Home Page (Available: www.genhomepage.com)

This is another ideal site for the beginner. It is the ultimate page for beginning genealogists, with guides, libraries, software, maps and geography. Ancestry.com sponsors this starter site.

Genealogy Online (Available: www.genealogy.org)

This is a "must see" site with unique links to genealogy chat rooms and other online databases. It offers access to the free Ancestry.com databases plus a listing of the top 200 genealogy Web sites. It also provides a list of family history records and databases, organized and listed by state.

Genealogy Today (Available: www.genealogytoday.com)

This is a good starting place for anyone who is just getting started with genealogy. Seasoned researchers will find something they can use, too. Unique features include finding lost relatives on a first name basis, free tools for organizing research, knowledge base with old occupations and illnesses, registries, mailing lists, and support groups for adoptees.

Repositories of Primary Sources (Available: www.uidaho.edu/special-collections/Other.Repositories.html)

If you want to know which archives and libraries have major collections of primary source documents, check this Web site. It lists over 5,000 other Web sites, which describe their institution's holdings of manuscripts, archives, rare books, historical photographs, and other primary sources. All links are regularly tested for accuracy and appropriateness.

Ethnic Sites

Christine's Genealogy Web Site (Available: http://ccharity.com)

This is Christine Cheryl Charity's comprehensive collection of African American genealogical resources. It features lots of links to other sites and is an excellent source on African American research.

Hispanic Genealogical Center (Available: www.hispanicgenealogy.com)

This is a good place to start a search for Hispanic ancestors. They offer databases on families of northern Mexico, south Texas, California, and New Mexico. It has hundreds of links to other Hispanic genealogy sites.

JewishGen: The Home of Jewish Genealogy (Available: www.jewishgen.org)

This site features a discussion group, information files, searchable databases, special interest groups, and much more. This is a great beginning point for genealogists of Jewish ancestry.

Native American Genealogy
(Available: http://members.aol.com/bbbenge/front.html)

This site has many links to other Native American genealogy sites. It is a good springboard to more specific types of information.

General Databases

Database of Illinois Civil War Veterans
(Available: www.sos.state.il.us/departments/archives/datcivil.html)

This is a searchable database of Civil War veterans from Illinois. It is from a 1900ñ1901 publication that originated from the rosters maintained during the Civil War by the Illinois Adjutant General. The names of approximately 250,000 men, organized into 175 regiments, are found on this database.

Bible Records Online (Available: www.biblerecords.com)

This is a wonderful site for researchers who have looked everywhere else. It indexes nearly 1,000 Bibles with over 3,000 unique names. The search engine works well. It also has links to other online Bible records.

Irene's Genealogy Resources
(Available: www.thecore.com/~hand/genealogy/links/resource.html)

This site offers links to genealogy resources in five categories: books, graveyards, help resources, lookups, and research resources. It contains a good section on using the U.S. Federal Census.

RAND Genealogy Club
(Available: www.rand.org/contact/personal/Genea)

The RAND Genealogy Club is a group of RAND employees who provide this page to share information about genealogical resources. The site has an interesting list of helpful genealogy links.

Putting It All Together

When I use the Internet for research here is what I do. I start by opening my genealogy program and bringing up the ancestor on whom I want to focus. Then I logon to the Internet and open FamilySearch, Ancestry.com, GenServ, and HeritageQuest. With these resources open on my computer, first I do a search for the name I have selected on each of the Web sites I have open. If I find something, I check for the information on the other sites. It is possible that the same person has submitted the information I find in one or more of the databases. When I find something I can use, I put it in a temporary file until I can corroborate or verify the information.

Here is a worthwhile searching tip. Start with the name and add other qualifiers one at a time. Don't try to restrict the search too narrowly by adding everything you know about the person. If the database doesn't have as much information as you have, it won't return a hit, even though the name you are looking for is there.

Suggestions for Researchers

1. If you don't have a genealogy program on your computer, download Personal Ancestral File. It is free and it works fine.
2. Learn how to import and export GEDCOM files so you can share your genealogy with others.
3. Subscribe to one of the commercial sites on the Internet. If you are short on cash start with GenServ. Their membership fee is only $12.00 a year.
4. Join a mailing list, just to see how they work. You don't have to stay on it forever.

Summary

Anyone who tries to do genealogy today without a computer is working hard and not smart. Computers are affordable for most people and all libraries. They should all be hooked up to the Internet if users want to get the most out of their investment. People who come to libraries should find at least one public access computer to use for genealogy research, searching the Internet, or word processing. Computers are wonderful tools and people should use them to make their work easier.

Bibliography (Ratings Guide explanation follows last citation)

Clifford, Karen. 2001. *The Complete Beginner's Guide to Genealogy, the Internet, and Your Genealogy Computer Program.* Baltimore, MD: Genealogical Publishing Company.

This guide is a wonderful tool for anyone who uses the Internet for genealogical research. It combines traditional techniques and resources with accessing the Internet. It is specifically designed to facilitate beginning researchers to build complete family histories. **PPP**

David A. Fryxell. Simply the Best: 101 Best Web Sites *Family Tree Magazine* (August), 20–30.

Helm, Matthew L., and April Leah Helm. 2001. *Genealogy Online for Dummies: A Reference for the Rest of Us.* 3rd ed. New York: Wiley Publishing.

Keeping up with the changes in online genealogy is nearly impossible. Online genealogy changes so much every year that revising a guide like this one almost means starting over from scratch. The authors do a good job of covering what is on the Internet for genealogists. The CD that comes with the book provides samples of several genealogy programs for the computer and one complete, fully functional program. **PP**

Hendrickson, Nancy. 2003. *Finding your Roots Online.* Cincinnati, OH: Betterway Books.

This book is a step-by-step tool designed for beginning, as well as seasoned, researchers. It presents real example of using the Internet for research. The author's understandable method covers the essentials of sound genealogical research. Researchers will learn how to get the most out of Internet resources and recognize when a research problem can't be solved online. **PP**

Kovacs, Diane K. 2002. *Genealogical Research on the Web.* New York: Neal-Schuman Publishers.

This book does a good job of teaching the beginner how to get started with basic research. It shows you how to use the Internet to find and use genealogical reference and documentation. It details how to find living family members and fellow researchers, and how to secure their assistance in extending one's ancestral lines. Genealogical Research on the Web has lots of anecdotal material that give life to the points the author is making. **PPP**

Lemmon, Stephen. 2001. *Personal Ancestral File 5 Features.* Hurricane, UT: The Studio. Videocassette.

This video presents detailed instructions for anyone who wants to use Personal Ancestral File. It teaches navigation of the software to make it easy to add and manipulate data. It also demonstrated how to print a variety of reports and import and export files. **P**

McClintock, Jan. 1999. *Internet Genealogy: What You Can and Cannot Do.* (Available: www.leisterpro.com/doc/Articles/IntGen/InternetGenealogy.html)

This is an excellent article on using the Internet for genealogical research. Because you cannot type in a name and get your family history back to Adam, it is good to find out how to do some of the basics. It is a "must read" for anyone who is just beginning to use the Internet as a research tool.

McClure, Rhonda R. 2000. *The Complete Idiot's Guide to Online Genealogy.* Indianapolis, IN: Macmillan.

This book shows the beginner how to get started in genealogical research and then moves to how to use computers and the Internet to locate data about ones ancestors. The last part of the book provides direction on creating genealogy Web pages. Easy to read, this book will help researchers focus on their own research. **PPP**

Porter, Pamela Boyer, et. al. 2003. *Online Roots: How to Discover your Family History and Heritage with the Power of the Internet.* Nashville: Rutledge Hill Press.

The author is a Certified Genealogical Records Specialist. She shares her expertise with other researchers in this book. She puts in plain words how to search on the Internet, how to evaluate the worth of what you discover, and techniques to make complete use of the resources of the Internet. Issues addressed include:

- evaluating the sources,

- examining modern lists and resources,

- finding leads to primary sources, and

- locating photographs on the web.

Using the Internet can be difficult. *Online Roots* makes your hunt more effective. **P**

Ratings Guide

The ratings for each bibliography describe not only what each resource contains, but also how it might fit into the library collection. Some of the materials are more appropriate for larger libraries with substantial budgets, and others belong in collections of any size—even in the personal research collection. To help you identify materials most appropriate for your collection, each resource is marked as either "L" for libraries and "P" for personal. They are ranked from one letter for recommended, two letters for preferred, and three letters for essential.

Chapter 12

Getting Help from Professional Researchers

Nearly all genealogists want to do their own research—mostly because it is the least expensive way to do it. They also carry in their heads tidbits of information they may have heard or seen somewhere, but never wrote them down. These clues may be the key to solving a brick wall in the search for their ancestors. So, it is reasonable to think, "If I have to write all of this stuff down just to give it to a professional, why bother?"

Also lurking at the back of the genealogist's mind could be the fear of a long-term financial commitment with no promise of any result.

What to Look for in This Chapter

Even the most experienced genealogists will need the help of a professional researcher sometime. In the long run it may be the least expensive way to go. In this chapter we will explore the reasons for paying someone to look up some information for you. We will also tell you how to locate individuals who may be willing to do research.

Hiring a Professional Genealogist

Seeking the help of a professional researcher can be either a first step or a last resort. People who are just getting started with their genealogy may need someone with experience, who knows his or her way around research facilities, to do a survey for them. Or, an experienced researcher may be at the "end of his or her rope" and doesn't know where to turn. Some family researchers with overseas ancestors may not speak or read the language. They may need to turn to a professional in the country of origin for help. In any case, hiring someone else to do your genealogical research is not uncommon. In some cases, it may be better to call on a professional researcher that lives in the area of your research and pay a modest fee, than to spend a thousand dollars or more to travel to the area and do the research yourself. On one occasion my mother traveled from Arizona to Missouri to find information on her great-grandmother. She spent over a thousand dollars and came home empty-handed. Years later I found the information she was looking for through an e-mail connection.

The easiest way to find a professional researcher is through libraries and archives. Every major research facility can probably supply a list of people who will do research for a fee. Even small institutions like local public libraries can probably furnish names and addresses of a few people in the community who will do research.

In a personal e-mail (July 29, 2003), Don Litzer, a reference librarian, relates the following anecdote:

> "There is a person in our community that offers her services as a professional genealogist. She is experienced, conversant in local resources, and a regular library user. If we encounter a patron whose genealogical information needs, extend beyond the normal services of the library we refer them to a professional who lives in the area. They need to specifically ask us for the contact information. We have to be careful not to endorse a particular professional researcher. So, we provide the names of several qualified researchers."

This is a good way introduce library patrons to the opportunity of hiring a professional genealogist.

Main Concerns

People who consider hiring a professional genealogist most often ask the same types of important questions.

1. How much will it cost?

Professional services could be as simple as pulling an exact citation and making a copy of it. This service could cost as little as $10.00. Most professionals charge between $15.00 and $35.00 per hour, plus copying and mailing expenses. Translations may cost as much as $50.00 per hour. Scanning a document and sending it as an e-mail attachment will cost about $5.00 plus the charge for research. Most researchers will have a minimum of $100.00 just to get started, unless you just want a quick look-up.

Many professional genealogists advertise their services in genealogical periodicals like *Everton's Family History Magazine, Heritage Quest, Forum*, and others. Several Web sites list genealogy professionals. GenealogyPro.com (Available: www.genealogypro.com) is a directory of independent genealogists and other related professionals. Genealogy Quest (Available: www.genealogy-quest.com) is a genealogy bureau that connects professional genealogists with genealogists who need the help of a professional. Anyone can use the Internet or a magazine to contact a professional to determine his or her fees and the area of expertise.

2. Can I rely on the information I get?

Generally, yes, but professional researchers are humans, and they can make mistakes. Asking for photocopies of original sources whenever possible is one way to verify the information they dig up for you. Make sure they cite their sources and provide a copy of the text they find.

3. How do I find a professional genealogist I can trust?

The most important question in hiring a professional genealogist is "How do I determine if he or she is qualified to do the job I want him or her to do?" Several organizations accredit or certify researchers. The people on their lists can generally be trusted to do a good job. Genealogists can contact these organizations for the names of qualified researchers in their area of interest.

Many professional genealogists are listed through their certifying or accrediting organizations. Contact one or more of the groups listed in this section for a list of their professional genealogists. Contact the top recommended individuals. If the person you contact lacks the expertise in a particular area of research, he or she will probably refer you to another researcher who has the appropriate skills.

The genealogist who is hiring a professional needs to ask for the credentials of the individual. Check the education and training, professional affiliations, publications, foreign languages (if relevant), and access to records of the professional. If the research involves uncommon problems, ask what expertise the professional has in dealing with the specific issues. After you screen the researcher, as with any contract, you need to establish three components of your agreement: costs, tasks, and deadlines.

Be sure to discuss fees in the first query letter. Find out how much the professional will charge and the method of payment required. Most professionals want some money up front and then work on an hourly basis after that. It is a good idea to set a dollar limit with the researcher. It is just good business to have a mutual understanding about your budget before any work is done.

Once you agree upon the fees, you and the researcher will need to agree on exactly what the researcher is expected to do. This requires letting the researcher know what you want. Will he or she work on only one or two ancestral lines or will he research all of them?

Finally, establish a time frame, or series of checkpoints for completing the identified tasks. Allow the researcher a reasonable amount of time to do the work.

4. What can I do before hiring a professional?

The best way to get your money's worth from a professional is to do your own homework first. You need to bring together all of the facts you have on the individual. In one of the workshops I do, I suggest that you interview your ancestor. Fill out the Ancestor Interview Form (see Figure 8.1).

The next step is to identify your sources. You might have a census record, or a marriage certificate, or a death certificate. You should also tell the professional all of the places you have searched but didn't find anything. If you have any personal knowledge or family traditions that may or may not be true, give that information to the professional, as well.

Sandy Day, Genealogy Librarian at the Schiappa Library in Steubenville, Ohio, offers the following advice (via personal e-mail, July 29, 2003):

> "Before hiring a professional, find out exactly what the fee is. (Do they charge by the hour or only by services provided? Most charge by the hour but some charge base fee for doing a particular search such as seeking vital records in a courthouse.)

> "Find out if they will send you a detailed description of sources they have researched. (Similar to a bibliography.)

"Find out approximately how long it will be before you hear from them. (Surely most have given you an estimate of when you should hear back from them.)

"If you have performed some preliminary work yourself, make sure you let the researcher know this. (Example: If you are requesting census work and already have performed some of this on your own, make sure they do not duplicate your work since you would be paying them for something you already have!)

"Lastly, be precise and brief. (Let the researcher know exactly what you are seeking, no generalizations here! Also even though they may require background info, too much of this can bog down what they are supposed to be seeking for you!)"

Mary Douglass, CGRS, a Certified Genealogical Records Specialist in Salina, Kansas, shared the following (via personal e-mail, August 7, 2003):

"The amount of information provided by the client is varied. More knowledgeable clients will ask for specific information about one person, giving a location and time frame. These requests are usually simple record retrieval jobs. I still get a lot of 'find everything for X in Kansas'. Then I have to work with the client to see what she or he really wants.

"I also do lineage papers for admission to a patriotic society. This is an entirely different category of research. Sometimes the client will provide an entire genealogy. I have to find the documentation for it. And sometimes their lineage is in error. Then I have to determine the correct lineage. That is a very sensitive area.

"Distance is usually the main reason my clients contact me. While I live in Salina, Kansas, I have yet to work in Saline County for a client. I cover most of north central and northwest Kansas. Some clients want the assurances that come from working with a board certified professional.

"Most of my research is done in courthouses around Kansas, libraries, newspaper, and/or cemeteries. Lineage papers require more correspondence and use of the Internet.

"Results depend on the client's needs and what records were available. I report on negative as well as positive searches.

"I send the client a detailed report explaining what records I searched and why, how I interpreted those records and photocopies of the records so the client may make his own interpretation. I also include maps of the area, historically and current. Part of my report is a suggestion for further research.

"I charge $35.00 per hour with an initial retainer of $100.00, plus expenses. All this is detailed on my contract—see my Web site.

"Most of my customers are very pleased and frequently retain me for further work. Some have become long-term clients, coming back for more research years after our initial contract.

"In my years of taking clients, I have been "stiffed" on fees enough times to require an initial retainer.

"New researchers rely heavily on the Internet, rather than using the traditional record repositories or courthouses, libraries, etc.

"I consider client work an opportunity to improve the research skills of the client by showing him or her, the 'why' as well as the 'how' of what I do for them.

"Genealogists are the nicest people on earth!"

Michael John Neill (Neill, 2003) has published an article on the Internet, entitled, "Hiring A Professional Genealogist." The article offers some valuable insights for anyone who is considering hiring a professional researcher.

Certifying or Accrediting Organizations

Board for Certification of Genealogists

Founded in 1964, the Board for Certification of Genealogists (BCG) (Available: www.bcgcertification.org) has promoted expertise and high standards among professional genealogists. Board-certified genealogists must pass rigorous tests and subscribe to a code of ethics. To ensure that their skills are continually updated, certified genealogists are reevaluated every five years. The board has developed specific and discriminating examinations in six categories. BCG is independent of any society, although its trustees and judges are always national leaders in the field.

The Roster of Board Certified Genealogist is available from the board. It details qualifications and services available from each genealogist.

Association of Professional Genealogists

The Association of Professional Genealogists (APG) (Available: www.apgen.org) was founded in 1979 to promote standards and ethics in the genealogical research, and now claims over 1,400 members worldwide. Members include family historians, professional researchers, librarians, archivists, writers, editors, consultants, computer specialists, and many others.

APG has an online directory that includes biographies of its members, along with their services, research and geographic specialties. This directory is available on APG's Web site (Available: www.apgen.org/directory/index.php).

International Accreditation

International Commission for the Accreditation of Professional Genealogists (ICAPGEN) (Available: www.icapgen.org/Programs/aglist.htm) has a list of accredited genealogists who have passed the accreditation examinations. Accreditation indicates that an individual has passed the accreditation examination and has agreed to abide by ethical standards. They must renew their accreditation every five years.

ProGenealogists Group

The ProGenealogists Family History Research Group (Available: www.progenealogists.com) conducts genealogy research at the Family History Library in Salt Lake City and in archives worldwide. These professionals specialize in researching and documenting family histories. They are accredited by a variety of organizations.

Genealogists looking for a professional researcher can also use one of the Web's all-purpose search engines and type in "+genealogists +professional +(state)" (fill in the state where you want to have someone do research). They will get more names than they can check out in an hour or so.

Everton's Family History Magazine

Every year in the September/October issue of *Everton's Family History Magazine*, they publish a pullout directory of professional researchers. The directory provides the name of the professional, contact information, and their experience in years. The directory also includes a long list of area or subject specialties offered by the researcher.

Suggestions for Librarians

1. Create a notebook or file that lists professional genealogists.
2. Create a list of local genealogists who will do research for a fee.

Suggestions for Researchers

*   If you have run up against a brick wall in your research, seriously consider hiring a professional to help you get around it.

*   Take the time to explore the cost of hiring a professional. You may find the cost affordable and worth the effort.

*   "Interview" the ancestor who represents your most difficult brick wall. Organizing what you already know may help the professional you hire, or you if you choose not to hire someone.

Summary

It is not unreasonable to hire someone to do genealogical research. In fact it could be the smartest, least expensive, and most efficient option of all. Librarians need to have information about hiring a professional to give their patrons access to this option. There are several good reasons to consider hiring a professional genealogist:

*   Genealogy records are in a foreign language.

*   Political obstacles prevent normal access to the records.

*   Access to the records is limited to members or those with appropriate credentials.

*   Travel distance is too great or too costly to make on-site access impossible.

*   Research skills for certain types of records are weak.

*   Physical or visual disability makes research difficult or impossible.

*   Verifying information is necessary before publishing a book.

*   Resolving conflict in data is required.

- Time is short and a deadline is at hand.

- Every possible record has been searched, and research has reached a "brick wall."

Bibliography (Ratings Guide explanation follows last citation)

Everton's Family History Magazine (Staff). 2003. Direct Connect: 2003 Directory of Professional Researchers. *Everton's Family History Magazine* (September/October): 98a.

Every year in the fall, Everton's publishes a directory of professional researchers. This is one way to get a current list.

Mills, Elizabeth S. 2001. Professional Genealogy: *A Manual for Researchers, Writers, Editors, Lecturers, and Librarians.* Baltimore, MD: Genealogical Publishing Company.

A different professional researcher has written each chapter of this hefty tome. Chapter topics include professional preparation, ethics, research skills, writing, editing, and publishing.
Those who hire a professional researcher expect high standards, skill, and experience. Professional genealogists mirror all of these traits as they take on a wide-range of activities, including archival administration and preservation, book selling, broadcasting, editing, lecturing, publishing, software development, and teaching.
This book is a must for anyone who engages in these activities for hire. **PPP**

Neill, Michael, John. Hiring A Professional Genealogist. *Ancestry Daily News* (Summer 2003). Available: www.rootdig.com/professional.

This Web page gives a good overview of the reasons for hiring a professional and how to do it.

Ratings Guide

The ratings for each bibliography describe not only what each resource contains, but also how it might fit into the library collection. Some of the materials are more appropriate for larger libraries with substantial budgets, and others belong in collections of any size—even in the personal research collection. To help you identify materials most appropriate for your collection, each resource is marked as either "L" for libraries and "P" for personal. They are ranked from one letter for recommended, two letters for preferred, and three letters for essential.

PART III

HANDY GENEALOGICAL
RESOURCES AND WORKSHEETS

TOOL KIT 1
THE RESOURCE BIBLIOGRAPHY

The resource bibliography is a list of all the works that are annotated at the end of each chapter. It is a good start for a collection in a public library. We offer some suggestions on how to use this list of genealogical materials.

Resource Bibliography

Anderson, Robert Charles. 1999. *The Great Migration: Immigrants to New England, 1634–1635*. Boston: Great Migration Study Project, New England Historic Genealogical Society.

Baggett, Joan J. 1998. *Genealogical Research for the Beginner: Why, Where, How*. Tampa, FL: J&P Genealogical Research.

Banks, Paul N., and Roberta Pilette, eds. 2000. *Preservation: Issues and Planning*. Chicago: American Library Association.

Bentley, Elizabeth Petty. 1999. *The Genealogist's Address Book*. Baltimore, MD: Genealogical Publishing Company.

Bentley, Elizabeth Petty. 2001. *Directory of Family Associations*. Baltimore, MD: Genealogical Publishing Company.

Best, Laura. 2003. *Genealogy for the First Time: Research Your Family History*. New York: Sterling Publishing.

Burroughs, Tony. 2003. *Finding Your Family History in the Attic*. Pleasant Grove, UT: 123 Genealogy. Videocassette.

Carmack, Sharon DeBartolo. 2000. *A Genealogist's Guide to Discovering Your Immigrant and Ethnic Ancestors*. Cincinnati, OH: Betterway Books.

Carmack, Sharon DeBartolo. 2002. *Your Guide to Cemetery Research*. Cincinnati, OH: Betterway Books.

Carmack, Sharon DeBartolo. 2003. *You Can Write Your Family History*. Cincinnati, OH: Betterway Books.

Carson, Dian, ed. 2002. *Directory of Genealogical and Historical Societies in the U.S. and Canada*. Niwot, CO: Iron Gate Publishing.

Clark, Murtie J. 1996. *The Pension Lists of 1792–95; With Other Revolutionary War Pension Records*. Baltimore, MD: Genealogical Publishing Company.

Clifford, Karen. 2001. *The Complete Beginner's Guide to Genealogy, the Internet, and Your Genealogy Computer Program*. Baltimore, MD: Genealogical Publishing Company.

Coletta, John Philip. 2003. *Finding Your Italian Roots: The Complete Guide for Americans*. Baltimore, MD: Genealogical Publishing Company.

Croom, Emily Anne. 1996. *Unpuzzling Your Past Workbook: Essential Forms and Letters for All Genealogists*. Cincinnati, OH: Betterway Books.

Croom, Emily Anne. 2000. *The Sleuth Book for Genealogists: Strategies for More Successful Family History Research*. Cincinnati, OH: Betterway Books.

Croom, Emily Anne. 2003. *The Genealogist's Companion and Sourcebook*. Cincinnati, OH: Betterway Books.

Croom, Emily Anne. 2003. *Unpuzzling Your Past: The Best Selling Basic Guide to Genealogy*. Cincinnati, OH: Betterway Books.

Crowe, Elizabeth Powell. 2001. *Genealogy Online*. New York: Osborne/McGraw-Hill.

Crume, Rick. 2002. Leaders of the Stacks. *Family Tree Magazine* (October): 26.

Daughters of the American Revolution. 2003. *DAR Patriot Index*. Washington, DC: National Society of the Daughters of the American Revolution.

Dollarhide, William, and Ronald Bremer. 1998. *America's Best Genealogy Resource Centers*. Bountiful, UT: HeritageQuest.

Eakle, Arlene H., and Linda E. Brinkerhoff. 2002. *Family History for Fun and Profit: The Genealogy Research Process*. Tremonton, UT: The Genealogical Institute.

Everton Publishers (Staff), ed. 2002. *The Handybook for Genealogists: United States of America*. 10th ed. Logan, UT: Everton Publishers.

Everton's Family History Magazine (Staff), ed. 2003. Direct Connect: 2003 Directory of Professional Researchers. *Everton's Family History Magazine* (September/October): 98a.

Family Chronicle (Staff), ed. 2003. *500 Brickwall Solutions to Genealogy Problems, 2003*. Toronto: Mooreshead Magazines.

Fleming, Ann Carter. 1997. *Teaching Genealogy: Tips and Techniques for Successful Adult Classes*. Valley Forge, PA: Pennsylvania Cradle of a Nation. Audiocassette.

Galford, Ellen. 2001. *The Genealogy Handbook: The Complete Guide to Tracing Your Family Tree*. Pleasantville, NY: Reader's Digest.

Greenwood, Val. D. 2000. *The Researcher's Guide to American Genealogy*. Baltimore, MD: Genealogical Publishing Company.

Hall-Ellis, Sylvia D., and Frank W. Hoffman. 1999. *Grantsmanship for Small Libraries and School Library Media Centers*. Englewood, CO: Libraries Unlimited.

Helm, Matthew L., and April Leah Helm. 2001. *Genealogy Online for Dummies: A Reference for the Rest of Us*. 3rd ed. New York: Wiley Publishing.

Hendrickson, Nancy. 2003. *Finding Your Roots Online*. Cincinnati, OH: Betterway Books.

Hill, Mary E. Vassel. 2000. FamilyRoots Organizer. Hurricane, UT: The Studio. Videocassette.

Hinckley, Kathleen W. 1999. *Locating Lost Family Members and Friends: Modern Genealogical Research Techniques for Locating the People of Your Past and Present*. Cincinnati, OH: Betterway Books.

Hinckley, Kathleen W. 2002. *Your Guide to The Federal Census For Genealogists, Researchers, and Family Historians*. Cincinnati, OH: Betterway Books.

Holt, Marilyn Irvin. 1994. *The Orphan Trains: Placing Out in America*. Lincoln, NE: University of Nebraska Press.

Howells, Cyndi. 2001. *Cyndi's List: A Comprehensive List Of 70,000 Genealogy Sites on the Internet*. Baltimore, MD: Genealogical Publishing Company.

Hunter, Julius K. 2000. *Digging For Family Roots: A Beginner's Guide to African American Genealogical Research*. St. Louis, MO: Julius K. Hunter & Friends African American Research Collection in the St. Louis County Library.

Johnson, Richard S., and Debra Johnson Knox. 1999. *How to Locate Anyone Who Is or Has Been in the Military: Armed Forces Locator Guide*. 8th ed. Spartanburg, SC: MIE Publishing.

Jones, Henry Z. 1993. *Psychic Roots: Serendipity and Intuition in Genealogy*. Baltimore, MD: Genealogical Publishing Company.

Kemp, Thomas Jay. 2000. *The Genealogist's Virtual Library: Full-Text Books on The World Wide Web*. Wilmington, DE: Scholarly Resources.

Kemp, Thomas Jay. 2003 *Virtual Roots 2.0: A Guide to Genealogy and Local History On the World Wide Web*. Wilmington, DE: Scholarly Resources.

Knox, Debra Johnson. 2003. *WWII Military Records: A Family Historian's Guide*. Spartanburg, SC: MIE Publishing.

Kovacs, Diane K. 2002. *Genealogical Research On The Web*. New York: Neal-Schuman Publishers.

Lemmon, Stephen. 2001. *Personal Ancestral File 5 Features*. Hurricane, UT: The Studio. Videocassette.

Lennon, Rachal Mills. 2002. *Tracing Ancestors Among the Five Civilized Tribes: Southeastern Indians Prior to Removal*. Baltimore, MD: Genealogical Publishing Company.

McClure, Rhonda R. 2000. *The Complete Idiot's Guide to Online Genealogy*. Indianapolis, IN: Macmillan.

McClure, Rhonda R. 2003. *Finding Your Famous and Infamous Ancestors: Uncover the Celebrities, Rogues, and Royals in Your Family Tree*. Cincinnati, OH: Betterway Books.

McManus, Stephen, Thomas Churchill, and Donald Thompson. 2003. *Civil War Research Guide: A Guide for Researching Your Civil War Ancestor*. Mechanicsburg, PA: Stackpole Books.

Melnyk, Marcia Yannizze. 2000. *The Weekend Genealogist: Timesaving Techniques for Effective Research*. Cincinnati, OH: Betterway Books.

Melnyk, Marcia Yannizze. 2002. *The Genealogist's Question and Answer Book: Solutions and Advice for Maximizing Your Research Results*. Cincinnati, OH: Betterway Books.

Mills, Elizabeth S. 1997. *Evidence! Citation and Analysis for the Family Historian*. Baltimore, MD: Genealogical Publishing Company.

Mills, Elizabeth S. 2001. *Professional Genealogy: A Manual For Researchers, Writers, Editors, Lecturers, and Librarians*. Baltimore, MD: Genealogical Publishing Company.

Neagles, James C. 1990. *The Library of Congress: A Guide to Genealogical and Historical Research*. Salt Lake City, UT: Ancestry Publishing.

Neill, Michael, John. Hiring A Professional Genealogist. *Ancestry Daily News* (Summer 2003). Available: www.rootdig.com/professional.

Nevius, Erin. 2003. *The Family Guide Book to Europe: Your Passport to Tracing Your Genealogy Across Europe*. Cincinnati, OH: Betterway Books.

Ogden, Sherelyn. 1999. *Preservation Of Library and Archival Material: A Manual*. Andover, MA: Northeast Document Conservation Center.

Pfeiffer, Laura Szucs. 2000. *Hidden Sources:_Family History in Unlikely Places*. Orem, UT: Ancestry Publishing.

Porter, Pamela Boyer, et. al. 2003. *Online Roots: How to Discover Your Family History and Heritage With the Power of the Internet*. Nashville: Rutledge Hill Press.

Quillen, W. Daniel. 2003. *Secrets of Tracing Your Ancestors*. Cold Spring Harbor, NY: Open Road Publishing.

Renick, Barbara. 2003. *Genealogy 101: How to Trace Your Family's History and Heritage.* Nashville: Rutledge Hill Press.

Rice, Donal, and Anne Collins. 2000. *How to Trace Your Family History: A Brief Guide to Sources of Genealogical Research for Beginners.* Dublin, Ireland: Dublin Corporation Public Libraries.

Rose, James M., and Alice Eichloz. 2003. *Black Genesis: A Resource Book for African-American Genealogy.* Baltimore, MD: Genealogical Publishing Company.

Schmal, John P., and Donna S. Morales. 2002. *Mexican-American Genealogical Research: Following the Paper Trail to Mexico.* Bowie, MD: Heritage Press.

Shaefer, Christina K. 1997. *Guide to Naturalization records of the United States.* Baltimore, MD: Genealogical Publishing Company.

Smith, Franklin Smith, and Emily Anne Croom. 2003. *A Genealogist's Guide to Discovering Your African-American Ancestors: How to Find and Record Your Unique Heritage.* Cincinnati, OH: Betterway Books.

Smith, Juliana Szucs. 2003. *The Ancestry Family Historian's Address Book: A Comprehensive Lists of Local, State, and Federal Agencies and Institutions and Ethnic and Genealogical Organizations.* Orem, UT: Ancestry Publishing.

Smolenyak, Megan. 2002. *Honoring Our Ancestors: Inspiring Stories of the Quest for Our Roots.* Orem, UT: Ancestry Publishing.

Sperry, Kip. 2003. *Abbreviations and Acronyms: A Guide for Family Historians.* Provo, UT: Ancestry Publishing.

Szucs, Loretto Dennis. 2000. *Ellis Island: Tracing Your Family History Through America's Gateway.* Provo, UT: Ancestry Publishing.

Szucs, Loretto Dennis, and Sandra Hargraves Leubking, eds. 1997. *The Source: A Guidebook of American Genealogy.* Salt Lake City, UT: Ancestry Publishing.

Thorndale, William, and William Dollarhide. 2000. *Map Guide to the U.S. Federal Censuses 1790–1920.* Baltimore, MD: Genealogical Publishing Company.

United States. National Archives and Records Administration. 2000. *National Archives Microfilm Resources for Research: A Comprehensive Catalog*. Washington, DC: National Archives and Records Administration.

United States. National Archives and Records Administration. 1995. *Guide to Federal Records in the National Archives of the United States*. 3 vols. Washington, DC: National Archives and Records Administration.

United States. National Archives and Records Administration. 1999. *Holocaust-Era Assets: A Finding Aid to Records at the National Archives at College Park, MD*. Washington, DC: National Archives and Records Administration.

Warren, Paula Stuart. 2002. Navigating the National Archives. *Family Tree Magazine* (October): 40.

Warren, Paula Stuart, and James W. Warren. 2001. *Your Guide to the Family History Library*. Cincinnati, OH: Betterway Books.

Woodtor, Dee Palmer. 1999. *Finding a Place Called Home: A Guide to African-American Genealogy and Historical Identity*. New York: Bantam Books.

TOOL KIT 2
NATIONAL ARCHIVES REGIONAL COLLECTIONS

National Archives—Northeast Region (Boston)
380 Trapelo Road
Waltham, MA 02154-6399
Phone: 866-406-2379
Fax: 781-663-0154
Hours: Mon. through Fri. and first Sat., 8:00 a.m. to 4:30 p.m.

Serves Connecticut, Maine, Massachusetts, New Hampshire, Rhode Island, and Vermont.

National Archives—Northeast Region
10 Conte Drive
Pittsfield, MA 01201-8230
Phone: 413-236-3604
Fax: 413-236-3609
Hours: Mon. through Fri., 8 a.m. to 4 p.m.
Wed., 8 a.m. to 9 p.m.
Closed weekends and federal holidays

National Archives—Northeast Region
201 Varick Street
New York, NY 10014-4811
Phone: 212-401-1620
Fax: 212-401-1638
E-mail: newyork.archives@nara.gov
Hours: Mon. through Fri., 8:00 a.m. to 4:30 p.m., third Sat. (microfilm only, not naturalization records), 8:30 a.m. to 4:00 p.m.

Serves New Jersey, New York, Puerto Rico, and the Virgin Islands—federal census records for all states and New York passenger arrivals on microfilm, also naturalization records for New York, New Jersey, and Puerto Rico.

National Archives—Mid-Atlantic Region
900 Market Street, Room 1350
Philadelphia, PA 19107
Phone: 215-606-0100
Fax: 215-606-0116
E-mail: Philadelphia.archives@nara.gov

Hours: Mon. through Fri., 8:00 a.m. to 5:00 p.m., second Sat., 8:00 a.m. to 4:00 p.m.

Serves Delaware, Pennsylvania, Maryland, Virginia, and West Virginia—primarily genealogical records.

National Archives—Great Lakes Region
7358 South Pulaski Road
Chicago, IL 60629-5898
Phone: 312-353-0162
Fax: 773-948-9050
Hours: Mon. and Wed. through Fri., 8:00 a.m. to 4:15 p.m., Tues., 8:00 a.m. to 8:30 p.m.

Serves Illinois, Indiana, Michigan, Minnesota, Ohio, and Wisconsin.

National Archives—Southeast Region
East Point, GA 30344-2593
Phone: 404-763-7477
Fax: 404-763-7059
Hours: Mon. and Wed. through Fri., 7:30 a.m. to 4:30 p.m., Tues., 7:30 a.m. to 9:30 p.m.

Serves Alabama, Georgia, Florida, Kentucky, Mississippi, North Carolina, South Carolina, and Tennessee.

National Archives–Central Plains Region
2312 East Bannister Road
Kansas City, MO 64131-3011
Phone: 816-268-8000
Fax: 816-268-8037
E-mail: kansascity.archives@nara.gov
Hours: Mon. through Fri., 8:00 a.m. to 4:30 p.m., third Sat., 9:00 a.m. to 4:00 p.m.

Serves Iowa, Kansas, Missouri, and Nebraska.

National Archives Southwest Region
501 West Felix Street
PO Box 6216
Fort Worth, TX 76115-3405
Phone: 817-334-5525
Fax: 817-334-5511
Hours: Mon. through Fri., 8:00 a.m. to 4:00 p.m., Wed., 8:00 a.m. to 9:00 p.m.

Serves Arkansas, Louisiana, New Mexico, Oklahoma, and Texas.

National Archives—Rocky Mountain Region
Denver Federal Center, Building 48
West 6th Avenue and Kipling Street
PO Box 25307

Denver, CO 80225-0307
Phone: 303-236-0817 or 303-236-9354
Fax: 303-407-5707
Hours: Mon. through Fri., 7:30 a.m. to 3:45 p.m., Wed., 7:30 a.m. to 4:45 p.m.

Serves Colorado, Montana, North Dakota, South Dakota, Utah, and Wyoming.

National Archives—Pacific Region
1000 Commodore Drive
San Bruno, CA 94066-2350
Phone: 650-238-3500
Fax: 650-238-3511
Hours: Mon. through Fri., 8:00 a.m. to 4:00 p.m., Wed., 8:00 a.m. to 8:00 p.m.

Serves California, except southern California; Hawaii; Nevada, except Clark County; and the Pacific Ocean area—federal court records, Bureau of Indian Affairs records, and Chinese immigration records.

National Archives—Pacific Southwest Region
24000 Avila Road
First Floor–East Entrance
Laguna Niguel, CA 92677-3497
Phone: 949-360-2641
Fax: 949-360-2624
Hours: Mon. through Fri., and first Sat., 8:00 a.m. to 4:30 p.m.

Serves Arizona, the southern California counties of Imperial, Inyo, Kern, Los Angeles, Orange, Riverside, San Bernardino, San Diego, San Luis Obispo, Santa Barbara, and Ventura, and Clark County, Nevada.

National Archives Pacific Alaska Region
6125 Sand Point Way NE
Seattle, WA 98115-7999
Phone: 206-526-6501
Fax: 206-526-6545
Hours: Mon. through Fri., 7:45 a.m. to 4:00 p.m., Tues., 5:00 a.m. to 9:00 p.m.

Serves Idaho, Oregon, and Washington—federal census for all states, and regional federal records.

National Archives Alaska Region
Federal Office Building
654 West Third Avenue, Room 012
Anchorage, AK 99501-2145
Phone: 907-271-2441
Fax: 907-271-2442
E-mail: Alaska.archives@nara.gov
Hours: Mon. through Fri., and first Sat., 8:00 a.m. to 4:00 p.m.

Serves Alaska.

TOOL KIT 3
GETTING STARTED HANDOUTS

Ancestor Interview Form

Question	Answer	Verified	Approximate	Next Step
Name	_____			_____
Birth date	_____	☐	☐	_____
Birth place	_____	☐	☐	_____
Marriage date	_____	☐	☐	_____
Marriage place	_____	☐	☐	_____
Death date	_____	☐	☐	_____
Death place	_____	☐	☐	_____
Cause / death	_____	☐	☐	_____
Spouse	_____	☐	☐	_____
Father	_____	☐	☐	_____
Mother	_____	☐	☐	_____
Children	_____	☐	☐	_____
Occupation	_____	☐	☐	_____
Religion	_____	☐	☐	_____
School	_____	☐	☐	_____
Places lived	_____	☐	☐	_____
Other	_____	☐	☐	_____
Other	_____	☐	☐	_____

Tool 3.1 Ancestor Interview Form

Checklist of Personal Genealogical Sources

___ Abstracts of title
___ Administrations of wills
___ Annulment decrees
___ Automobile insurance
___ Bankruptcy filings
___ Birth announcements
___ Burial reports
___ Cemetery records
___ Church membership lists
___ Church transfers
___ Club membership records
___ Contracts
___ Court judgments
___ Criminal convictions
___ Deeds
___ Drivers license
___ Employment applications
___ Family Bible
___ Family histories
___ Fire insurance policies
___ Funeral home receipts
___ Guardianship documents
___ Honor roll recognition
___ Hunting license
___ Income tax records
___ Job transfers
___ Land grants
___ Letters
___ Loan applications
___ Marriage applications
___ Medical checkups
___ Military disability papers
___ Military pension
___ Military service medals
___ Ministerís records
___ Motor vehicle registration
___ Newspaper clippings
___ Passenger lists
___ Pension applications
___ Personal property tax records
___ Probate records
___ Property settlements
___ Real estate tax records
___ Scholarship applications
___ Scrapbooks
___ Service awards
___ Tax notices
___ Union dues book
___ Water rights
___ X-rays

___ Accident reports
___ Adoption papers
___ Apprenticeship diplomas
___ Awards
___ Baptism certificate
___ Blessing certificates
___ Business license
___ Charitable donations
___ Church minutes
___ Citizenship papers
___ College applications
___ Correspondence
___ Court minutes
___ Customs records
___ Diplomas
___ Economic records
___ Employment termination
___ Family group sheets
___ Family records
___ Firearm registration
___ Genealogical records
___ Health records
___ Hospital receipts
___ Immigrant records
___ Institutional records
___ Journals, diaries
___ Land patents
___ Library cards
___ Marine insurance
___ Marriage certificates
___ Medical records
___ Military discharge
___ Military records
___ Military service record
___ Mission reports
___ National Guard records
___ Obituaries
___ Passports
___ Personal interviews
___ Personnel records
___ Professional certificates
___ Property surveys
___ Report cards
___ School tax records
___ Secondary school registration
___ Sextons records
___ Tombstone rubbings
___ Vaccination records
___ Wedding books
___ Yearbooks

___ Achievements
___ Anniversary announcements
___ Auction receipts
___ Baby books
___ Biographies
___ Bonds
___ Case files
___ Christening certificate
___ Church records
___ Club dues
___ Confirmation certificates
___ Court dockets
___ Court subpoenas
___ Death certificates
___ Divorce documents
___ Elementary school registration
___ Engagement announcements
___ Family heirlooms
___ Farm records
___ Funeral programs
___ Graduation programs
___ Historical society membership
___ Hospital records
___ Immunization certificates
___ Insurance papers
___ Judicial summons
___ Legal papers
___ Life insurance
___ Marriage announcements
___ Marriage licenses
___ Military citations
___ Military firearms
___ Military separation papers
___ Military uniform
___ Mortgages
___ Naturalization logbooks
___ Ordination certificates
___ Pedigrees charts
___ Personal papers
___ Probate inventories
___ Property leases
___ Publications
___ Retirement applications
___ School transcripts
___ Selective service cards
___ Social security card
___ Traffic tickets
___ Visas
___ Wills

Tool 3.2 Checklist of Personal Genealogical Sources

Pedigree Chart

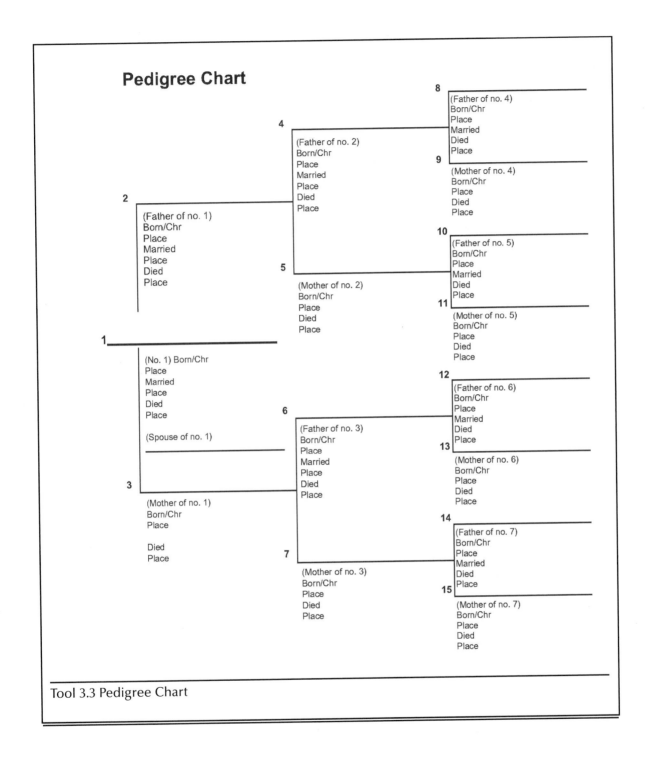

2
(Father of no. 1)
Born/Chr
Place
Married
Place
Died
Place

4
(Father of no. 2)
Born/Chr
Place
Married
Place
Died
Place

8
(Father of no. 4)
Born/Chr
Place
Married
Died
Place

9
(Mother of no. 4)
Born/Chr
Place
Died
Place

5
(Mother of no. 2)
Born/Chr
Place
Died
Place

10
(Father of no. 5)
Born/Chr
Place
Married
Died
Place

11
(Mother of no. 5)
Born/Chr
Place
Died
Place

1
(No. 1) Born/Chr
Place
Married
Place
Died
Place

(Spouse of no. 1)

3
(Mother of no. 1)
Born/Chr
Place

Died
Place

6
(Father of no. 3)
Born/Chr
Place
Married
Place
Died
Place

12
(Father of no. 6)
Born/Chr
Place
Married
Died
Place

13
(Mother of no. 6)
Born/Chr
Place
Died
Place

7
(Mother of no. 3)
Born/Chr
Place
Died
Place

14
(Father of no. 7)
Born/Chr
Place
Married
Died
Place

15
(Mother of no. 7)
Born/Chr
Place
Died
Place

Tool 3.3 Pedigree Chart

275

Family Group Sheet

HUSBAND'S NAME _____
Born (Date) _____ (Place)_____
Married (Date)_____ (Place)_____
Died (Date) _____ (Place)_____   Your Name & Address

Father of Husband_____
Born (Date)_____ (Place) _____
Married (Date)_____ (Place)_____
Died (Date)_____ (Place)_____   Sources, Notes, Etc.

Mother of Husband _____
Born (Date)_____ (Place)_____
Married (Date)_____ (Place)_____
Died (Date)_____ (Place)_____

WIFE'S NAME_____
Born (Date)_____ (Place)_____
Died (Date)_____ (Place)_____

Father of Wife_____
Born (Date)_____ (Place)_____
Married (Date)_____ (Place)_____
Died (Date)_____ (Place)_____

Mother of Wife _____
Born (Date)_____ (Place)_____
Died (Date)_____ (Place)_____

CHILDREN	BORN Date Place	DIED Date Place	MARRIED To whom Date
1 M F			
2 M F			
· 3 M F			
4 M F			
5 M F			
6 M F			
7 M F			
8 M F			
9 M F			

Tool 3.4 Family Group Sheet

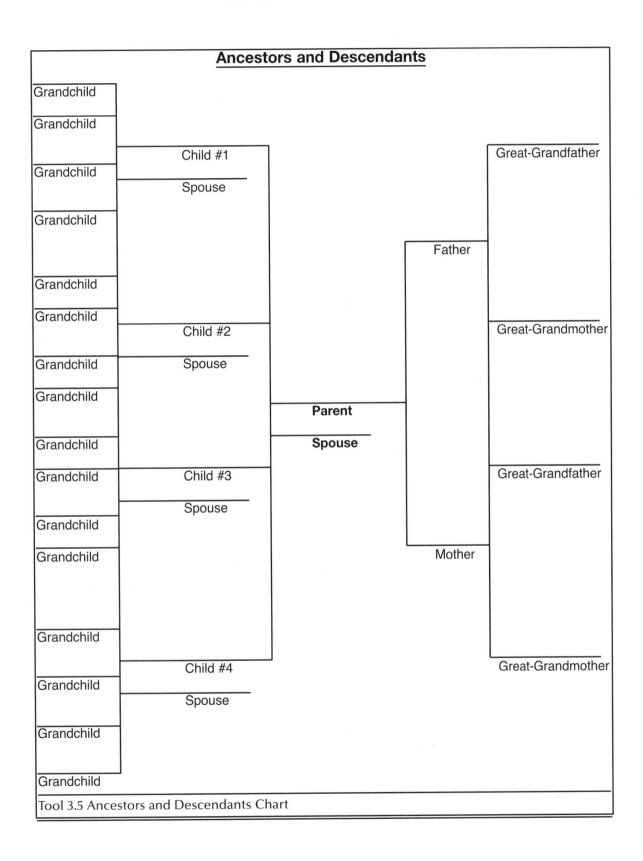

Ancestors and Descendants

Grandchild

Grandchild

Grandchild

Child #1

Spouse

Great-Grandfather

Grandchild

Grandchild

Grandchild

Father

Grandchild

Grandchild

Great-Grandmother

Child #2

Spouse

Grandchild

Parent

Grandchild

Spouse

Grandchild

Grandchild

Child #3

Great-Grandfather

Spouse

Grandchild

Grandchild

Mother

Grandchild

Great-Grandmother

Child #4

Grandchild

Spouse

Grandchild

Grandchild

Tool 3.5 Ancestors and Descendants Chart

Checklist of Web Sites

Ancestor's Name _____

Web site	Address	Contains
FamilySearch	www.familysearch.org	Genealogies, databases, and indexes
Ancestry	www.ancestry.com	Genealogies, census images, databases
HeritageQuest	www.heritagequestonline.com	Census images, virtual library
RootsWeb	www.rootsweb.com	Genealogies, surname list
USGenWeb	www.usgenweb.org	State and county data
Roots-L	www.rootsweb.com/roots-l	Mailing lists
CyndisList	www.CyndisList.com	Search engine to genealogy sites
Searchable Death Indexes	http://home.att.net/~wee-monster/deathrecords.html	Links to searchable death data
Google	www.google.com	Global search engine
Switchboard	www.switchboard.com	National telephone directory
Best Genealogy Links on the WWW	www.geocities.com/Heartland/1637	Links to major genealogy sites
GENDEX WWW Genealogical Index	www.gendex.com/gendex	Index to genealogies on the Web
GenServ Genealogical GEDCOM Server	www.genserv.com	Searchable online GEDCOM datafiles
Genealogy.org	www.genealogy.org	Genealogies, census, datafiles
Making of America	www.hti.umich.edu/m/moagrp	Digital library of primary sources
LIBDEX Library Index	www.libdex.com	Index to 18,000 libraries
Vital Records Index	www.vitalrec.com	Links to finding vital records
Family History Library Catalog	www.familysearch.org/Eng/Library/FHLC/frameset_fhlc.asp	Catalog to the holdings of the Family History Library
FuneralNet Directory	www.funeralnet.com/search.html	Directory of funeral homes
AccessGenealogy.com	www.accessgenealogy.com	Links to online genealogies

Tool 3.6 Checklist of Web Sites

Oral History Interview

Questions for a taped interview with a family member

1   What is your name? (Maiden name?)
2   What is the date of your birth?
3   Where were you born?
4   Who were your parents?
5   Where were they born?
6   Who did you marry?
7   When were you married?
8   What are the names of your children?
9   What are the names of your brothers and sisters?
10   As a child, what was the first event you remember?
11   What did you do during the day before you went to school?
12   What was a typical day like after you started school?
13   What was your favorite subject in school?
14   As a child what did you want to grow up to be?
15   What did you like to do for fun?
16   What job did you work at for most of your life?
17   What one thing did you always wish you could have done but never did?
18   Tell me what you can remember about your grandparents.
19   Tell me how you met your husband [wife].
20   Tell me about your courtship and marriage.
21   Do you have any secrets that you don't mind talking about now?
22   Tell me about the places you lived as a child and as an adult.
23   What was the most important invention in your lifetime?
24   If you could live your life again, what single thing would you do differently?
25   If you could pass on one piece of wisdom from your life, what would it be?

Tool 3.7 Oral History Interview Checklist

TOOL KIT 4
KEEPING YOUR RESEARCH ORGANIZED

Research Log

Ancestor's Name _____

Objective			Approximate Date		Locality	
Date of Search Number	Location/ Call Numbers	Description of Source (Author, title, year, pages)		Comments/Results (Purpose of search, years, names)		Document

Additional notes:

Tool 4.1 Research Log

Data Extraction Form

Surname   _____

Title of document   _____
Volume   _____
Date   _____
Page numbers   _____
Author   _____
City of publication   _____
Publisher   _____
Date of publication   _____

Date of research   _____
Location of research   _____
Call # or film #   _____

Notes

Page #   Information Extracted

Tool 4.2 Data Extraction Form

Family Bible Extraction Form

Births

Name	Date	Mother	Father	Family Connection

Deaths

Name	Death Date	Birth date	Age	Family Connection

Marriages

Groom	Bride	Marriage Date	Groom's Parents	Bride's Parents

Tool 4.3 Family Bible Extraction Form

Cemetery Research Outline

Name of Cemetery

Location

Inscription on Tombstone

Photo of grave

Description of Tombstone

Headstone

Footstone

Artwork

Grave appearance

Inscription on Tombstone

Photo of grave

Description of Tombstone

Headstone

Footstone

Artwork

Grave appearance

Tool 4.4 Cemetery Research Outline

283

Biographical Sketch Outline

Name	_____	_____
Parents	_____	_____
Birth	Date	_____
	Place	_____
Education	_____	_____
	_____	_____
Residences	_____	_____
	_____	_____
Siblings	_____	_____
	_____	_____
Military	_____	_____
	_____	_____
Marriage	Spouse	_____
	Date	_____
	Place	_____
Children	_____	_____
	_____	_____
	_____	_____
Illnesses	_____	_____
	_____	_____
Religious events	_____	_____
	_____	_____
Family moves	_____	_____
	_____	_____
Jobs	_____	_____
	_____	_____
Family events	_____	_____
	_____	_____
Property owned	_____	_____
	_____	_____
Court events	_____	_____
	_____	_____
Death	Date	_____
	Place	_____
Burial	Date	_____
	Place	_____
Anecdotes	_____	_____
	_____	_____
	_____	_____
	_____	_____

Tool 4.5 Biographical Sketch Outline

Tool Kit 5

Additional Research Checklists

Checklist for Planning a Research Trip

Item	Notes	Cost
Dates of trip	_____	_____
Primary destination	_____	_____
Other research facilities on your way	_____	_____
Mode of transportation	_____	_____
Buy bus or airline ticket	_____	_____
Have vehicle serviced	_____	_____
Lodging (# of nights @ $_____ +18%)	_____	_____
Meals/food (# of meals_____)	_____	_____
Sightseeing	_____	_____
Shopping	_____	_____
Visits to family/friends (gifts)	_____	_____
Research expenses (admission fees, etc.)	_____	_____
Resource purchases (books, forms, etc.)	_____	_____
Total Cost Estimate		_____

Preparation
- ☐ Names to research _____
- ☐ Specific information to find _____
- ☐ Visit Web site of library _____
- ☐ Search online catalog for surnames _____
- ☐ Search online catalog by place _____
- ☐ Call to someone who works at library _____
- ☐ Print out list of resources to check _____
- ☐ Organize and prioritize resources list _____

List of things to pack
- ☐ Clothes _____
- ☐ Extra comfortable shoes _____
- ☐ Data you have on the families already _____
- ☐ Roll of quarters for coin-operated copiers _____
- ☐ Pencils _____
- ☐ Legal notebook pad _____
- ☐ Magnifying glass _____
- ☐ Extra file folders _____

Tool 5.1 Checklist for Planning a Research Trip

Checklist for Genealogical Research 1700–1750

Ancestor's Name _____

Birth _____

Where _____

Death _____

Where _____

Check These Research Tools	Where did you search?	What did you find?	What's the next step?
FamilySearch.org	☐ _____	_____	_____
Town records	☐ _____	_____	_____
Church records	☐ _____	_____	_____
Making of America	☐ _____	_____	_____
RootsWeb.com	☐ _____	_____	_____
Ancestry.com	☐ _____	_____	_____
HeritageQuest Online	☐ _____	_____	_____
Periodical Source Index	☐ _____	_____	_____
GenServ.com	☐ _____	_____	_____
State archives	☐ _____	_____	_____
Marriage certificate	☐ _____	_____	_____
Court records	☐ _____	_____	_____
Family Bible records	☐ _____	_____	_____
Cemetery records	☐ _____	_____	_____
Barbour Collection	☐ _____	_____	_____
The Great Migration	☐ _____	_____	_____

Tool 5.2 First Places to Look: Checklist for Genealogical Research 1700-1750

First Places to Look
Checklist for Genealogical Research 1750–1800

Ancestor's Name _____

Birth _____

Where _____

Death _____

Where _____

Check These Research Tools Where did you search?   What did you find?   What's the next step?

1790 Federal census ☐ _____   _____   _____

Town records ☐ _____   _____   _____

Church records ☐ _____   _____   _____

FamilySearch.org ☐ _____   _____   _____

RootsWeb.com ☐ _____   _____   _____

Ancestry.com ☐ _____   _____   _____

DAR Patriot Index ☐ _____   _____   _____

Periodical Source Index ☐ _____   _____   _____

USGenWeb ☐ _____   _____   _____

Revolutionary War Land Bounty Index ☐ _____   _____   _____

Marriage certificate ☐ _____   _____   _____

Court records ☐ _____   _____   _____

Family Bible records ☐ _____   _____   _____

Cemetery records ☐ _____   _____   _____

Obituaries ☐ _____   _____   _____

Barbour Collection ☐ _____   _____   _____

Tool 5.3 First Places to Look: Checklists for Genealogical Research 1750-1800

First Places to Look
Checklist for Genealogical Research 1800–1850

Ancestor's Name _____

Birth   _____

Where   _____

Death   _____

Where   _____

Check These Research Tools	Where did you search?	What did you find?	What's the next step?
1800 Federal census	☐ _____	_____	_____
1810 Federal census	☐ _____	_____	_____
1820 Federal census	☐ _____	_____	_____
1830 Federal census	☐ _____	_____	_____
1840 Federal census	☐ _____	_____	_____
FamilySearch.org	☐ _____	_____	_____
Land records	☐ _____	_____	_____
Land bounty records	☐ _____	_____	_____
Probate records	☐ _____	_____	_____
Death certificate	☐ _____	_____	_____
Marriage bonds	☐ _____	_____	_____
Birth certificate	☐ _____	_____	_____
Cemetery records	☐ _____	_____	_____
Court records	☐ _____	_____	_____
Military records	☐ _____	_____	_____

Tool 5.4 First Places to Look: Checklist for Genealogical Research 1800-1850

First Places to Look
Checklist for Genealogical Research 1850–1900

Ancestor's Name _____
Birth _____
Where _____
Death _____
Where _____

Check These Research Tools Where did you search?   What did you find? What's the next step?

1850 Federal census ☐ _____   _____ _____

1860 Federal census ☐ _____   _____ _____

1870 Federal census ☐ _____   _____ _____

1880 Federal census ☐ _____   _____ _____

Ellis Island database ☐ _____   _____ _____

Civil War Pension Apps. ☐ _____   _____ _____

State death indexes ☐ _____   _____ _____

Immigration letters of intent ☐ _____   _____ _____

Probate records ☐ _____   _____ _____

Death certificate ☐ _____   _____ _____

Marriage certificate ☐ _____   _____ _____

Birth certificate ☐ _____   _____ _____

Cemetery records ☐ _____   _____ _____

Court records ☐ _____   _____ _____

FamilySearch.org ☐ _____   _____ _____

Tool 5.5 First Places to Look: Checklist for Genealogical Research 1850-1900

First Places to Look
Checklist for Genealogical Research 1900–1950

Ancestor's Name _____

Birth _____
Where _____
Death _____
Where _____

Check These Research Tools	Where did you search?	What did you find?	What's the next step?
1900 Federal census	☐ _____	_____	_____
1910 Federal census	☐ _____	_____	_____
1920 Federal census	☐ _____	_____	_____
1930 Federal census	☐ _____	_____	_____
Ellis Island database	☐ _____	_____	_____
World War I Draft Registration	☐ _____	_____	_____
Social Security Death Index	☐ _____	_____	_____
Google.com ("First/Last Name")	☐ _____	_____	_____
Switchboard.com (Living relatives)	☐ _____	_____	_____
Death certificate	☐ _____	_____	_____
Marriage certificate	☐ _____	_____	_____
Birth certificate	☐ _____	_____	_____
Cemetery records	☐ _____	_____	_____
PERSI (Periodical Source Index)	☐ _____	_____	_____
School records	☐ _____	_____	_____

Tool 5.6 First Places to Look: Checklist for Genealogical Research 1900-1950

First Places to Look
Checklist for Genealogical Research 1950–2000

Ancestor's Name _____
Birth _____
Where _____
Death _____
Where _____

Check These Research Tools	Where did you search?	What did you find?	What's the next step?
Social Security Death Index	☐ _____	_____	_____
Switchboard.com (Living relatives)	☐ _____	_____	_____
Obituaries	☐ _____	_____	_____
Google.com ("First/Last Name")	☐ _____	_____	_____
World War I Draft Registration	☐ _____	_____	_____
World War II Military Records	☐ _____	_____	_____
State Death Indexes	☐ _____	_____	_____
Newspaper index	☐ _____	_____	_____
RootsWeb.com	☐ _____	_____	_____
Death certificate	☐ _____	_____	_____
Marriage certificate	☐ _____	_____	_____
Birth certificate	☐ _____	_____	_____
Cemetery records	☐ _____	_____	_____
High school yearbook	☐ _____	_____	_____
School records	☐ _____	_____	_____

Tool 5.7 First Places to Look: Checklists for Genealogical Research 1950-2000

Checklist for Accessing Printed Information in Distant Libraries	
_____	Search LIBDEX (www.libdex.com) for library in the area where ancestor lived.
_____	Search online catalog of library for surname of ancestor.
_____	Identify titles that may contain information about ancestor.
_____	Request the title through interlibrary loan at your library.
_____	If the book is not available through interlibrary loan, do the following.
_____	Contact library to request a copy of index pages for your surname in the book.
_____	Ask them how much they charge or offer to pay.
_____	Review the photocopies of the pages from the index.
_____	Identify which pages are most likely to have information on your ancestor.
_____	Submit a second request to the library for the specific pages that you want.
_____	Wait for the pages to arrive.
_____	Send a check and a thank you note.

Tool 5.8 Checklist for Accessing Printed Information in Distant Libraries

Tool Kit 6

Federal Census Worksheets

Census Questions	1790	1800	1810	1820	1830	1840
Name of head of house	X	X	X	X	X	X
Address		X				
Free white males under 16 years	X					
Free white males 16 years and up	X					
Free white females under 16 years	X					
Free white females 16 years and up	X					
Slaves	X	X	X			
Free white males under 10 years		X	X	X		
Free white males 10 and under 16		X	X	X		
Free white males 16 and under 26		X	X	X		
Free white males 26 and under 45		X	X	X		
Free white males 45 and up		X	X	X		
Free white females under 10 years		X	X	X		
Free white females 10 and under 16		X	X	X		
Free white females 16 and under 26		X	X	X		
Free white females 26 and under 45		X	X	X		
Free white females 45 and up		X	X	X		
Free white males between 16 and 18				X		
Male slaves under 14 years				X		
Male slaves 14 to 26				X		
Male slaves 26 to 45				X		
Male slaves 45 and up				X		
Female slaves under 14 years				X		
Female slaves 14 to 26				X		
Female slaves 26 to 45				X		
Female slaves 45 and up				X		
Free male colored persons under 14 years				X		
Free male colored persons 14 to 26				X		
Free male colored persons 26 to 45				X		
Free male colored persons 45 and up				X		
Free female colored persons under 14 years				X		
Free female colored persons 14 to 26				X		
Free female colored persons 26 to 45				X		
Free female colored persons 45 and up				X		
All other persons except Indians not taxed		X	X	X		
Occupation				X	X	X

Tool 6.1 Federal Census Questions at a Glance 1790–1840

Census Questions	1790	1800	1810	1820	1830	1840
Free white males under 5 years					X	X
Free white males 5 and under 10					X	X
Free white males 10 and under 15					X	X
Free white males 15 and under 20					X	X
Free white males 20 and under 30					X	X
Free white males 30 and under 40					X	X
Free white males 40 and under 50					X	X
Free white males 50 and under 60					X	X
Free white males 60 and under 70					X	X
Free white males 70 and under 80					X	X
Free white males 80 and under 90					X	X
Free white males 90 and under 100					X	X
Free white males 100 and up					X	X
Free white females under 5 years					X	X
Free white females 5 and under 10					X	X
Free white females 10 and under 15					X	X
Free white females 15 and under 20					X	X
Free white females 20 and under 30					X	X
Free white females 30 and under 40					X	X
Free white females 40 and under 50					X	X
Free white females 50 and under 60					X	X
Free white females 60 and under 70					X	X
Free white females 70 and under 80					X	X
Free white females 80 and under 90					X	X
Free white females 90 and under 100					X	X
Free white females 100 and up					X	X
Male slaves under 10 years					X	X
Male slaves 10 to 24					X	X
Male slaves 24 to 36					X	X
Male slaves 36 to 55					X	X
Male slaves 55 to 100					X	X
Male slaves ages 100 and up					X	X
Female slaves under 10 years					X	X
Female slaves 10 to 24					X	X
Female slaves 24 to 36					X	X
Female slaves 36 to 55					X	X
Female slaves 55 to 100					X	X
Female slaves ages 100 and up					X	X
White persons deaf and dumb under 14					X	
White persons deaf and dumb 14 under 25					X	
White persons deaf and dumb 25 and up					X	
White persons who are blind					X	
White persons foreigners not naturalized				X	X	X
Name and age of Revolutionary War pensioner						X

Tool 6.1 Federal Census Questions at a Glance 1790–1840

Census Questions	1850	1860	1870	1880	1890	1900	1910	1920	1930
Address						X	X	X	X
Name of head of household	X	X	X	X		X	X	X	X
Names of other persons in home	X	X	X	X		X	X	X	X
Relationship to household head				X		X	X	X	X
Age	X	X	X	X		X	X	X	X
Date of birth, month and year						X			
Month born if under one year			X	X					
Sex	X	X	X	X		X	X	X	X
Single				X		X	X	X	X
Married				X		X	X	X	X
Widowed/divorced				X		X	X	X	X
Number of years married						X	X		
Mother of how many children						X	X		
Number of children living						X	X		
Color (Race)	X					X	X	X	X
Color (White, Black, Mulatto)		X	X						
Color (White, Black, Mulatto, Chinese, Indian)				X		X			
Occupation	X	X	X	X		X	X	X	X
Number of weeks/ months not employed				X		X	X		X
Sick or disabled on day enumerators visit				X					
Value of real estate owned	X	X	X						X
Value of personal property		X	X						
Own or rent home						X	X	X	X
Own home free of mortgage						X	X	X	
Does this family live on a farm?						X	X	X	X
Place of birth of this person	X	X	X	X		X	X	X	X
Place of birth of father				X		X	X	X	X

Tool 6.2 Federal Census Questions at a Glance 1850–1930

Census Questions	1850	1860	1870	1880	1890	1900	1910	1920	1930
Place of birth of mother				X		X	X	X	X
Father foreign born			X						
Mother foreign born			X						
Native tongue of this person								X	X
Native tongue of this person's parents								X	X
Married within the year	X	X	X	X		X			
Age at first marriage									X
In school within the year	X	X	X	X			X	X	X
Over 21 and unable to read/write	X	X	X						
Cannot read			X	X					
Cannot write			X	X					
Can read						X	X	X	
Can write						X	X	X	
Can speak English						X	X	X	X
Deaf, dumb, blind, insane, idiotic, pauper, or convict	X	X	X	X			X		
Males eligible to vote			X						
Males not eligible to vote			X						
Year of immigration to U.S.						X	X	X	X
Number of years in U.S.						X			
Naturalization						X	X	X	X
Year of naturalization								X	
Survivor of Union/Confederate Army/Navy							X		
Veteran of U.S. Military and expedition									X
Own a radio set									X

Tool 6.2 Federal Census Questions at a Glance 1850–1930

Name: _____

Date of birth: _____   Date of death: _____

In household of:	Males		Females	Males						Females				
Indicate age group of this person	To 16	16 and up	Females	0-10	10-16	16-18	16-26	26-45	45 & up	0-10	10-16	16-26	26-45	45 & up
1790-County State Name:														
1800-County State Name:														
1810-County State Name:														
1820-County State Name:														

In household of:	Males													Females													Aliens	S. Rev. W.
Indicate age group of this person	0-5	5-10	10-15	15-20	20-30	30-40	40-50	50-60	60-70	70-80	80-90	90-100	100 & up	0-5	5-10	10-15	15-20	20-30	30-40	40-50	50-60	60-70	70-80	80-90	90-100	100 & up		
1830-County State Name:																												
1840-County State Name:																												

Dwelling #	Family #	Head of Family	Age	Sex	Color	Occupation	Value of real estate	Value of personal estate	Place of Birth	Married this year	School this year	Can't read/write	Deaf, blind, insane, etc.
1850 – County:		State:				Post Office:							
1860 – County:		State:				Post Office:							

Tool 6.3 Federal Census Chronology 1790–1860

Dwelling #	Family #	Name of each person whose place of abode on June 1, 1870 was in this family	Age	Sex	Color	Occupation	Value of real estate	Value of personal estate	Place of birth	Father foreign	Mother foreign	Month if b. yr.	Month if m. yr.	School this year	Can't read/write	Deaf, blind, etc.	Male Citizen	Can't vote

1870 - County: State: Post Office:

Dwelling #	Family #	Name of each person whose place of abode on June 1, 1880 was in this family	Age	Sex	Color	Relationship to head o this family	Occupation	Mos. unemployed	Deaf, blind etc.	Attended school	Can't read/write	Place of birth of this person	Place of birth of father	Place of birth of mother

1880 - County: State: Post Office:

Dwelling #	Family #	Name of each person whose place of abode on June 1, 1900 was in this family	Relation to head of household	Color	Sex	Month of birth	Year of birth	Age	Marital status	# of yrs. married	M. of # of children	# of living children	Place of birth of this person	Place of birth of father	Place of birth of mother	Immigration Year	# yrs. in U.S.	Naturalization	Occupation

1900 - County: State: Post Office:

Tool 6.4 Federal Census Chronology 1870–1900

298

REQUESTING INFORMATION

Requests for Information		
Ancestor or Surname _____		
Person queried	**Summary of query**	**Response**
Name Address E-mail Phone	Date	Date
Name Address E-mail Phone	Date	Date
Name Address E-mail Phone	Date	Date
Name Address E-mail Phone	Date	Date

Tool 7.1 Requests for Information Summary Chart

Sample Letter

Social Security Administration
Office of Earnings Operations
FOIA Workgroup
300 N Greene Street
PO Box 33022
Baltimore, Maryland 21290

Re: Freedom of Information Act Request

Dear Freedom of Information Officer,

I am writing this request under the Freedom of Information Act, 5 U.S.C. Section 552. I hereby request a copy of the SS-5, Application for Social Security Card for the following individual:

NAME
###-##-####
Birth:
Death:

This person is my father. He is deceased, having been listed in the Social Security Administration's Death Master File. I understand the fee for this service is $27.00 for copy of original SS-5 application. Included is a check for $27.00 made out to the Social Security Administration to cover any administrative costs required by this request.

Please respond to my request upon receipt of this initial correspondence. Thank you for your attention and assistance.

Sincerely,
Requestor Name
Street
City, State, Zip
Daytime Phone Number:

Tool 7.2 Sample Letter to Social Security Administration

TOOL KIT 8

WEB AND COMPUTER RESOURCES

Genealogy Program Comparison Table

Program	Description/Features	Cost	Demo version
Ages!	This is an easy-to-use, full-featured genealogy software. It has an intuitive user interface, allows for multiple parents, any number of generations, integrated note-manager, flexible date format, is GEDCOM compatible, and offers multiple printout options. Web site: www.daubnet.com/english/ages.html	$35.00	Shareware version allows up to 50 individuals.
Ancestral Quest	This program is for anyone engaged in genealogy research. Data entry is easy; keyboard shortcuts, and super-fast mouse navigation make data entry a snap. The program is compatible with PAF database and is GEDCOM compatible. Web site: www.ancquest.com/aqindex.htm	$29.95	Demo version allows up to 120 names.
Ancestry Family Tree	Automatically searches about 2 billion names at Ancestry.com to find the best matches in a person's family tree. Lets users publish a family tree online. Accommodates photos and multimedia. GEDCOM compatible. http://aft.ancestrycom	$19.95	Free for seven days.
Brothers Keeper 6	The database can hold up to 10 million names. The program can attach sources to events and pictures to people. The print preview is a nice feature. Printing includes ancestor charts, descendant box charts, timelines, birthday and anniversary lists, family group sheets with pictures, and it can print a book with an index. GEDCOM import/export compatible. Web site: www.bkwin.org.	$45.00 to register software	Shareware. Try it before you buy it.
Cumberland Family Tree	This is a versatile and easy-to-use program that features a variety of reports, GEDCOM import/export, and HTML publishing. Focuses on creating a family history book and customizing individual reports. Web site: www.cf-softwarecom.	$45.00	Shareware for 45-day free trial.

Tool 8.1 Genealogy Program Comparison Table

Program	Description/Features	Cost	Demo version
DoroTree	This is the family tree software for Jewish genealogists. It is easy-to-use with complete bilingual capabilityóEnglish and Hebrew. It includes direct Internet access to Jewish genealogy sites. Special features include Yahrzeit reports, Holocaust commemoration, and Hebrew-Gregorian date conversion. Users can create Web pages and store multimedia. Web site: www.dorotree.com/features.html	$59.00	None
Family Tree Legends	This is a powerful and easy-to-use program. Features include a smart matching interface that allows users to collaborate with other researchers, GEDCOM merge and find duplicates, and spell checking. Web site: www.familytreelegends.com.	$39.95	None
Family Tree Maker	This is one of the most popular genealogy programs available. The data entry wizard makes it easy to add information. Store any number of facts for each individual. Add photos, sound, video, and text. Display a wide array of trees, printouts, and formats. Web site: www.genealogy.com/soft_ftm.html	$24.00 to $49.00 Amazon. com has the best price	None
Gene Macintosh Software	User can store family data and notes, draw and print family trees and pedigree charts, create web pages from the database, and exchange GEDCOM data with users of other genealogy programs. Gene is capable of handling complicated databases with thousands of names, multiple marriages and divorces, adoptions, illegitimate children, and intermarriage between relatives. www1.ics.uci.edu/~eppstein/gene	$15.00 (single user); site license $300.00	Shareware
Generations Family Tree	Engaging tutorials make it easy to get started. Fill in the blanks for uncomplicated data entry. Stores facts for every individual in the database. Includes a 350-million name database. Program has SnapShot Express, a photo restoration and enhancement software. Web site: www.broderbund.com/Product.asp?OID=4147943	$9.99 to $29.99	None

Tool 8.1 Genealogy Program Comparison Table *continued*

Program	Description/Features	Cost	Demo version
GenoPro	Users can draw a complete family tree, add pictures, generate and print family reports, and analyze compiled data. GEDCOM compatible. Gold (paid) version eliminates advertising. Web site: www.genoprogoldcom.	Free to $24.00	Gold version Free download version includes advertising.
Great Family	This program makes it fast and easy to create and edit a family tree. It is also great for generating Web pages with pictures and extra text. Navigation is easy and intuitive. Imports/exports GEDCOM files. Includes family tree organizing tools. Web site: www.greatprogs.com/greatfamily	$29.93	30-day free trial.
Legacy Family Tree	Multifunctional, multi-featured program, that lets users see up to eight families at a time, and have two family files open at the same time. Drag and drop features make it easy to copy from one file to another. Pop-up lists make it easy to select the next view. GEDCOM compatible. One of the most comprehensive genealogy programs available. Web site: www.legacyfamilytree.com/Features.asp	$19.95 to $49.95 depending on version	Standard version is available as a free download.
Mac Family Tree	This program for Macintosh computers helps users document, store, and display information about their families. They can draw and print family trees, lists, cards, and heritage charts. Data is exported as html documents to build a Web page. GEDCOM 5.5 is the native file format. Web site: www.onlymac.de/html/macfamilytree.html	$29.95	Free demo download.
The Master Genealogist	Used by professional researchers and beginning genealogist alike, this is one of the most powerful family history programs available. Users can manage volumes of research, organize research trips, keep track of correspondence, or publish a book. Most data fields have no limits. Genealogists can include photographs, sources, events, multiple names per person, relationships, and user-defined events and flags. The program can generate a wide variety of displays, reports, and printouts. Web site: www.whollygenes.com/tmg5.htm	$79.00	Download for a 30-day free trial.

Tool 8.1 Genealogy Program Comparison Table *continued*

Program	Description/Features	Cost	Demo version
Personal Ancestral File	PAF helps users put in order their family history records. It produces on-screen and printed copies of pedigree charts, family group records, and other reports. The program can accommodate a variety of naming conventions. Accommodates multimedia and GEDCOM imports/exports. Easiest of all programs to use. It has online lessons for beginners. Web site: www.familysearch.org/eng/paf	$6.00 for CD-ROM version	Free download of fully functioning program.
Reunion	Reunion is a genealogy software program for Macintosh computers. Reunion lets users publish family tree information with elegant graphics. It makes creating Web pages a snap. Reunion creates large, high-resolution, graphic charts that allow for easy editing of boxes, lines fonts, and colors. Wall charts are a specialty. GEDCOM compatible. Web site: www.leisterpro.com/index.shtml	$99.00	Download free demo version, which allows up to 35 people.
RootsMagic	Comprehensive yet easy-to-use, this is a new full-featured genealogy program. User can have multiple databases open at the same time and drag and drop data from one program to another. Integrated backup and restore helps safeguard data. Web site: www.rootsmagiccom.	$29.95	Download free demo version, which allows up to 50 people.

Tool 8.1 Genealogy Program Comparison Table *continued*

Tool 8.2 Libraries and Archives Web Directory

In Chapter 5 you saw a list of libraries and archives with contact information—names, addresses, telephone numbers, and so forth. In this appendix we provide a list of electronic contact points using the same list as in Chapter 5. You can use these electronic addresses to contact any of the libraries or archives. You can also use the CD-ROM that accompanies this book to find hyperlinks that you can click on to take you directly to the desired Web site.

All Web site addresses are accurate and live, but we all know that Web addresses are subject to unpredictable changes. If you get an error message while trying to use one of the Web addresses we have provided, go to a search engine and do a search on the name of the institution you are trying to find. You should be able to find the updated address.

Organization of the Information

I first identify the name of the organization. After that I present the Web and e-mail addresses. If they have a special page to help you ask for services from them, I include it in this area. The final paragraph of each repository is for suggestions on using the electronic addresses to help you get to the information you want.

Alabama

Birmingham Public Library

Tutwiler Collection of Southern History and Literature
Web site: www.bponline.org/sou/Genealogy.htm
Online Catalog: www.jclc.org/services/opacmenu.html
List researchers: www.bplonline.org/sou/oldsite/Researchers.htm
Check the Web site for research fees.

Anniston Public Library

Alabama Room
E-mail: alroom@anniston.lib.us
Web site: www.anniston.lib.al.us/alaroom.htm
Online Anniston Telephone Directories 1914 to 1923:
www.anniston.lib.al.us/archive/index.htm
The online telephone directories are a real treasure.

Huntsville-Madison County Public Library

Archives and Heritage Room
Archives: www.hpl.lib.al.us/departments/archives
Heritage Room: www.hpl.lib.al.us/departments/hhr
Online catalog: www.hpl.lib.al.us/ibistro
Use the Contact Form on their Web site to request information.

Mobile Public Library

Local History and Genealogy Department
E-mail: lhgmgr@mplonline.org
Web site: www.mplonline.org/directory.html
Online catalog: www.mplonline.org/catalog.htm
Use e-mail to contact the Genealogy Department.

Wallace State Community College

Wallace State Library
E-mail: genws@hiwaay.net

Web site: www.wallacestate.edu/library.html
Use e-mail to contact the Genealogy Department.

University of Alabama

William Stanley Hoole Special Collections
E-mail: archives@bama.ua.edu
Web site: www.lib.ua.edu/libraries/hoole/about
Online catalog: http://library.ua.edu
Search the online catalog for access to resources.

Alaska

Alaska Historical Library

State Office Building
E-mail: asl@eed.state.ak.us
Web site: www.library.state.ak.us/hist/hist.html
Online catalog:
http://199.33.240.110/uhtbin/cgisirsi.exe/c6LsmXrTw3/139330043/60/1180/X
The Web site has some good online guides to genealogical research in Alaska.

Alaska State Archives

Archives
E-mail: archives@eed.state.ak.us
Web site: www.archives.state.ak.us
Contact the agency for access from a distance.

University of Alaska Library Anchorage

Archives and Manuscripts Department
E-mail: ayarch@uaa.alaska.edu
Web site: www.lib.uaa.alaska.edu/archives
The Collections List is the gateway to the collection.

University of Alaska Fairbanks

Rasmuson Library
Web site: www.uaf.edu/library
Use the Web site to access resources and services.

Arizona

Arizona State Library

Archives and Public Records
Genealogy Collection
E-mail: archive@lib.az.us
Web site: www.dlapr.lib.az.us/archives
Arizona Biographical Database: www.lib.az.us/Bio/bio_Search.cfm
The Arizona Biographical Database is a wonderful tool.

West Valley Genealogical Society Library

Genealogy Library
Web site: www.rootsweb.com/~azwvgs/Index.htm
Obituaries Project: www.rootsweb.com/~azwvgs/ObitProject.htm
The Obituaries Project is limited, but a very nice online tool.

Arizona State University Libraries

Arizona Collection
Web site: www.asu.edu/lib/archives/arizona.htm
Online collections: www.asu.edu/lib/archives/digicoll.htm
Arizona Jewish Historical Society Oral History Project:
www.asu.edu/lib/archives/shema/shema.htm
The Arizona Jewish Historical Society Oral History Project is a wonderful site.

University of Arizona

Special Collections
Web site: www.library.arizona.edu/branches/spc/homepage/index.html
Online catalog: http://sabio.library.arizona.edu/search
Use the Web site to explore the resources and services of the library.

Arkansas

Arkansas State History Commission Archives

Archives
Web site: www.ark-ives.com/using_archives/index.php
Contact a local researcher for access to the collection.

Fort Smith Public Library

Genealogy Department
E-mail: genealogy@fspl.lib.ar.us
Web site: www.fspl.lib.ar.us/genmain.html

Online catalog: http://fsmollie.fspl.lib.ar.us

Their Web site has lots of links for genealogical research.

University of Arkansas Library

Special Collections

Web site: http://dante.uark.edu/specialcollections

Use their online requests forms to ask for copies of documents.

Pine Bluff/Jefferson County Library

Genealogy Collection

Web site: http://pbjc-lib.state.ar.us/genealogy.htm

Online catalog: http://pbjc-lib.state.ar.us/highland/highland.htm

The library staff will do searches pertaining to Jefferson County.

California

California State Library

Sutro Library Branch

E-mail: sutro@library.ca.gov

Web site: www.onelibrary.com/Library/calslsut.htm

Online catalog: www.library.ca.gov

The Web site gives a good summary of their resources and services.

California State Library

California History Room

E-mail: cslcal@library.ca.gov

Web site: www.library.ca.gov/html/genealogy.cfm

Microfilm is available on interlibrary loan.

Tuolumne County

Genealogical Society Library

E-mail: info@tcgsonline.org

Web site: www.tchistory.org/gen_soc.html

The Web site has membership information. Send an e-mail.

Los Angeles Public Library

The History and Genealogy Department

E-mail: history@lapl.org

Web site: www.lapl.org/central/history.html

Online catalog: http://catalog1.lapl.org

The online research guides will help you access local information.

Huntington Beach Public Library

Genealogy Collection
Web site: www.hbpl.org/collections_genealogy.htm
Search the online catalog learn about their resources.

Carlsbad City Library

Genealogy Division
Georgina Cole Library
E-mail: mvano@ci.carlsbad.ca.us
Web site: http://ci.carlsbad.ca.us/cserv/genealog.html
Online catalog: http://web2.ci.carlsbad.ca.us
They have an impressive list of research guides online.

Sons of the Revolution Library

Library
E-mail: sr@walika.com
Web site: www.walika.com/sr/library.htm
Send them an e-mail if you think they can help you.

Colorado

Colorado State Archives

Archives
Web site: www.colorado.gov/dpa/doit/archives
Out-of-State Requests: $25.00 per search.

Colorado Historical Society

Stephen H. Hart Library
E-mail: research@chs.state.co.us
Web site: www.coloradohistory.org/chs_library/library.htm
Online catalog: www.coloradohistory.org/chs_library/catalog.htm
Most resources available on request to library visitors.

Colorado State Library

Library
Web site: www.cde.state.co.us/index_library.htm
Contact the agency for availability of research services.

Denver Public Library

Western History and Genealogy Department
Web site: www.denver.lib.co.us/whg/index.html

Online catalog: http://catalog.denver.lib.co.us/cgi-bin/cw_cgi?getBasicTerms+25185
Contact the reference staff for availability of research services.

Boulder Public Library

Carnegie Library for Local History
Web site: www.boulder.lib.co.us/branch/carnegie.html
Online catalog: http://nell.boulder.lib.co.us/search
Contact the agency for availability of research services.

Pikes Peak Library District

Regional History and Genealogy Resources
Web site: http://library.ppld.org/SpecialCollections/localHistoryGenealogy.asp
Online catalog: http://catalog.ppld.org/uhtbin/cgisirsi
Contact the agency for availability of research services.

Connecticut

Connecticut State Library

History and Genealogy
Web site: www.cslib.org/handg.htm
Online catalog: http://csulib.ctstateu.edu/search~blolclilplrlal
The Web site has links to some unique resources.

Connecticut Historical Society

Museum, Library and Education Center
One Elizabeth Street at Asylum Avenue
E-mail: Ask us@chs.org
Web site: www.chs.org/library/geneal.htm
The Web site is a good index to the resources they have.

Godfrey Memorial Library

Genealogy Collection
E-mail library@godfrey.org
Web site: www.godfrey.org/index.html#builders
Online catalog: www.librarycom.com/cgi-
bin/opac.exe/login?library=Godfrey%20Memorial%20Library&checkbox=checkbox
Their online catalog has many biographies and obituaries.

New Haven Colony Historical Society

Library
Web site: http://members.aol.com/dtrofatter/nhcol.htm
Check the Web site for contact information.

Stamford Historical Society

Research Library
E-mail: history@stamfordhistory.org
Web site: www.stamfordhistory.org/libr_1.htm
Research fees: www.stamfordhistory.org/libr_fees.htm
Use the Web site to find out what they have.

Delaware

Historical Society of Delaware

Library
E-mail: hsd@.hsd.org
Web site: www.hsd.org/library.htm
For a fee they will do a preliminary search of their resources.

Delaware State Archives

Hall of Records
Delaware Public Archives
E-mail: archives@state.de.us
Web site: www.state.de.us/sos/dpa/default.shtml
You can send an e-mail request for specific information.

Wilmington Institute Library

Library
Web: site: www.dla.lib.de.us/Dir_Data/Wilmington%20Institute%20Library.html Check
their Web site for detailed information on their services.
Hagley Museum and LibraryResearch Library
Web site: www.hagley.lib.de.us
Online catalog: http://209.71.104.75/cgi-bin/Pwebrecon.cgi?DB=local&PAGE=First
Check the online catalog for relevant resources.

Dover Public Library

Delaware Room
Web site: www.doverpubliclibrary.org
Search the Web site for detailed genealogical services.

District of Columbia

Historical Society of Washington, DC and City Museum

Kiplinger Research Library
E-mail: info@citymuseumdc.org
Web site: www.citymuseumdc.org/Library/Library_index.asp
Online catalog: www.citymuseumdc.org/ Do_Research/index.asp
Check the online catalog for access to resources.

District of Columbia Public Library

Washingtoniana Collection
Web site: www.dclibrary.org/washingtoniana
Online catalog:http://citycat.dclibrary.org/uhtbin/cgisirsi/F4WHxALplq/9200009/60/54/X
Contact the library for availability of research services.

Historical Society of Washington DC

Library of Washington History
Web site: www.loc.gov/rr/main/religion/dch.html
They will accept telephone and mail requests for information.

Florida

Orange County Library System

Genealogy Department
Web site: www.ocls.lib.fl.us/Locations/DRI/Genealogy/genealogy_department.asp
Online catalog: www.ocls.info/library_catalog.asp
Open and free to the public. Check with the reference department for services to out-of-state patrons.

Miami-Dade Public Library System

Genealogy Department
Web site: www.mdpls.org/info/locations/main/gd.asp
Online catalog: http://webcatalog.mdpls.org/ipac20/ipac.jsp? profile=dial#f
Most materials do not circulate.

Tampa-Hillsborough Library

Genealogy Department
Web site: www.hcplc.org/hcplc/ig/genealogy.html
Online catalog: http://ipac.hcplc.org/ipac20/ipac.jsp?profile=dial#focus
Check the online catalog.

Jacksonville Public Library

Genealogy Collection
Web site: http://jpl.coj.net/English/library/main.html#GEN
Most materials do not circulate.

Florida Department of State

Division of Library and Information Services
Florida State Archives
Web site: http://dlis.dos.state.fl.us/barm/fsa.html
Online catalog: http://dlis.dos.state.fl.us/barm/rediscovery/default.asp
World War I Service Records: www.floridamemory.com/Collections/WWI
Check the World War I Service Records online search engine.

Indian River County Main Library

Florida History and Genealogy Department
E-mail: pcooper@indian-river.lib.fl.us
Web site: http://indian-river.lib.fl.us
Online catalog: http://geoweb.indian-river.lib.fl.us:8000
Mail order requests: www.rootsweb.com/~flindian/mainlib.htm
Follow the directions on the page for mail order requests.

Georgia

Georgia Department of Archives and History

Archives
Web site: www.sos.state.ga.us/archives
Online catalog: www.sos.state.ga.us/archives/index/sa.htm
Check for research service or professional researchers.

Georgia Historical Society Library

Library and Archives
E-mail: ghslib@georgiahistory.com
Web site: www.georgiahistory.com/Lib_and_Archives.html
Web page as a link to the Savannah Jewish Archives.

Macon-Bibb County Public Libraries

Washington Memorial Library
E-mail: washingg@mail.bibb.public.lib.ga.us
Web site: www.co.bibb.ga.us/library/G&H.htm
Online catalog: http://pines.public.lib.ga.us
The Web site lists the resources of the library.

Augusta Genealogical Society Library

AGS Library
Web site: www.augustagensociety.org/library.htm
They do not conduct research or answer inquiries for nonmembers.

Atlanta-Fulton Public Library System

Georgia Local and Family History Collections
Web site: www.af.public.lib.ga.us/central/gagen/index.html
Online catalog: http://afplweb.af.public.lib.ga.us/cgi-bin/cw_cgi?getBasicTerms+26428
Their online Guide to the Genealogy Collection is a good place to start.

Ellen Payne Odom Genealogy Library

Research Library
E-mail: alastair@electricscotland.com
Web site: www.electricscotland.com/familytree
Send them e-mail to find out what they have.

Hawaii

Hawaii State Archives

Historical Records Branch
E-mail: archives@Hawaii.gov
Web site: www.hawaii.gov/dags/archives/welcome.html
Services and fees are listed on their Web site.

Hawaii State Library

Hawaii and Pacific Section
Web site: www.hawaii.gov/hidocs
Online catalog: http://ipac.librarieshawaii.org/ipac20/ipac.jsp?profile=#focus
They have an index to newspapers on their Web site.

Hamilton Library, University of Hawaii

Genealogy Page
Web site: www.hawaii.edu/emailref/internet_resources/Genealogy.htm
Online catalog: http://uhmanoa.lib.hawaii.edu
Visit the library or use their online links to Internet genealogy sources.

Bishop Museum Library

Research Library
E-mail: library@bishopmuseum.org
Web site: www.bishopmuseum.org/research/cultstud/libarch
Send them an e-mail to learn how they can help you.

Hawaiian Historical Society Library

Library Services
Web site: www.hawaiianhistory.org/lib/libmain.html
Online catalog: www.hawaiianhistory.org/search.html
The Web site gives a good summary of library services for genealogists.

Idaho

Idaho State Historical Society

Library and Archives
Web site: www.idahohistory.net/library_archives.html
Web site and catalog: www.idahohistory.net
They have a comprehensive index to cemeteries on their Web page.

University of Idaho Library

Special Collections and Archives
Web site: www.lib.uidaho.edu/special-collections
Online catalog: http://ui.wash-id.net/cgi-bin/Pwebrecon.cgi?DB=local&PAGE=First
They have an online guide to using the Archives.

North Idaho College

Library
Web site: www.nic.edu/library
Online catalog: http://nic.wash-id.net/cgi-bin/Pwebrecon.cgi?DB=local&PAGE=First
Search the online catalog to see if they have resources you can use.

Brigham Young University-Idaho

Arthur Porter Special Collections
E-mail: familyhistory@byui.edu
Web site: http://abish.byui.edu/specialCollections/spchome.htm
Online catalog: http://abish.byui.edu/specialCollections/search.cfm
Family History Resource indexes:
http://abish.byui.edu/specialCollections/fhc/FamilyHistory.htm
The Family History Resource indexes are powerful tools—marriages, deaths, and obituaries.

Illinois

Arlington Heights Memorial Library

Kathrine Shackley Room for Local History and Genealogy

Web site: www.ahml.lib.il.us/genealogy.asp
Online catalog: http://iii.ahml.info
They will not do extensive research.

South Suburban Genealogical and Historical Society

Library
E-mail: ssghs@usa.net
Web site: www.rootsweb.com/~ssghs
Quick cemetery lookups are available through the Web site.

Illinois State Archives

Norton Building
Web site: www.sos.state.il.us/departments/archives/archives.html
This is one of the best state-based genealogy Web sites in the U.S.

Lincoln Library

Sangamon Valley Collection
Web site: http://lincolnlibrary.rpls.lib.il.us/llhome5.htm
Online catalog: www.rpls.ws/web2/tramp2.exe/log_in?setting_key=LincolnLibrary
Try their e-mail reference service available from their Web site.

Peoria Public Library

Genealogy Department
Web site: www.peoria.lib.il.us/genealogy.htm
E-mail page: www.peoria.lib.il.us/reference%20questions/eReference.htm
The Web Page does a good job of telling you what is in the collection.

The Newberry Library

Research Library
E-mail: reference@newberry.org
Web site: www.newberry.org/nl/newberryhome.html
Online catalog: www.newberry.org/nl/collections/virtua.html
Genealogy Services: www.newberry.org/nl/genealogy/L3gservices.html
The genealogy services page details the services they provide to genealogists.

Indiana

Indiana State Archives

Family History Department
E-mail: arc@icpr.state.in.us
Web site: www.in.gov/icpr/archives/family
Web site has links to birth, marriage and death certificates, plus homestead awards database, and a naturalization database.

Indiana State Library

Genealogy Division
Web site: www.statelib.lib.in.us/www/isl/whoweare/genealogy.html
Online Resources from the Genealogy Division:
www.statelib.lib.in.us/www/isl/whoweare/genealogy.html
The online resources include a cemetery locator and a marriage index.

Kokomo-Howard County Public Library

Department of Genealogy and Local History Services
Web site: www.kokomo.lib.in.us/genealogy/index.html
Online databases: www.kokomo.lib.in.us/genealogy/index.html#databases
Check out their long list of online databases—a wonderful resource.

St. Joseph County Public Library

Local History/Genealogy
E-mail: local.history@sjcpl.org
Web site: www.libraryforlife.org/aboutsjcpl/departments/localhistory/localhistory.html
Online catalog: http://sjcpl.lib.in.us/onlinecatalog/onlinecatalog.html
Online obituary index: www.libraryforlife.org/databases/obituary/obituary.html
The obituary index (1920-1999) is a great resource.

Willard Library

Regional and Family History Department
E-mail: willard@willard.lib.in.us
Web site: www.willard.lib.in.us/genealogy.html
See their Web page for remote access.

Iowa

State Historical Society of Iowa–Des Moines

Library Archives Bureau
Web site: www.iowahistory.org
Online catalog: http://infohawk.uiowa.edu/F?func=file&file_name=find-b&local_base=iow06
State Historical Society maintains a list of professional researchers who provide services.

State Historical Society of Iowa–Iowa City

Centennial Building
Web site: www.iowahistory.org
Online catalog: http://infohawk.uiowa.edu/F?func=file&file_name=find-b&local_base=iow06
Search the Web site to find out about services and resources.

Kansas

Kansas State Historical Society

Research Library and Archives
E-mail: information@kshs.org
Web site: www.kshs.org
Search engine for newspapers: www.kshs.org/library/news.htm
Search engine for Kansas places: www.kshs.org/genealogists/places
All newspapers on microfilm circulate through interlibrary loan.

Johnson County Library

Genealogy Department
E-mail: bakerb@jcl.lib.ks.us
Web site: www.jocolibrary.org
Genealogy page: www.jocolibrary.org/index.asp?DisplayPageID=726
Online catalog:
http://ibistro2.jocolibrary.org/uhtbin/cgisirsi/bRCGaXsbmB/234290575/60/1180/X
Their Internet genealogy page has some interesting links.

Wichita Public Library

Genealogy Department
Kansas Reference, and Local History Collection
E-mail: REF-GLH@WICHITA.LIB.KS.US
Web site: www.wichita.lib.ks.us/genhist/index.html
Their Web site gives a good summary of the collection.

Iola Public Library

Raymond L. Willson Genealogy Collection
E-mail: iolaref@alltel.net
Web site: www.iola.lib.ks.us
Online catalog: http://216.96.90.98/winnebago/index.asp?lib=???
Check their online catalog for holdings.

Riley County Genealogical Society

Library
E-mail: rcgs03@cox.net
Web site: www.rileycgs.com
Their Web page is the gateway to their resources and services.

Kentucky

Kentucky Department of Libraries and Archives

Library and Archives
Web site: www.kdla.ky.gov
Online catalog: http://kdla.kyvl.org
Check their Web site for services to out-of-state customers.

Daviess County Public Library

Kentucky Room
E-mail: dcpl700@dcpl.lib.ky.us
Web site: www.dcpl.lib.ky.us/kyroom.htm
Online catalog: http://208.47.93.179/webclient.html
Check their online catalog for access to the collection.

Kentucky Historical Society

History Center
Web site: http://history.ky.gov/Research/Research_Collections.htm
Online resources: http://history.ky.gov/Research/Online_Resources.htm
Check the online resources.

Western Kentucky University

Kentucky Library
Web site: www.wku.edu/Library/dlsc/ky_lib.htm
Online catalog: http://topcat2000.wku.edu/cgi-bin/Pwebrecon.cgi?DB=local&PAGE=First
Check their online catalog for access to the collection.

The National Society of the Sons of the American Revolution

Library
Web site: www.sar.org/geneal/library.htm
Online catalog: http://sar.library.net
The Society will supply a list of contract researchers.

Louisiana

New Orleans Public Library

Louisiana Division
E-Mail: cbhamer@bellsouth.net
Web site: http://nutrias.org
Online catalog: http://nutrias.org/ipac.htm
Check the online indexes of vital records.

Louisiana State Archives

Archives
E-mail: archives@sos.louisiana.gov
Archive Web site: www.sec.state.la.us/archives/archives/archives-index.htm
Confederate Pension Application Index Database:
www.sos.louisiana.gov/archives/gen/cpa-index.htm
New Orleans Ship Passenger List Online Index:
www.sos.louisiana.gov/archives/gen/nln-ship_pass-index.htm
Check out the online database indexes.

State Library of Louisiana

Louisiana Section Reference Desk
E-mail: ladept@pelican.state.lib.us
Web site: www.state.lib.la.us/Dept/LaSect/index.htm
Check the Web site for remote access.

Diocese of Baton Rouge

Historical Archives
E-mail: archives@diobr.org
Web site: www.diobr.org/departments/archnives/index.htm
Follow the request procedures outlined on their Web page.

East Baton Rouge Parish Library

Bluebonnet Regional Branch
Genealogy Department
Web site: www.ebr.lib.la.us/ie.htm
Online catalog: www.ebr.lib.la.us:8000
Check the online catalog to see what the have.

Maine

Maine State Library

State House Station #64
Genealogy Resources
Web site: www.maine.gov/msl/services/reference/gen_resources.htm
Online catalog: http://ursus.maine.edu
They have a list of professional genealogist on their Web site.

Maine State Archives

Research Room
Web site: www.state.me.us/sos/arc/research/homepage.htm

Research Room Privileges Application: www.state.me.us/sos/arc/forms/Register.pdf
Marriages online index:
http://thor.dafs.state.me.us/pls/archives/archdev.marriage_archive.search_form
Deaths online index:
http://thor.dafs.state.me.us/pls/archives/archdev.death_archive.search_form
Check the online marriage and death databases.

University of Maine

Fogler Library
Web site: www.library.umaine.edu
Online catalog: http://130.111.64.3
Search the online catalog to see if they have material on your ancestors.

Maine Historical Society

Research Library
E-mail: info@mainehistory.org
Web site: www.mainehistory.org/library_genealogy.shtml
Online catalog: www.mainehistory.org/library_search.shtml
See their page: www.mainehistory.org/library_research.shtml
Check out their Web site for access to online data.

Penobscot Maritime Museum

Stephen Phillips Memorial Library
E-mail: library@penobscotmarinemuseum.org
Online index to family names collection: www.penobscotmarinemuseum.org/Jones.htm#Jones
Check out their family names index. They charge $25.00 per request for a search of the files.

Maryland

Maryland State Archives

Family History Research
E-mail: archives@mdarchives.state.md.us
Web site: www.mdarchives.state.md.us
For visitors: www.mdarchives.state.md.us/msa/refserv/html/visit.html
All requests from a distance must be submitted by mail, fax, or e-mail. No phone requests.

Frederick County Public Libraries

C. Burr Artz Public Library, Maryland Room
E-mail: www_fcpl@co.frederick.md.us
Web site: www.fcpl.org
Online catalog: www.fcpl.org/uhtbin/cgisirsi/CLms2TbCrY/70620107/60/1180/X
Consult this page for access from a distance:

www.fcpl.org/01_inf/01_3_mdrm/01_3_01.html#collection
See Web site for access from a distance.

Maryland Historical Society

Research Library
Web site: www.mdhs.org/explore/library.html
Online catalog: http://207.67.203.36/m60006
Search the online catalog for relevant material.

Enoch Pratt Free Library

Special Collections
E-mail: SLRC@epfl.net
Web site: www.epfl.net/slrc/special_collections
Online catalog: http://pac.epfl.net/uhtbin/cgisirsi/7Tvt3Km5Ju/10920167/60/1180/X
Researchers are encouraged to contact the Special Collections Librarian before they visit.

Dorchester County Public Library

Central Library—Genealogy/Local History
E-mail: infodesk@dorchesterlibrary.org
Web site: www.dorchesterlibrary.org/genealogy.html
Send specific questions to their e-mail address.

Massachusetts

Massachusetts Archives

Archives at Columbia Point
E-mail: archives@sec.state.ma.us
Web site: www.state.ma.us/sec/arc/arcgen/genidx.htm
Use the Web address to find out how to access their resources.

Massachusetts Historical Society Library

Research Library
E-mail: Library@masshist.org
Web site: www.masshist.org/library
Online catalog: www.masshist.org/library/abigail.cfm
A $10.00 fee must accompany mail-in request for photocopies.

Connecticut Valley Historical Museum Library

Library and Archive Collections
Web site: www.quadrangle.org/library-archive.htm
Online catalog: www.masscat.org
Search the online catalog to find out if they have something you can use.

Plymouth Public Library

History/Genealogy
E-mail: mregan@ocln.org
Web site: www.plymouthpubliclibrary.org/history.htm
Local History and Genealogy Web Sites: www.plymouthpubliclibrary.org/history5.htm
Check out the Local History and Genealogy Web Sites for some interesting data.

Michigan

Detroit Public Library

Burton Historical Collection
E-mail: dporemba@detroit.lib.mi.us
Web site: www.detroit.lib.mi.us.burton
Online catalog: http://webpac.wayne.edu/webpac-bin/wgbroker?new+-access+top.dpl
Inquiries may be made by phone, mail (including e-mail), and in person.

Michigan Library and Historical Center

Library of Michigan
Web site: www.michigan.gov/hal/0,1607,7-160-17449_18635—-,00.html
This is a great Web site. They have some very good online indexes.

Clarke Historical Library

Central Michigan University
Mount Pleasant, Michigan 48859
Web site: http://clarke.cmich.edu
Online resources: http://clarke.cmich.edu/online.htm
The Web site has a number of full-text files and exhibits, including county histories.

University of Michigan

Bentley Historical Library, Reference Unit
E-mail: bentley.ref@umich.edu
Web site: www.umich.edu/%7Ebhl
Online catalog: http://mirlynweb.lib.umich.edu/WebZ/umAuthorize?sessionid=0
Use the link, "Guide to Use of the Bentley Historical Library" on their Web page.

Minnesota

Minnesota Historical Society

Library and Collections

E-mail: kathryn.otto@mnhs.org
Web site: www.mnhs.org/library/index.html
Online catalog: www.pals.msus.edu/cgi-bin/pals-cgi?palsAction=
newSearch&setWeb=MHSCATT
The powerful online catalog has links to additional sources and Web sites.

University of Minnesota

Immigration History Research Center
University of Minnesota
E-mail: wurlx001@umn.edu
Web site: www1.umn.edu/ihrc
Online catalog: www1.umn.edu/ihrc/search.htm#top
Fees for remote access: www1.umn.edu/ihrc/patron.htm
See the remote access page for details about services and fees.

Iron Range Research Center

Research Center
E-mail: yourroots@ironworld.com
Web site: www.ironrangeresearchcenter.org
Searchable online database:
www.ironrangeresearchcenter.org/scripts/runisa.dll?irrrb:searchresults
This Web site has fantastic online databases

Minnesota Genealogical Society Library

Research Library
E-mail: Lbesch@worldnet.att.net
Web site: www.mngs.org
Online catalog: http://webmandarin.sirs.com/mgs
List of surname being researched by MGS members: www.mngs.org/surname.html
The surname list is a good place to start.

Minneapolis Public Library

Resources for Genealogical Research
Web site: www.mpls.lib.mn.us/genealogy.asp
Online catalog: http://mplwebcat.mpls.lib.mn.us
The online catalog is a good index to the collection.

Mississippi

Mississippi Department of Archives and History

Archives and Library
E-mail: refdesk@mdah.state.ms.us

Web site: www.mdah.state.ms.us/arlib/arlib_index.html
Online search: http://mdah.state.ms.us/arlib/contents/er/index.html
This is a good Web site for genealogical researchers.

Evans Memorial Library

Research Library
E-mail: eml@tombigbee.lib.ms.us
Web site: www.tombigbee.lib.ms.us/evans/index.html
Use the Web site to find out how to use the collection.

Mississippi State University

Mitchell Memorial Library
Special Collections Department
E-mail: sp_coll@llibrary.msstate.edu
Web site: http://library.msstate.edu/sc
Online catalog: http://library.msstate.edu/Web2/tramp2.exe/log_in?setting_key=mitchell
The best way to access this collection is to go there and use it. Otherwise contact a professional researcher.

Missouri

St. Louis County Library

Julius K. Hunter and Friends African American Research Collection
St. Louis County Library
Web site: www.slcl.lib.mo.us/slcl/sc/jkh/sc_jkh_fd.htm#dbase
Online catalog: http://199.181.178.210
The online catalog will tell you what resources they have.

St. Louis County Library

Local History and Genealogy
Web site: www.slcl.lib.mo.us/slcl/sc/sc-genpg.htm
Online catalog: http://199.181.178.210
This is an excellent Web site for genealogists.

Missouri State Archives

Archives
E-mail: archref@sosmail.state.mo.us
Web site: www.sos.mo.gov/archives
Online catalog: http://msa.library.net
Online databases: www.sos.mo.gov/archives/resources/ordb.asp
Online birth and death index: www.sos.mo.gov/archives/resources/birthdeath
This is a great site. Don't miss it if you have Missouri ancestors. Check out the online birth and death indexes.

State Historical Society of Missouri

Research Library
E-mail: BoeckmanL@umsystem.edu
Web site: www.system.missouri.edu/shs
Out-of-state request form: www.system.missouri.edu/shs/outofstate.htm
Use the out-of-state request form to access the resources from a distance.

Montana

Montana Historical Society

Library and Archives
E-mail: MHSLibrary@state.mt.us
Web site: www.his.state.mt.us/departments/Library-Archives
Online catalog: www.his.state.mt.us/departments/Library-Archives/catalogs.html
Use the Web site to discover if they have something that will help with your research.

Montana State Library

Library
Web site: http://msl.state.mt.us
Online catalog:
http://mtscprod.msl.state.mt.us/uhtbin/cgisirsi/ULVIPfvE01/275890068/60/1180/X
Use the online catalog to find out if they have the materials you need.

Parmly Billings Library

Library
E-mail: refdesk@billings.lib.mt.us
Web site: www.billings.lib.mt.us
Online catalog: www.billings.lib.mt.us:8080/ipac-cgi/ipac.exe
Lewis and Clark links: www.billings.lib.mt.us/l-c.html
The Lewis and Clark links are especially helpful to researchers.

Great Falls Genealogical Society Library

High Plains Heritage Center
E-mail: gfgs@mt.net
Web site: www.rootsweb.com/~mtmsgs/soc_gfgs.htm
Send them an e-mail to find out they can help you.
Butte—Silver Bow Public Library   Library
Web site: www.co.silverbow.mt.us/library.htm
Check out this Web site if you have Montana ancestors.

Nebraska

Nebraska State Historical Society

Library/Archives
E-mail: lanshs@nebraskahistory.org
Web site: www.nebraskahistory.org/lib-arch
Online catalog: www.nebraskahistory.org/databases/librarycatalog.htm
Newspapers on microfilm are available through interlibrary loan.

Nebraska State Genealogical Society Library

Beatrice Public Library
E-mail: lriedesel@beatrice.lib.ne.us
Society Home Page: www.rootsweb.com/~nesgs
Library Home Page: www.beatrice.lib.ne.us
Send an e-mail to learn about services from a distance.

Omaha Public Library

Genealogy Department
Web site: www.omaha.lib.ne.us/aboutus/locations/gen.html
Online catalog: http://catalog.omaha.lib.ne.us/ipac20/ipac.jsp?profile=web&menu=search
Web Links page: www.omaha.lib.ne.us/subjects/genealogy/genealogy.html
The Web Links page has some worthwhile genealogy links.

American Historical Society of Germans from Russia

Research Library
E-mail: ahsgr@aol.com
Web site: www.ahsgr.org
This is a good Web site for such narrowly focused research.

Nevada

Nevada State Library and Archives

Genealogical Resources
Web site: http://dmla.clan.lib.nv.us/docs/nsla/services/genealres.htm
Use the Web site to help you find a professional.

Nevada Historical Society

Research and Reading Room
Web site: http://dmla.clan.lib.nv.us/docs/museums/reno/his-soc.htm
Use the Web site to help you find a professional.

New Hampshire

New Hampshire State Library

Genealogy Section
E-mail: zmoore@library.state.nh.us
Web site: www.state.nh.us/nhsl/history/index.html
Online catalog: www.state.nh.us/nhsl/nhupac.html
The online catalog is a good remote access point for researchers who live a distance away.

New Hampshire Department of State

Division of Vital Records Administration
Web site: www.nh.gov/sos/vitalrecords/LIBRARY.html
The Web site contains some New Hampshire specific links.

New Hampshire Historical Society

Tuck Library
Web site: www.nhhistory.org/library.html
Online catalog: http://nhhistory.library.net
Reproduction pricelist: www.nhhistory.org/reproductionprices.html
Their Web site is full of good information for researchers.

Manchester Public Library

New Hampshire Room and Genealogy
E-mail: coneil@ci.manchester.nh.us
Web site: www.ManchesterNH.gov/CityGov/LIB/Adult/NHRoom.html
Send an e-mail message to find out what they can do for you.

New Jersey

Rutgers University Libraries

Special Collections, Genealogical Resources
Web site: www.libraries.rutgers.edu/rul/libs/scua/genealogy/genealogy.shtml
The Web site gives researcher good access the collection.

New Jersey State Archives

Archives
E-mail: archives.reference@sos.state.nj.us
Web site: www.state.nj.us/state/darm/links/archives.html
Online catalog: www.state.nj.us/state/darm/links/webcat/genealogy.html
Searching fees and instructions: www.state.nj.us/state/darm/links/reference.html#collections
Refer to the Web site for searching fees and instructions.

The New Jersey Historical Society

Library
E-mail: contact@NJHS@jerseyhistory.org
Web site: www.jerseyhistory.org
Researchers are encouraged to use their card catalogs and then ask a reference if they still have questions.

Newark Public Library

The New Jersey Information Center
E-mail: njreference@npl.org
Web site: www.npl.org/Pages/Collections/njic.html
Online catalog: www.npl.org/Pages/Catalog/index.html
Send an e-mail to discover how they can help you.

Joint Free Public Library of Morristown-Morris Township

Local History and Genealogy Department
E-mail: jochem@main.morris.org
Web site: www.jfpl.org/gene.htm
Online catalog: http://web2.morris.org
The online catalog can tell you if they have materials that could help you.

New Mexico

New Mexico State Records and Archives

Archival and Historical Services Division
E-mail: archives@rain.state.nm.us
Web site: www.nmcpr.state.nm.us
Online catalog: http://164.64.110.201/webcat/front-nm.htm
Check out their Web pages to determine if they could have the information you need.

Rio Grande Valley Library System

Special Collections Library
E-mail: SpecialCollections@cabq.gov
Web site: www.cabq.gov/library/specol.html
Online catalog: http://albuq.cabq.gov
All materials are available for in-house use only. Photocopying is allowed.

New Mexico State Library

Library Services
E-mail: southwest@stlib.state.nm.us
Web site: www.stlib.state.nm.us
Online catalog: http://salsa.stlib.state.nm.us/ipac20/ipac.jsp?profile=nms#focus
Contact them to find out how to access the collection from a distance.

Carlsbad Public Library

Library
Web site: http://elin.lib.nm.us/cpl/index.htm
Online catalog: http://webcat.elin.lib.nm.us/uhtbin/cgisirsi
Use the online catalog to find out what they have.

University of New Mexico Zimmerman Library

Center for Southwest Research
E-mail: cswrref@unm.edu
Web site: www.unm.edu/~cswrref/engcollect.html
Online archives: http://elibrary.unm.edu/oanm
Use the online catalog to plan your research tip.

New York

New York Genealogical and Biographical Society Library

Family History
E-mail: library@nygbs.org
Web site: www.newyorkfamilyhistory.org
Records Search Service Request Form: www.nygbs.org/info/searchorder.html
Online Resources: www.nygbs.org/info/online.html
The $60.00 membership fee is worth the money, even if you just use the online services.

New York State Archives

New York State Education Department
E-mail: archref@mail.nysed.gov
Web site: www.archives.nysed.gov/aindex.shtml
Online catalog: http://nysl.nysed.gov:80/uhtbin/cgisirsi/UbDloSUzSi/129260119/60/56/X
The Web site is a powerful tool for researchers.

Rochester Public Library

Monroe County (NY) Library System
Web site: www.libraryweb.org/genealogy.html
Online catalog: www.libraryweb.org/tutorials/libra/index.html
Check out the Web site for online resources and databases.

North Carolina

North Carolina State Archives

Public Services Branch

E-mail: archives@ncmail.net
Web site: www.ah.dcr.state.nc.us/sections/archives/arch/gen-res.htm
The search and handling fee for out-of-state requests is $20.00 per inquiry. See their fee schedule page for additional services and products.

State Library of North Carolina

Genealogical Services
Genealogy Web page: http://statelibrary.dcr.state.nc.us/iss/gr/genealog.htm
Genealogy Questions via e-mail: http://statelibrary.dcr.state.nc.us/forms/Famref.htm
Genealogical materials do not circulate. Though researchers may ask questions by e-mail, following the guidelines.

Public Library of Charlotte and Mecklenburg County

Carolina Room
Web site: www.plcmc.lib.nc.us/libloc/maincarolina.asp
Online catalog: www.plcmc.lib.nc.us/catalog/default.asp
Contact them for the best way to access the collection.

Olivia Raney History Library

History Library
Web site: www.wakegov.com/locations/oliviaraneyhistorylibrary.htm
They have some unique online resources at their Web site.

Rowan Public Library

History Room
E-mail: info@co.rowan.nc.us
Web site: www.lib.co.rowan.nc.us/HistoryRoom/default.htm
Online Catalog: www.youseemore.com/RowanPLint/default.asp
This library takes genealogical research seriously and their Web site reflects it.

North Dakota

North Dakota State Library

Research Library
Web site: http://ndsl.lib.state.nd.us
Online catalog: www.odin.nodak.edu/cgi-bin/pals-cgi?palsAction=restart&documentName=selectre.html
Check out their Web site for details about their services.

State Archives and Historical Research Library

North Dakota Heritage Center
E-mail: archives@state.nd.us

Web site: www.state.nd.us/hist/sal/gen.htm
Charges for reference services: www.state.nd.us/hist/sal/charge.htm
Refer to the page, "Charges for Reference Services."

University of North Dakota Chester Fritz Library

Family History and Genealogy Room
University Avenue and Centennial Drive
E-mail: library@mail.und.nodak.edu
Web site: www.und.edu/dept/library/Collections/Famhist/home.html
Online Catalog: http://webcat.odin.nodak.edu
Send them an e-mail to find out about services from a distance.

Bismarck Mandan Historical and Genealogical Library

Library
Web site: www.rootsweb.com/~nddunn
Though it lacks detail, the Web site is a good place to begin research from a distance.

Ohio

Public Library of Cincinnati and Hamilton County

Genealogy Department
Genealogy Department: www.cincinnatilibrary.org/info/main/hi.asp
Online catalog: http://catalog.cincinnatilibrary.org
This is a premier genealogical research library. The Web site is full of information for researchers.

Rutherford B. Hayes Presidential Library

Spiegel Grove
E-mail: hayeslib@rbhayes.org
Web site: www.rbhayes.org
Online catalog: http://maurice.bgsu.edu/screens/opacmenu.html
Start with the Web site to prepare for a trip to this library.

Ohio Historical Society

Archives and Library
Web site: www.ohiohistory.org/resource/archlib/index.html
Contact form: www.ohiohistory.org/contact.html
Online catalog: www.ohiohistory.org/occ/menu.html
Use the Contact Form to get started with research at this library.

Ohio Genealogical Society

Library
E-mail: ogs@ogs.org

Web site: www.ogs.org (Great Web site)
Online catalog: http://65.40.73.196:210/m3/apps/m3opac/ogs
For a society library their Web site is better than most.

Ohio State Library

Genealogy Services
E-Mail: genhelp@sloma.state.oh.us
Web site: http://winslo.state.oh.us/services/genealogy
Online catalog: http://slonet.state.oh.us
Their online catalog comprehensive and user-friendly.

Oklahoma

Oklahoma Historical Society

Research Division
E-mail: statemuseum@ok-history.mus.ok
Web site: www.ok-history.mus.ok.us/lib/lrdintro.htm
They require a research fee of $20.00 for out-of-state inquiries before research can begin. The in-state fee is $5.00. Copy charges and postage will be billed.

Oklahoma Department of Libraries

Allen Wright Memorial Library
Web site: www.odl.state.ok.us/index.html
Online catalog: http://catalog.odl.state.ok.us
Most materials can be borrowed by interlibrary loan through a local public library.

Tulsa City-County Public Library

Genealogy Center
Web site and online catalog: www.tulsalibrary.org/genealogy
The staff can answer short questions by phone or letter. The staff cannot do look-ups or extensive research.

Lawton Public Library

Family History Room
Web site: www.cityof.lawton.ok.us/library/genealogy.htm
Open and free to the public. Contact the library for remote access.

Tulsa Genealogical Society

Library
E-mail: tgslibrary@cox.net
Web site: www.tulsagenealogy.org/library
Send them an e-mail to request research services.

Oregon

Genealogical Forum of Oregon

Library
E-mail: info@gfo.org
Web site: www.gfo.org/library.htm
The Web site is full of finding tools and indexes.

Oregon State Archives

Genealogy Records
E-mail: reference.archives@state.or.us
Web site: http://arcweb.sos.state.or.us/banners/genealogy.htm
The Web site has some online birth and death records for Portland.

Oregon Historical Society

Museum and Research Library
E-mail: orhist@ohs.org
Web site: www.ohs.org
Research Assistance Fees: www.ohs.org/collections/reseach-assistance.cfm
Check the page "Research Assistance Fees" for research from a distance.

University of Oregon

Knight Library
Web site: http://libweb.uoregon.edu
Access to the online catalog is on their Web site.

Rogue Valley Genealogical Society

Research Library
E-mail: info@vggslibrary.org
Web site: www.rvgslibrary.org
Send an e-mail for more information about their services.

Pennsylvania

Historical Society of Pennsylvania

Research and Collection
Web site: www.hsp.org/default.aspx?id=2
Online catalogs: www.hsp.org/default.aspx?id=3
Research by Mail: www.hsp.org/default.aspx?id=134
Check out the Research by Mail page for access from a distance.

Genealogical Society of Pennsylvania

Research Room
E-mail: gsppa@aol.com
Web site: www.libertynet.org/gspa/library.html
Web page for requesting a search: www.libertynet.org/gspa/GSPInquiryProcs2.htm
See the Web site for requesting a search if you cannot get to the library.

Library Company of Philadelphia

Research Room
E-mail: Refdept@librarycompany.org
Web site: www.librarycompany.org
Online catalog: http://lcp-agent.auto-graphics.com/agent/SearchPages.asp?myses=176&w=A&cuid=lcp&cusrvr=themis&s=LD
The Web site is a gateway to a myriad of other historical sources and images.

Carnegie Library of Pittsburgh

Pennsylvania Department
E-mail: padept@carnegielibrary.org
Web site: http://216.183.184.20/locations/pennsylvania/genealogy
Web page for contacting the Pennsylvania Department:
http://216.183.184.20/locations/pennsylvania/contact.cfm
Use the Web page to contact the Pennsylvania Department.

Lancaster County Historical Society

Research Library
E-mail: lchs@ptd.net
Web site: www.lancasterhistory.org
Online catalog: http://pilot.sshe.edu:8072/cgi-bin/Pwebrecon.cgi?DB=local&PAGE=First
Access the Web site to learn of a wide variety of services.

Historical Society of Western Pennsylvania

Library and Archives
E-mail: hswp@hswp.org
Web site: www.pghhistory.org/archv_lib/library.htm
Online catalog: http://digital.library.pitt.edu/hswp
The Web site has information on research services and fees.

Rhode Island

Rhode Island Historical Society

Research Library
Web site: www.rihs.org/libraryhome.htm

Research Request Form: www.rihs.org/FORM%20res%20svc.htm
Use the Research Request Form to access the library from a distance.

Rhode Island State Library

Library
E-mail: statelibrary@sec.state.ri.us
Web site: www.state.ri.us/library/web.htm
Online Catalog: www.library.state.ri.us/dbtw-wpd/opac/opac.htm
Send an e-mail to find out about remote access.

Providence Public Library

Rhode Island Collection
Web site: www.provlib.org/accessinfo/ricollect/ricollect.htm
Online catalog: www.provlib.org/librarycatalog.htm
Access the collection through the Web site.

Rhode Island State Archives

State Archives and Public Records Administration
E-mail: reference@archives.state.ri.us
Web site: www.state.ri.us/archives
Web page for probate forms: www.state.ri.us/archives/probateforms.htm
Fill out the probate request form and send it in to find out the charges.

Westerly Public Library

Memorial and Library Association
Web site: www.clan.lib.ri.us/wes
Check out their Web page for more information.

South Carolina

South Carolina Department of Archives and History

Archives and History Center
Web site: www.state.sc.us/scdah/homepage.htm
Search the Web site to learn more about their resources and services.

South Carolina Historical Society

Library
Web site: www.schistory.org
Research Services: www.schistory.org/researchservices.htm
Check the Research Services page for more about access from a distance.

Heritage Library Foundation

The Heritage Library-Hilton Head
E-mail: webmaster@heritagelib.org
Web site: www.heritagelib.org
Online catalog: www.librarycom.com/heritage
No charge for e-mail or telephone lookups.

Camden Archives and Museum

Library/Research Collections
Web site: www.mindspring.com/~camdenarchives/index.html
The Web page has links to some online data.

The Huguenot Society of South Carolina

Library
E-mail: huguenot@cchat.com
Web site: www.huguenotsociety.org
If you have Huguenot ancestors send them an e-mail to find out about their resources.

South Dakota

South Dakota State Historical Society

South Dakota State Archives
Web site: www.sdhistory.org/arc/archives.htm
Online catalog: www.sdhistory.org/soc/bkcatlog03.htm
Online Newspaper Database: www.sdhistory.org/arc/newspaper/default.asp
The Newspaper Database is an outstanding index.

South Dakota State Library

Genealogy Research
Web site: www.sdstatelibrary.com/research/#Genealogy
Online Catalog: http://webpals.sdln.net/cgi-bin/pals-cgi?palsAction=restart&documentName=selectre.html
The online catalog is a good starting point for research from a distance.

Rapid City Public Library

Library
Web site: http://rcplib.sdln.net
Online catalog: http://webpals.sdln.net/cgi-bin/pals-cgi?palsAction=newSearch&setWeb=RCPCAT_
Search the catalog for materials relevant to your research.

Siouxland Libraries

Sioux Falls Public Library
Web site: www.siouxland.lib.sd.us/library/index.asp
Look for the online catalog from their Web site.

Alexander Mitchell Library

Special Collections
E-mail: ampl@dsln.net
Web site: http://ampl.sdln.net/Special%20Collections.htm
Online catalog: http://nickel.sdln.net/webpals
Use the online catalog to find appropriate titles and contact the library for access.

Tennessee

Tennessee State Library and Archives

Tennessee History and Genealogy
Web site: http://state.tn.us/sos/statelib/pubsvs/intro.htm
Online catalog: http://tns-verso.auto-graphics.com/verso/public/public_opac.htm
Online instructions for ordering copies of documents:
www.state.tn.us/sos/statelib/pubsvs/mailstat.htm
Follow the online instructions for ordering documents.

Memphis-Shelby County Public Library

History Department
E-mail: hisref@memphis.lib.tn.us
Web site: www.memphislibrary.org/history/index.html
Online catalog: www.memphislibrary.org/libcat/librarycatalog.htm
Their Web site has links to African American popular Web sites.

Knox County Public Library

McClung Collection
Web site: www.knoxlib.org/departments/ethc/mcclung/mcc-gen.php
Online Catalog: http://cat.knoxlib.org/uhtbin/cgisirsi/ XLvs317a0c/245080333/60/1180/X
The Web site explains fee-based services.

Chattanooga-Hamilton County Public Library

Local History and Genealogy Department
Web site: www.lib.chattanooga.gov/localHist/localHist.html
Web site for mail service: www.lib.chattanooga.gov/services.html#mail
Use the Web site for mail service for access from a distance.

Tennessee Historical Society

War Memorial Building
E-mail: tnhissoc@tennesseehistory.org
Web site: www.tennesseehistory.org
Send them an e-mail for more detailed information.

Texas

Texas State Library and Archives Commission

Library and Archives
E-mail: geninfo@tsl.state.tx.us
Web site: www.tsl.state.tx.us
Online catalog: http://star.tsl.state.tx.us/uhtbin/cgisirsi/xhMDNycHoV/305240007/60/68/X
Send an e-mail to find out how to access the state archives.

Houston Public Library

Clayton Library, Center for Genealogical Research
Web site: www.hpl.lib.tx.us/clayton
Online catalog: http://catalog.houstonlibrary.org/search~b1a1o1c1i1
Online databases are accessible through the Houston Public Library Power Card, available to all Texas residents.

Dallas Public Library

History and Social Science Genealogy Section
Web site: http://dallaslibrary.org/CHS/cgc.htm
Online catalog: http://catalog.dallaslibrary.org
The best way to access this outstanding collection is go to the library.

Carnegie Center of Brazos Valley History

Bryan College Station Public Library System
Web site: www.bcslibrary.org
Look for their online catalog from their Web page.

The Fort Worth Public Library

Genealogy, Local History and Archives
E-mail: genlhst@fortworthlibrary.org
Web site: www.fortworthlibrary.org/genlhst.htm
Online catalog: www.fortworthlibrary.org/opac.htm
Obituary Index 1966-1993: http://198.215.16.250/webpacj/webclient.html
Use the Obituary Index to find an obituary.

The Grapevine Public Library

Genealogy Resources
Web site: www.grapevine.lib.tx.us/genpage.asp
Online catalog: http://catalog.grapevine.lib.tx.us/#focus
Local vital records index online: www.grapevine.lib.tx.us/gvsearch.asp
Check their online vital records database for information.

Utah

Marriott Library, University of Utah

Special Collections
Web site: www.lib.utah.edu
Special Collections: www.lib.utah.edu/spc/wam/uthist.html
Online Catalog: www.lib.utah.edu/information/unis/index.html
The online catalog will tell you what they have.

Utah State Archives and Records Services

Archives
E-mail: archivesresearch@utah.gov
Web site: www.archives.utah.gov
Online catalog: http://archives.utah.gov/catbegin.htm
Use the Web site to learn more about their services.

Utah State Historical Society

Family History Resources
E-mail: cergushs@utah.gov
Web site: http://history.utah.gov/library/familyhist.html
Searchable burial database: http://webapps.dced.state.ut.us/burials/execute/searchburials
Online catalog: http://usld.ipac.dynixasp.com/ipac20/ipac.jsp?profile=history
Check out the online access to burials and newspapers.

Brigham Young University

Utah Valley Regional Family History Center
E-mail: byu-familyhisotrycenter@email.byu.edu
Web site: http://uvrfhc.lib.byu.edu
Researchers can check to see if the Utah Valley Regional Family History Center has the film by entering the film number into the search engine.

Vermont

Vermont Historical Society

Library
E-mail: vhs@vhs.state.vt.us
Web site: www.vermonthistory.org/libinfo.htm#genealogy
Send them an e-mail to find out how they can help you.

Vermont State Archives

Archives, Redstone Building
Web site: http://vermont-archives.org/admin/referenc.htm
Online catalog: http://arccat.uvm.edu
The online catalog is the best starting point for this archive.

Vermont Department of Libraries

Library
E-mail: questions@dol.state.vt.us
Web site: http://dol.state.vt.us
Online catalogs: http://web2.dol.state.vt.us
The Web site has links to lots of good information.

Brooks Memorial Library

Genealogy and Local History Room
E-mail: brattlib@brooks.lib.vt.us
Web site: www.brooks.lib.vt.us
Online catalog: www.brooks.lib.vt.us/catalog.htm
Online queries to: www.brooks.lib.vt.us/ancestorask.html
Online queries cost $10.00 per hour.

Virginia

Library of Virginia

Genealogical Research
E-mail via Web page: www.lva.lib.va.us/whatwedo/libemailform.asp
Web site: www.lva.lib.va.us/whatwehave/gene/index.htm
Online catalog: http://ajax.lva.lib.va.us/F/?func=file&file_name=find-b
Send them an e-mail to find out if they have the resources you need.

Virginia Historical Society

Research Collections
Web site: www.vahistorical.org/research/main.htm

Online catalog: http://vhs3.vahistorical.org/star/x.starmarc.html
Check the Web site for A Guide to African American Manuscripts.

Fairfax County Public Library

Virginia Room
E-mail: va_room@fairfaxcounty.gov
Web site: www.co.fairfax.va.us/library/branches/vr/default.htm
Online catalog:
http://fcplcat.co.fairfax.va.us/uhtbin/cgisirsi/coaPs8VpF5/149200024/60/1180/X
Check out their excellent Web site for resources you can use.

University of Virginia

Manuscripts and Rare Books Collection
Web site: www.lib.virginia.edu/manuscripts.html
Contact them before making a research trip.

Jones Memorial Library

Library
Web site: www.jmlibrary.org
Online catalog: www.ci.lynchburg.va.us/fiberoptic/electron.htm
Check out their Web site.

Washington

Fiske Library

Research Library
Web site: www.fiske.lib.wa.us
Their shelf list indexes holdings by state.

Tacoma Public Library

Northwest Room
Web site: www.tpl.lib.wa.us/v2/NWROOM/Nwroom.htm
Online catalog: http://192.103.195.14/uhtbin/cgisirsi.exe/x/0/49
Use the online catalog to find out what they have.

Spokane Public Library

Genealogy Research
Web site: www.spokanelibrary.org/research/genealogy/default.asp
Catalog: http://web2.spokanelibrary.org
Use their online catalog to see if they have something you can use.

Washington State Archives

Archives
E-mail: archives@secstate.wa.gov

Web site: www.secstate.wa.gov/archives
Searchable database: www.secstate.wa.gov/history/search.aspx
Washington census and naturalization records are available electronically on their searchable database.

Seattle Genealogical Society

Research Library
Web site: www.rootsweb.com/~waseags
Check out their page on Research Services.

West Virginia

West Virginia Division of Culture and History

Archives and History Section, Capitol Complex
Web site: www.wvculture.org/index.html
Their Web site is one of the very best.

West Virginia and Regional History Collection

West Virginia University (Morgantown)
Web site: www.libraries.wvu.edu/wvcollection/genealogy.htm
They offer interlibrary loan through their Web site.

Marshall University

James E. Morrow Library, Special Collections
Web site: www.marshall.edu/library/morrow.asp
Online catalog: www.miles.marshall.edu:8000/cgi-bin/chameleon
Local Newspaper Index: www.miles.marshall.edu:8000/cgi-bin/chameleon?skin=lni
The Local Newspaper Index is a good online resource.

Berkeley County Historical Society

Genealogical Resources
Web site: www.bchs.org/genealogy.html
Their Web site provides a good list of what they have.

Wisconsin

Vesterheim Genealogical Center

Naeseth Library
Web site: www.vesterheim.org/genealogy.html
Norwegian Research Questionnaire: www.vesterheim.org/Genealogy2001/imquest.html

Fill out the request for research and send it to them.
Wisconsin Historical Society Library-Archives
Web site: www.wisconsinhistory.org/libraryarchives
Online catalog: www.wisconsinhistory.org/Libraryarchives/catalogs
Search the catalog for relevant materials.

Milwaukee County Historical Society

Research Library
E-mail: mchs@prodigy.net
Web site: www.milwaukeecountyhistsoc.org
The Web site has links to indexes of naturalization records, coroner's reports, and probate records.

Milwaukee Public Library

Library
Web site: www.mpl.org
Online catalog: http://countycat.mcfls.org
Genealogy page: www.mpl.org/files/great/bookmark.cfm?Category=12
They have a long list of online services.

Brown County Public Library

Local History and Genealogy
Web site: www.co.brown.wi.us/library/history-genealogy/index.shtml
Look for their online catalog from their Web site.

Wyoming

Laramie County Library System

Genealogy and Local History
Web site: www.lclsonline.org/adult_services/genealogy/index.html
Online Catalog: http://wyld.state.wy.us/larm
They offer interlibrary loan through their Web site.

Wyoming State Archives

Barrett Building
E-mail: wyarchive@state.wy.us
Send them an e-mail to learn about their services.

Wyoming State Library

Library
Web site: www-wsl.state.wy.us
Online catalog for Wyoming libraries:

http://wyld.state.wy.us
Use the statewide online catalog for bibliographic access to library collections across the state.

Albany County Public Library

Wyoming Room
Web site: http://acpl.lib.wy.us/services/collections.html#genealogy
Online catalog: http://wyld.state.wy.us/uhtbin/cgisirsi/XON05naaYX/8790036/60/1180/X
Use the online catalog to find out if what they have can help you.

INDEX

ABOUT THE AUTHOR

James Swan has worked in school, academic, or public libraries since 1964. He has been a genealogist for about the same time. His research has taken him to both coasts and lots of repositories in between. In 1977 he was named director of the Central Kansas Library System and the Great Bend Public Library, where he has been since. He has spoken and written books for librarians on a wide variety of topics. He also teaches genealogy classes for the public. *The Librarian's Guide to Genealogical Services and Research* is his sixth book. Swan has also self-published two family history books. He holds a BA and MLS from Brigham Young University.